SPECULUM ANNIV

London Church Courts and Society on the Eve of the Reformation

SPECULUM ANNIVERSARY MONOGRAPHS

SEVEN

London Church Courts and Society on the Eve of the Reformation

Richard M. Wunderli

THE MEDIEVAL ACADEMY OF AMERICA 1981

The publication of this book was made possible by funds contributed to the Medieval Academy during the Semi-Centennial Fund Drive.

LCC: 79-89571
ISBN: 910956-71-5
Printed in the United States of America

For Georgiana and Tom

BLANK PAGE

Contents

Figures and Tables

Figures

Tables

BLANK PAGE

Acknowledgments

It is a humbling task to write an acknowledgments page for one's first book. I am made to realize how much many other people have contributed directly to my work. It is also a gratifying task, because I may now publicly thank those same people. Without their encouragement, assistance, and judicious criticism, this book would not exist.

Although this monograph is largely a reworked version of my doctoral dissertation, it had its genesis many years before I began my Ph.D. work. The topic was first suggested to me in 1965 by Professor F. R. H. DuBoulay of the University of London. In the early 1970s it became a Ph.D. dissertation at Berkeley. There it was read and critiqued by three professors—three very different minds, each with a uniquely different approach to the past: Professor Robert Brentano, who more than anyone else is responsible for my development as a historian; Professor Thomas G. Barnes, who by example compelled me to find in local history a piece of a larger story; and Professor John T. Noonan, Jr., who after many careful readings of my work finally impressed upon me (one who has difficulty with legal thought) what "law" is all about. All three men have been kind, always helpful, and generous with their time and encouragement. I owe more to them than I could ever repay.

My manuscript in typescript was then filtered through many different minds, each of which was responsible for shaping a portion of the monograph: Professors Michael Sheehan, Charles Donahue, and Richard Helmholz, and Dr. Marjorie McIntosh. The editors of Speculum Anniversary Monographs, Luke Wenger and Siegfried Wenzel, have checked my work and saved me from many foolish blunders. I have usually taken my readers' advice. In a few instances, however, I have declined certain suggestions and, therefore, must take full responsibility for any errors.

Writing London history is an especially pleasing task, because one may live in London and avail oneself of its magnificent libraries. To Dr. A. E. J. Hollaender, formerly Keeper of the Manuscripts, Guildhall Library Muniment Room, and his excellent staff, I owe special thanks. I was also helped with unfailing courtesy by the staffs of the British Library, the Corporation of London Records Office, the Greater London Record Office, the Public Record Office, and Lambeth Palace Library.

I also wish to thank that exceptionally humane scholar, Professor Stephan Kuttner, Director of the Institute of Medieval Canon Law (Berkeley, California), for his help in so many ways: he helped me find canon law sources; he answered any questions touching canon law; and he hired me as a research fellow during a grim period of futile job seeking.

Finally I wish to acknowledge those who financially have made possible the research and writing of this work: the Ford Foundation (Special Career Fellowship) and the Maybelle McCleod Lewis Memorial Fellowship Fund.

Abbreviations

Acta correct.	Acta quoad correctionem delinquentium. Guildhall Library, London, MSS 9064/1–11.
Acta test.	Acta testamentorum. Guildhall Library, London, MSS 9168/1–8.
D.D.C.	*Dictionnaire de droit canonique*
Guild. Lib.	Guildhall Library, London. Muniment Room.
Journals	Corporation of London Records Office. Journals.
Letterbooks	Corporation of London Records Office. Letterbooks.
Lib. assign.	Liber assignationum. Greater London Record Office, DL/C/1,3.
Lib. exam.	Liber examinationum. Greater London Record Office, DL/C/205–208. Guildhall Library, MS 9065.
Port. Ward Present.	Ward Presentments, Portsoken Ward. Corporation of London Records Office, MS 242A.
P.R.O.	Public Record Office, London
Repertories	Corporation of London Records Office. Repertories.
X	Decretales. A. Friedberg, ed., *Corpus Juris Canonici,* 2 (Leipzig, 1879), edition and apparatus from the edition of Rome, 1582.

For more information about the manuscript sources, see the Bibliography on pp. 161–63.

BLANK PAGE

Introduction

When the first session of the Reformation Parliament met in London in November, 1529, a rather timid, directionless group of members began by attacking simple church "abuses." During the following seven years these same members of parliament were guided into legislating the English Reformation: they broke with the spiritual head at Rome and established Henry VIII as the "Supreme Head of the Church of England." Thus, by a series of legislative acts, England was brought into that European phenomenon, Reformation.[1]

"The one definite thing which can be said about the Reformation in England," wrote F. M. Powicke, "is that it was an act of state."[2] Indeed it was. But other conditions for Reformation were already present in England before 1529 that helped smooth the transition from the English Catholic Church to the Church of England. A. G. Dickens has dwelt at length on this fundamental question: Why were so many respectable Englishmen during the 1520s willing "to abandon their class prejudices against heresy and listen to Lutheranism, or even to more radical voices?" He found many leavening forces in pre-Reformation England that already were stretching and tearing at the social fabric.[3] My book is also about those social conditions preceding the English Reformation. It is not meant to be, however, a teleological study leading inescapably to the Reformation Parliament. Rather, I have analyzed a pre-Reformation ecclesiastical judicial system in London and have argued that records of these church courts give us good evidence of the secularization of people's attitudes in London just before the Reformation.

That much of European society became "secularized" during the early modern period is a commonplace among historians. Indeed, secularization is usually taken as one of the primary characteristics of a new, post-medieval age. It is a conceptual, abstract thread that forms the seam between medieval and modern in textbooks. My task is to

1. The best new work on the Reformation Parliament is Stanford Lehmberg, *The Reformation Parliament, 1529–1536* (Cambridge, 1970).
2. F. M. Powicke, *The Reformation in England* (New York, 1961), p. 51.
3. A. G. Dickens, *The English Reformation* (London, 1964), p. 64. Dickens devotes chapters 1–5 to outlining the "basic conditions which made possible" the English Reformation.

give the term concreteness, to explicate just how secularization as a process worked over a period of time and in a specific place. Professor Richard Helmholz through his study of English legal records has already pointed to the way that English society was becoming secularized during the first half of the sixteenth century.[4] My evidence for a specific locality—London—and a specific time will point to the same conclusion, and I will argue that before the English Reformation a profound shift in attitudes of lay people had already taken place.

G. R. Elton has observed that of all places in England during the 1530s, "London seemed almost the least distracted." He attributes this calmness primarily to London's proximity to the king's courts and administration.[5] I will argue from my evidence that the Londoners' lack of distraction at Reformation probably was due to changed lay attitudes rather than a brooding threat of the king's police powers. There was in pre-Reformation London, we shall see, a move away from—and a disenchantment with—church court jurisdiction by Londoners, and a corresponding appeal by the same men and women to secular authorities to hear "spiritual" suits. The move to secular authorities, like drifting sands which insensibly create new shapes, reordered loyalties to authority in pre-Reformation London. Church courts seem to have appeared to many Londoners after the 1490s lax and incapable of bringing wrongdoers to justice. Where Londoners felt that they could no longer find stringent justice in church courts, they sought justice in secular, city courts. Secular justice in the mayor's court was much harsher than church court justice. In pre-Reformation London, litigants seem to have come to expect the immediate results which the secular courts could provide. Hence, there was a shift in the "dynamic center" of overlapping legal systems, from ecclesiastical to secular—and with this shift a "re-formation" of laymen's loyalties, a secularization of attitudes.[6]

Church courts were never a purely ecclesiastical phenomenon. They were a part of an encompassing legal system that performed a peculiar form of social and moral control. The courts, in other words, must be understood within a system—a conceptual framework—made up of

4. Richard Helmholz, "Assumpsit and *Fidei Laesio*," *Law Quarterly Review* 91 (1975), 431.

5. G. R. Elton, *Policy and Police* (Cambridge, Eng., 1972), p. 160.

6. Image of a "dynamic center" from Leopold Pospíšil, *Anthropology of Law: A Comparative Theory* (New York, 1971), p. 343. See also A. B. Ferguson, *The Articulate Citizen and the English Renaissance* (Durham, N.C., 1965), p. 4, for the laity's search for remedy in the king's courts.

many other interlocking parts: rules of behavior (canon law, local custom), a system of compulsion to enforce these rules (church courts), attitudes of lay people toward court sanctions, and lay attitudes toward those normative rules that they wanted enforced or ignored.[7] It is easier to devise an abstract sociological model of a legal system than to fit real courts into abstract systems. In real life the many parts of a system do not fit neatly together. Thus, the picture of ecclesiastical jurisprudence that I construct in Chapter II is an untidy model made up of elements from modern legal theorists and of actual legal processes in pre-Reformation London.

The study of the actual behavior of church courts is a relatively new field. Little work has been done especially on the criminal side of the law. Only a handful of English church courts have been analyzed.[8] The paucity of our knowledge of these courts is justification enough for adding a monograph on the subject. We are just beginning to make sense of invaluable, unwieldy collections of English church court records. My findings on the behavior of London church courts often contradict the findings of other researchers working in different regions. Stephen Lander, for example, has argued that the church courts of Chichester before 1530 were undergoing administrative reform, and consequently had become active and popular; these same courts de-

7. I have been influenced especially by Alf Ross, *Towards a Realistic Jurisprudence: A Criticism of the Duality in Law,* trans. Annie I. Fausbøll (Copenhagen, 1946), see esp. pp. 147–48.

8. See Brian Woodcock, *Medieval Ecclesiastical Courts in the Diocese of Canterbury* (London, 1952); R. W. Dunning, "The Wells Consistory Court in the Fifteenth Century," *Proceedings of the Somerset Archaeological and Natural History Society* 106 (1961/2), 46–61; F. S. Hockaday, "The Consistory Court of the Diocese of Gloucester," *Transactions of the Bristol and Gloucestershire Archaeological Society* 46 (1925), 195–287; R. Marchant, *The Church under the Law: Justice, Administration and Discipline in the Diocese of York, 1560–1640* (Cambridge, Eng., 1969); Colin Morris, "A Consistory Court in the Middle Ages," *Journal of Ecclesiastical History* 14 (1963), 150–159, and "The Commissary of the Bishop in the Diocese of Lincoln," *Journal of Ecclesiastical History* 10 (1959), 50–65; C. I. A. Ritchie, *The Ecclesiastical Courts of York* (Arbroath, 1956); Ralph Houlbrooke, "The Decline of Ecclesiastical Jurisdiction under the Tudors," and Stephen Lander, "Church Courts and the Reformation in the Diocese of Chichester, 1500–1558," both in R. O'Day and F. Heal, *Continuity and Change: Personnel and Administration of the Church of England, 1500–1642* (Leicester, 1976); Margaret Bowker, ed., *An Episcopal Court Book for the Diocese of Lincoln 1514–1520,* Lincoln Record Society 61 (Lincoln, 1963), and her article, "Some Archdeacons' Court Books and the Commons' Supplication against the Ordinaries of 1532," in *The Study of Medieval Records: Essays in Honour of Kathleen Major,* ed. D. A. Bullough and R. L. Story (Oxford, 1971), pp. 282–316; and E. M. Elvey, ed., *The Courts of the Archdeacon of Buckingham, 1483–1523,* Buckinghamshire Record Society 19 (Aylesbury, 1975).

clined only during the 1530s as a result of attacks by government officials which "undermined their authority permanently." [9] In London, I have found, there was a similar—albeit minor—reform of church court procedures around the turn of the sixteenth century; but the decline of and loss of respect for church authority came also around the turn of the sixteenth century. The decline of London's courts, in other words, was a contributing factor to Reformation, not a result of it. Margaret Bowker, working with archdeacons' court books of Lincoln (c. 1480–1522) has found evidence supporting an earlier thesis of Michael Kelly, that the commons in 1532 were afraid of and objected to the effectiveness of church courts.[10] I will argue the opposite, that litigants had drifted away from London church courts long before the Reformation because of the haphazard, ineffective nature of ecclesiastical justice. There is no reason for London evidence to confirm evidence elsewhere. London was always the exception in England.

Those of us who have worked on church court records all agree upon one point: at some time during the early sixteenth century, English church courts declined in prestige and popularity; wherever and whenever this decline took place, it was caused in part by or was accompanied by a disenchantment with church court sanctions.[11] Sanctions, after all, are a *sine qua non* of a legal system.[12]

Because of limitations of surviving documentation, my research necessarily has been limited to London, the city and its suburbs. Documentation also limits the time scope. Earliest surviving church court records for London date from 1470 and continue sporadically through 1516. Because of the capricious survival of bureaucratic data, therefore, beginning and terminal dates for a study of London courts are wrenched arbitrarily out of time. The court records are inseparable

9. Lander, "Church Courts and the Reformation," p. 215.
10. Bowker, "Some Archdeacons' Court Books," pp. 282–316; Michael Kelly, "The Submission of the Clergy," *Transactions of the Royal Historical Society*, 5th Series, 15 (1965), 97–119. Cf. G. R. Elton, *Reform and Reformation: England, 1509–1558* (Cambridge, Mass., 1977), p. 9, who states that the "oppressive and omnipresent network of the ecclesiastical courts excited much hatred"; he further states that these popular clichés were unfounded.
11. See Lander, "Church Courts and the Reformation"; Houlbrooke, "The Decline of Ecclesiastical Jurisdiction," p. 245; and O'Day and Heal's introduction to *Continuity and Change*, p. 7.
12. Cf. especially E. A. Hoebel, *The Law of Primitive Man* (Cambridge, Mass., 1964), p. 26. He had in mind "physical coercion by a socially authorized agent," but the moral and social coercion of an ecclesiastical court (e.g., excommunication) may also be considered a sanction.

from the specific courts in which they were produced; I have reserved a discussion of the nature of these records for the following chapter on specific London courts.

I have felt compelled as well to go beyond legal history and legal systems into London's political and social structure. For, as Elton has correctly remarked, "Urban history has attracted hardly anyone so far, and London especially returns a blank." [13] In London's wards and parishes we must recover the methods and procedures by which wrongdoers were reported to the proper authorities for correction. And with the help of corollary evidence from city records, we can better make sense of the voluminous yet curt London church court records.

Because of the imposing and seemingly intractable mass of surviving London ecclesiastical court records, the human institution buried beneath scribal entries has become badly obscured. Yet these courts touched the lives of pre-Reformation Londoners as few other institutions could. My task, therefore, has been to recover this institution, and to fit it into London society, into a legal system, and into the flow of history before the English Reformation.

13. Elton, *Reform and Reformation*, p. 399.

BLANK PAGE

I

The Courts

During the late Middle Ages, the bishop of London had many courts which were held in his name and which sat in many different locations in the city of London and throughout the diocese. Bishops had the power to hear any case in their dioceses, but they had long since delegated this authority to professional legists. When a rare suit was heard by a bishop personally, his court was known as the Audience Court. We have no evidence of the activities of such a court in London; rather, our surviving evidence is from long-established, professionally staffed courts in which the bishop took no part in person.[1]

1. The Consistory Court

The bishop's highest court was his consistory, which convened weekly—sometimes biweekly—in the Long Chapel of St. Paul's Cathedral.[2] Its judge was the official-principal, who was a university-trained doctor of canon and/or civil law. Attached also to this court were the bishop's registrar (scribe of acts) and a group of apparitors who delivered court summonses.

We know very little about the activities of this court because so few records survive. There are only five deposition books and one actual court book, the "Liber assignationum" (1500–1505).[3] The Liber assignationum really belonged to the court lawyers, the proctors, for it records their appearances and schedules of future appearances. From this record we rarely can discern the nature of the case before the court. It does not give us actual arguments of proctors, only formal, routine pleadings; it does not give us judicial decisions, only a date for proctors to appear to hear a decision; it does not give us evidence or testimony, only assignments to proctors and court examiners to obtain depositions from witnesses. Actual testimony is contained in the deposition books, five of which survive for pre-Reformation London, but

1. A diagram of the church courts in London may be found in Figure 1 on p. 9.
2. See C. R. Cheney, *Handbook of Dates for Students of English History* (London, 1961), p. 74, for a discussion of how the London consistory calendar meshed with those of other London courts.
3. Lib. assign., DL/C/1; Lib. exam., DL/C/205–208; Guild. Lib. MS 9065.

none of which covers the years of the Liber assignationum, 1500–1505. Thus, they do not augment the Liber assignationum; but they do give us valuable examples of the types of cases heard in consistory—usually marriage and testamentary suits—and the types of questions posed to elicit certain points of law.

Court procedure alone distinguished the bishop's consistory from his lower courts. In consistory, cases followed an intricate course devised by medieval academic proceduralists; the procedure joined together elements from the older Roman Law with the newer canonic system. Thomas Oughton, an eighteenth-century canonist working with Elizabethan sources, divided this procedure comprehensibly into three phases: (1) *litis contestatio*, during which took place all preparatory actions before a suit was joined, such as issuance of court summonses, certification that they had been delivered, appointment of proctors (that is, representatives of litigants), presentation of a charge (a "libel" if a civil suit, an "article" if criminal), response to the charge by a defendant, and finally assignment of a trial date; (2) *probatio*, or the trial, during which witnesses were examined by a court examiner, their responses put in writing, and written depositions submitted to the court; and (3) *sentencia*, or the court sentence based on written depositions.[4] This neat tripartite procedure was not delineated as such by fifteenth-century canonists, but the sequence in the procedure outlined is what took place in court. After a sentence was pronounced, court expenses usually were charged to the losing party; this, however, was at the judge's discretion.

The Liber assignationum listed all the steps taken when the assistance of a proctor was needed, but it does not tell us the details of any one step in the procedure. Written depositions were kept in separate deposition books as described above, and sentences were kept in yet other books—none of which has survived.

All pleas and actions were in writing; each procedural step required a separate appearance in court; and postponements were allowed in order that interlocutory questions could be answered. Consequently, this full or "plenary" procedure was thorough and time-consuming. Cases moved along at a regular pace; during each session of court a case made its appearance along one of a progression of procedural steps. Cases in consistory often required several terms—usually over a

4. Thomas Oughton, *Ordo judiciorum* (London, 1738), pp. 31–37. For the early development of the various steps in procedure from the Roman Law model, see Jane Sayers, *Papal Judges Delegate in the Province of Canterbury, 1198–1254* (Oxford, 1971), pp. 42–99.

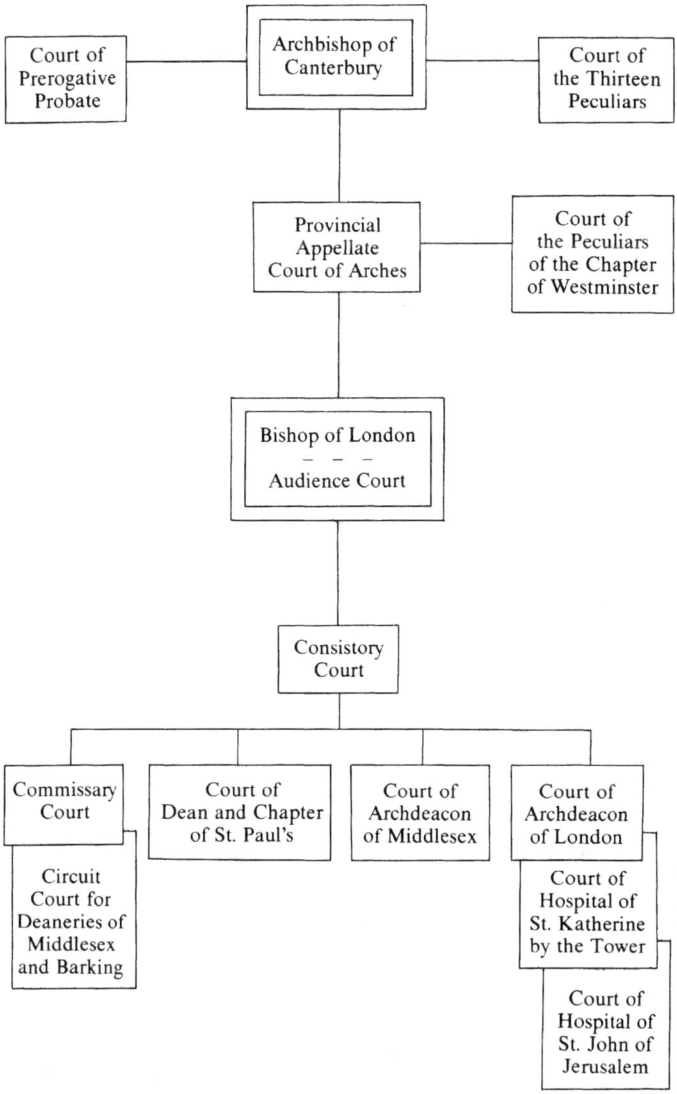

FIGURE 1

Church Courts in the City and Suburbs of London, c. 1500

year—to reach a conclusion. Because of this complex procedure, all litigants required professional help: proctors to represent them in court and advocates to plead the legal merits of their cases before a judge.

A few commissions to consistory court judges by London bishops have survived. From these commissions we have a clear idea of the broad jurisdiction of London officials-principal. Extant commissions invariably contain five separate clauses which define the official's delegated authority. His jurisdiction covered the entire diocese of London, including the city of London; his judicial authority was the same as the bishop's, that is, there were no appeals from consistory to the bishop, but rather from consistory to the archbishop; he was to hear all matters touching matrimony, divorce, and benefices; he was to inquire into, correct, and punish excesses, crimes, and transgressions wherever found; and he was ordered not to infringe on the powers of other officials, that is, of lower diocesan judges.[5]

2. The Commissary Court

In stark contrast to London's highly professional consistory court was the bishop's lower commissary court, whose chief magistrate was the commissary-general. The commissary court, like a modern-day magistrate's court, followed summary procedures; all pleadings were given *viva voce* in open court. Litigants, as a rule, were not represented by counsel; trial, therefore, was a direct confrontation between judge and litigant, without professional legists as mediators to define and shape the legal dispute. Guilt or innocence was not decided by a judge's scrutiny of written depositions, but rather by compurgation: to prove his "innocence"—actually his good reputation—a defendant needed only to produce three or four "honest" neighbors as compurgators or oath-helpers to swear in court that they believed the defendant's own oath of innocence. If a defendant failed his compurgation, he was pronounced guilty. If complications arose, for example, over questions concerning the honesty of compurgators, a case was immediately sent to consistory court, where the wheels of justice

5. Guild. Lib., Registers of Hill, Savage, Warham, and Barons, MS 9531/8, fols. 21r, 38r (Bishop Thomas Savage to Edward Vaughn and Bishop William Warham to William Mors). Vaughn's commission, with slight changes in the word order, is also in Lib. assign., fol. 1r–v. For other commissions, see Lib. assign., fols. 23r, 194r, 217r. See also the fifteenth-century formulary book, British Library, Harl. MS 2179, fol. 24v, for a commission to a London official-principal containing only two clauses: that the official's jurisidiction is the same as the bishop's; and that the official was not to infringe on the jurisdictions of other officials.

ground more finely but more slowly and expensively. For reasons which will be explained later, commissary court costs—scribes' and summoners' fees—were borne by defendants alone, whether innocent or guilty.

Assisting the commissary-general was a court scribe who kept a terse, daily record in a court book of appearances and pleadings of litigants. Today, eleven such court books survive, each of which is titled "Acta quoad correctionem delinquentium." [6] Entries in the court book contain similar information: first was entered the name of a defendant and the charge against him; at the same time, in the margin of the book, the scribe noted the defendant's parish and the name (often just the initial) of the summoner who was assigned to deliver the summons to the defendant. There then followed a record of appearances: the charge; a pleading to the charge; the success or failure of compurgation; any related pleadings; and the sentence of the judge if the case reached some conclusion. Unlike the consistory court book (the Liber assignationum), in which a case history is scattered through the folios, the commissary court book contains a complete case history encapsulated in a single abbreviated entry. A typical example is the following case of William Mariott:

> Sepulcri W Willielmus Mariott adulteravit cum Johanna Mason. emanavit littera viis et modis quia non potuit apprehendi. xxvi° die Januarij [1490] comparuit et negavit articulum et purgare se 4ª [apparently; inserted] die Jovis proximo. xxx° die Januarii comparuit et negavit articulum et purgavit se cum vicinis viz. Thoma Redenos, Johanne Atkynson et solvit feodum et dimittitur.[7]

Our earliest surviving commissary court book dates from 1470. The final book of the series ends in 1516. These records then fall silent until 1582. The terminal date, 1516, is especially unfortunate; two potentially valuable court books, for 1518 to 1526, and 1526 to 1529, have disappeared within the past 130 years. Consequently, we miss much

6. Acta correct., MSS 9064/1–11. These court books are cited hereafter by volume number (1–11) and folio. Sample folios are edited in Appendix B. See also the Bibliography of Manuscript Sources.

7. Acta correct., vol. 4, fol. 17v. The parish is St. Sepulcre, just outside the west gate of the city. The apparitor, "W", is William James. James could not find Mariott, who was then summoned by any "ways and means," *viis et modis;* that is, the summoner publicly announced the summons to court on the streets of Mariott's parish. For a statement of my editorial policy on all citations from the Acta Correct., see Appendix B, p. 149.

information from the 1520s which might have given us solid evidence of London church court activities during those crucial years preceding the Reformation Parliament. All that we possess of the two lost court books are a few select cases, published in 1847 as a series of church court precedents by the meticulous church historian Archdeacon William Hale.[8] When editing portions of the London court books, Hale skimmed off from thousands of cases only those which most interested him. Hale had a keen eye for unusual and colorful criminal cases, but his edited book of precedents is of little value in understanding the workaday business of ecclesiastical justice. If we are to understand fully the nature of London church courts, we must comprehend what routinely took place in court. Much of my research—and the heart of this monograph—therefore, is to be found in the routine, day-to-day acts of the commissary court from 1470 through 1516.

The jurisdiction of the bishop's commissary court was much more constricted than that of his consistory court. We possess a lone surviving commission from a London bishop to a commissary-general in which the limited jurisdiction of the commissary court is delineated. The commissary's jurisdiction extended only to the city of London and the deaneries of Middlesex and Barking (those parishes and villages immediately surrounding the city). The commissary-general was to correct and punish crimes and excesses.[9] And he was given full power over probate of wills: that is, the commissary court was the probate court for London.[10]

Thus, the commissary court was a city court, restricted largely to criminal cases and probate. By way of contrast, the higher consistory court was diocese-wide and heard primarily civil suits, although it could and did hear criminal and testamentary matters. Within the city of London, there were no hard lines of demarcation between the two courts. After the turn of the sixteenth century, as we shall see, much consistory business was heard in commissary court with an abbreviated, plenary-like procedure.[11]

8. William H. Hale, *A Series of Precedents and Proceedings in Criminal Causes Extending from the Year 1475 to 1640, Extracted from the Act-Books of Ecclesiastical Courts in the Diocese of London, Illustrative of the Discipline of the Church of England* (London, 1847).

9. Cf. the formulary book, British Library, Harl. MS 2179, fols. 25v–26r, in which a sample fifteenth-century commission to a London commissary-general included powers also to inquire into crime.

10. Guild. Lib., Register Kempe, MS 9531/7, fol. 222r: from Richard Lichfield, custodian of spiritualities, *sede vacante*, to William Lichfield (a relative?), dated 23 April 1489: also in Guild. Lib., Register of Wills, MS 9171/6, fol. 147v.

11. See chapters below on defamation and marriage suits. See also Appendix B, pp. 157–60, samples of Acta correct., vol. 11, fols. 322r, 327r.

Because of the commissary court's enormous volume of business, it sat several days per week—usually in St. Paul's Cathedral. I have tried to reconstruct a court calendar by plotting the days that the court sat for different years, but the results are disappointing. No obvious pattern emerges. The court sat anywhere from three to six days per week throughout the year. Court days were not always the same weekdays, although Wednesdays and Fridays were the busiest days for the court. Days on which the court was in recess are also baffling; they were not prominent saints' days. There seems not to have been a set court calendar, but rather court days seem to have been determined by the pressing work load, by the personal affairs and personal schedule of the judge, or by other London court calendars which precluded the commissary court from sitting.

The commissary judge also was responsible for the suburban deaneries of Middlesex and Barking, which were within his "general" commission, and he periodically went on circuit to these deaneries. The commissary-general took with him his scribe and certain apparitors (or "summoners") to villages like Stepney, Haringay, and West Ham—places which since have been swallowed into the Greater London Area and are marked today only by commuter train stops. One of the eleven surviving commissary court books is a separate court record for this circuit commissary court. Evidence from surviving probate records suggests that the commissary-general seems not to have gone on circuit after August 1528; rather, litigants from these suburban villages took their suits to London.[12]

Contemporary descriptions of actual church courts are rare. And descriptions by early Tudor Londoners concerning ecclesiastical justice are usually tainted by Reformation-minded hatred for court officers. Fortunately we possess a fifteenth-century comic, bawdy song in which an unidentified church court—a combination consistory and commissary court—is vividly described. The ballad lacks that Reformation animosity, and gives a sharp picture of court officers, various litigants, types of court procedure, and even the physical furniture of the court. In this picture of the court, the culprits are not the church court officers, but those more traditionally medieval rascals, a friar and a stepmother. The ballad recounts the story of a young boy named Jack who is charged in court for witchcraft; he is charged *viva voce* in court—like London's commissary court—by his stepmother and her friend, friar Topias. Jack, it so happened, had obtained a magic flute

12. The circuit court book is Acta correct., vol. 7 (for the years 1496–1500). The joining of the two courts of the commissary takes place in the records in Acta test., MS 9168/5, from fol. 59r.

with which he defended himself against his cruel stepmother and the friar; when he played his flute, all who heard were bewitched to laugh and dance uncontrollably. The ballad continues that on a court day (a Friday), the friar, the stepmother, and many other people

> floct to the court to heare eache case;
>   the Officiall was sett.
>
> Much civill matters were to doo,
> more libells read then one o tow
>   both against priest & clarke;
> Some there had testaments to proue
> some women there through wanton loue
>   which gott strokes in the darke.
>
> Each Proctor there did plead his case;
> when forth did stepp fryer Topias
>   and Iackes stepdame alsoe;
> "Sir Officiall," a-lowd said hee,
> "I haue brought a wicked boy to thee,
>   hath done me mightye woe;
>
> "he is a wiche, as I doe feare"
> . . . .
> "he is a Devill," quoth the wiffe,
> "& almost hath bereaued my liffe!"
> . . . .
> "Pipe on, Iack!" sayd the officiall,
> "& let me heare thy cuning all."
>   Iack blew his pipe full lowde
> That euery man start vp, & dancte;
> Proctors & preists, & somners pranct,
>   & all in that great crowde;
>
> Over the deske the officiall ran,
> & hopt Vpon the table, then
>   straight Iumpt vnto the flore.
> The fryer that danct as fast as hee,
> mett him midway, & dangerouslye
>   broke eithers face full sore.
>
> The register leapt from his pen,
> & hopt in the throng of men,
>   his inkhorne in his hande;
> with swinging round about his head,
> some he strucke blind, some almost dead,
>   some they cold hardly stand.

The proctors flung their bills about,
. . . .
The Somners, as they had beene woode,
leapt ore the formes & seates a goode,
  & wallowed on the earth.
Wenches that for their pennance came,
& other meeds of wordlye shame,
  danct euery one as fast.[13]

The scene ends in chaotic exhaustion when Jack stops blowing his pipe. The official equitably rules, after hearing Jack's side of the story, that Jack is not a witch and has a just cause against his stepmother and friar Topias.

Real courts obviously were not as chaotic as this. But London's commissary court was, like the above court, alive with proctors, priests, compurgators, prostitutes, summoners, and suitors—all jostling one another for a turn in court. And London's commissary court was, in fact, even more bawdy, more wildly rife with sexual offenders and defamatory sexual slurs.

3. Other London Church Courts

London diocese contained many other church courts whose activities must remain in darkness because their records have not survived. Each of the four archdeaconries in London diocese—London, Middlesex, Colchester, and Essex—had a court, but because of lack of records we rarely know so much as the name of an occasional judge.[14] Thus, surviving records have limited necessarily the scope of my research to the city of London and its suburbs.

The archdeaconries of London and Middlesex present a peculiar problem. Their jurisdictions overlapped that of London's commissary court, but we know little of the types of cases heard in the archdeacons' courts. We know that the archdeacon's court in London shared territorial jurisdiction with the commissary court because of certain entries which appear in commissary court records. When certain defendants were summoned to court, scribes noted that they introduced special pleas, *preventiones*, and were summarily dismissed from court. This was a plea by a defendant that he was under the jurisdiction of another

13. F. J. Furnivall, ed., *Bishop Percy's Folio Manuscript: Loose and Humorous Songs* (London, 1868), pp. 25–27.

14. In Acta correct., vol. 11, fol. 301r, it is noted that the archdeacon's court of London sat at the parish of St. Nicholas Macella.

court on the same charge; he proved his plea by exhibiting a certificate of *preventio* to that effect. Often the other court was noted in the records; more often than not it was the court of the archdeacon either of London or of Middlesex. Elizabeth Glaser, for example, was charged in court for pimping and prostitution; she produced in court her certificate of *preventio* and was dismissed—presumably without having to pay additional court costs:

> Elizabeth Glaser communis pronuba et communis meretrix. iii° die Decembris [1492] comparuit et negavit articulum et purgare se 7ª manu die Mercurii proximo. comparuit et introduxit prevencionem domini archidiaconi Londonensis.[15]

Elizabeth Glaser was from the parish of St. Mary Magdalene in Old Fish Street, which was within the commissary's jurisdiction as well. Curiously there seem to have been no boundaries separating an archdeacon's court from the commissary court; both seem to have been able to hear the same types of cases from the same London parishes.

Conflicting jurisdictions between diocesan and archidiaconal officials are not surprising; other dioceses faced the same problem. In the rambling diocese of Lincoln, for example, jurisdictional disputes during the late fourteenth and fifteenth centuries between archdeacons and bishops' commissaries were solved only by a hard-fought, sensible compromise; a similar jurisdictional conflict and agreement was reached in Chichester at about the same time.[16] What is striking in London is the apparent harmony between archdeacon and bishop's commissary-general. London episcopal records, which extend as far back as the early fourteenth century, give no hint of similar jealousy and strife between archdeacon and commissary; yet, as far as can be deduced from extant pleas of *preventio*, each official had similar judicial tasks among the same laity.

One explanation for this apparent harmony may lie in the enormous case loads facing London church courts. London's commissary court, at least, was far too busy to exclude other jurisdictions from its territory. Another and perhaps better reason for this harmony may be that there was a general, but not hard-and-fast, division of labor between the two courts. The archdeacons were responsible to ensure the proper physical condition of parish buildings, furniture, and ornaments. They

15. Acta correct., vol. 5, fol. 33v (35v in pencil). We do not know why she did not introduce the *preventio* on her first appearance.
16. Colin Morris, "The Commissary of the Bishop," pp. 50–65; Lander, "Church Courts and the Reformation," p. 216.

probably heard all legal disputes over the parish fabric because no such cases appear in either consistory or commissary court records. Parish churchwardens seem to have been answerable to their archdeacons rather than to the bishop's officers for parish monies and property. Churchwardens for St. Mary-at-Hill, for example, noted in their account book that their accounts for the year had been exhibited before the archdeacon of London for his approval.[17] Thus, the archdeacon's court seems to have had primary responsibility for the parish fabric, and occasionally it also heard litigation destined for the commissary. But strict definition of jurisdictions is not characteristic of London courts at this time.

Within the city and suburbs of London were at least five other ecclesiastical bodies with limited jurisdictions: the "peculiars" of the archbishop of Canterbury; the "peculiars" of the abbey and chapter of Westminster; the court of the dean and chapter of St. Paul's; and the courts of the priory hospitals of St. John of Jerusalem and St. Katherine's by the Tower. It is not readily clear who were suitors in these courts, whether the respective household officers (*familia*) of each religious corporation or the tenants of the corporations' properties. In the court of St. Paul's both tenants and cathedral officers were under the dean's jurisdiction. Tenants of the prebends and manors in St. Paul's, since at least 1287, had been freed from both bishop's and archdeacon's courts. The register of the statutes and customs of St. Paul's clearly shows the cathedral's territorial jurisdiction as well as its jurisdiction over its ministers.[18] In one recorded case—a plea to stop a probate action in commissary court—executors of a will argued successfully that the deceased, one Henry Stokes of St. Faith's parish, was a "virgarius in Ecclesia Cathedrali Sancti Pauli Londonensis," and that, therefore, the dean and chapter had rightful jurisdiction. It is not clear here if Stokes, as a *virgarius*, was a virgate-holder of St. Paul's or a verger in the cathedral; *virgarius* may mean either.[19] In either case his will belonged in the dean's court.

17. Guild. Lib., MS 1239/2, fol. 84r.
18. William S. Simpson, ed., *Registrum statutorum et consuetudinum ecclesiae cathedralis Sancti Pauli Londinensis* (London, 1873), pp. 16 (customs c. 1450), 89, and 221 (customs during deanship of John Colet, 1505–1519): "Decani officium et potestas est, ut omnibus Canonicis, Presbiteris, Vicariis, et omnibus in Ecclesia ministrantibus, seu maneriis vel prebendis morantibus, in animarum regimine, morum correccione et jurisdiccione premineat, et causas omnes ad Capitulum spectantes audiat . . . " (p. 16).
19. Acta test., MS 9168/3, fol. 56v; a similar case in MS 9168/2, fol. 6r. See also Acta correct., vol. 8, fol. 161v, and vol. 11, fol. 316r, in which defendants from St. Andrew Holborn in an adultery case were dismissed from court "quia fuerunt iurisdictionis decani et capituli Sancti Pauli."

The courts of the priory hospitals of St. Katherine and St. John of Jerusalem may not have actually held separate courts for those under their jurisdiction. The evidence is slim indeed; but evidence suggests that their courts, in fact, may have been joined to the court of the archdeacon of London. We have two stray bits of evidence: in 1512 Thomas Lovell, official of the court of the archdeacon, signified an excommunication in Chancery on behalf of the jurisdiction of St. John of Jerusalem;[20] and in 1490 another official of the archdeacon, John Milet, who was also a plaintiff in the defamation suit, was styled "officialem domini archideaconi Londonensis ac Commissarium generalem jurisdiccionis Sancte Katherine iuxta turrim Londonensis."[21] We do not know who was within the jurisdiction of these courts. St. John's (the Hospitallers) had an exclusive jurisdiction from the twelfth century, and St. Katherine's from perhaps the mid-fifteenth century.[22]

Within the city and suburbs of London were two small jurisdictions which were completely beyond the control of the bishop of London: the "peculiars" of the archbishop of Canterbury and of the abbey of Westminster. Thirteen city parishes owed their patronage to the archbishop of Canterbury and took their legal disputes to the dean of the peculiars, i.e., the rector of the parish of St. Mary of Arches (who was also the commissary of the official of Canterbury). A similar court was held for those belonging to certain Middlesex parishes that owed their patronage to the abbey of Westminster.

4. Court of Arches

Because of its location in England's capital, the archbishop's court of the peculiars early in its history came to attract appellate business from Canterbury province: soon there grew two separate courts of the arch-

20. P. R. O., Significations of Excommunication, C 85/126, #20 (25 August 1512). See also Acta correct., vol. 9, fol. 41v, in which defendants were dismissed from court "quia sunt in jurisdictionis domini Sancti Johannis."
21. Acta correct., vol. 4, fol. 97v. Margaret Rowland had defamed John Milet.
22. The best account of St. Katherine's is by M. Redden in the *Victoria County History: London*, I (London, 1909), 525–30; although originally founded in 1148, St. Katherine's received most of its privileges, perhaps even its rights of jurisdiction, from Henry VI after his secretary, Thomas Bekington, was made its master. For the priory of St. John of Jerusalem, Clerkenwell (just beyond the northwest walls of London in Middlesex), see especially Helena Chew's account in *Victoria County History: Middlesex*, I (London, 1969), 193–200; from the first papal recognition of the order of the Hospitallers in the early twelfth century, its members were exempted from local ordinaries' jurisdictions. I do not know why the archdeacon of London rather than Middlesex seems to have administered St. John's court.

bishop in London, the peculiars and an appellate court. The appellate court was held in the rear portion of St. Mary of Arches (or St. Mary-le-Bow) and was popularly known as the court of Arches (*curia de Arcubus*). Little may be stated with certainty about this court in Tudor England because no records from before the mid-sixteenth century have survived.[23] The imposing, silent shadow of the court of Arches, nevertheless, falls on other London church courts. The prestigious provincial court drew to London ambitious professional ecclesiastical lawyers, judges, and scribes, who also staffed London diocesan courts in the city.[24]

5. Numbers of Cases

The London consistory court heard only a small portion of total ecclesiastical suits in London; many more were heard by the lower commissary court. Exact numbers of consistory court cases over a long period of time are largely a matter of conjecture because of the court's meager surviving records. We have quantitative evidence only for 1500 to 1505, and numbers for these years undoubtedly were influenced by a terrible two-year plague which devastated all England during 1499 and 1500. Plague effects on the London consistory, however, are not clear. Although it is true that a drop in population and the social havoc wrought by the plague may have caused litigation to decrease, it is also true that large numbers of deaths meant increased testamentary and probate business for church courts. All that can be stated with certainty is that only forty to sixty new cases per year were introduced into the London consistory between 1500 and 1505. Cases usually continued for as long as a year, which meant that the court calendar was full.

A probable downward trend in consistory court litigation during the early sixteenth century can be deduced indirectly from commissary court evidence. Trial procedures and types of cases introduced into the lower commissary court—for which we have abundant records—mirror in important ways litigation in the higher consistory court. Certain conclusions which argue for a decline in consistory court business can be mentioned briefly here, although a full discussion of each point is reserved for following chapters: (1) Breach of faith suits (for petty debt) disappeared completely from London consistory and commis-

23. See M. Doreen Slatter, "The Records of the Court of Arches," *Journal of Ecclesiastical History* 4 (1953), 141.

24. Judges, advocates, proctors, and scribes from the Arches practiced in all London church courts and Admiralty. I am preparing a series of articles on the personnel of London ecclesiastical courts.

sary courts in the early sixteenth century; they were taken by suitors instead to the mayor's court, which was formally established in 1518 as the court of Requests. (2) At the same time many marriage suits, normally heard in consistory court, were taken by suitors instead to the commissary court. (3) During the first decade of the sixteenth century, a change of procedure in defamation suits in the commissary court allowed plaintiffs to prove with witnesses that they had been defamed; consequently, defamation suits were no longer appealed to the higher consistory court with its "long form" procedure; defamation suits normally tried in the bishop's consistory then were tried in the commissary court much more quickly and much less expensively.

The decline of consistory court business in London after the turn of the sixteenth century is largely conjectural, but we are certain of a parallel decline in ecclesiastical court litigation in a neighboring diocese. We know, from Brian Woodcock, of a downward trend in litigation in the Canterbury diocesan consistory court; this court heard both plenary and summary cases and combined in one court the functions of both the London consistory and commissary courts. The total number of cases introduced into the Canterbury consistory for the year 1486 was 693; by the year 1499 the number had fallen to 380 cases, by 1522 to 223 cases; and by 1535 only 93 cases were introduced in consistory.[25] Colin Morris, in his study of the Lincoln consistory, also found a decline in civil suits during the early sixteenth century.[26] The diocese of Chichester seems to be the exception; Stephen Lander has found that these diocesan courts were still "active and popular" until about 1530.[27] Decline in consistory court business—as there certainly was at Canterbury and Lincoln, and probably also at London—meant a decline as well in appeals to the provincial court of Arches.

When we approach the London commissary court looking for hard statistical evidence, we are more successful, because complete daily court records survive for thirty-four of the forty-six years between 1470 and 1516. Yearly numbers of alleged offenders fluctuated greatly, from a high of 1,515 reported cases in the year 1490 to a low of 229 just ten years later in 1500 (see Fig. 2). Such fluctations in court business have a gruesome kinship with the periodic plagues and epidemics that ravaged early Tudor London. Londoners experienced an outbreak of plague at least once every decade, and over one decade, 1511–1521,

25. Woodcock, *Medieval Ecclesiastical Courts*, pp. 59–60, 125.

26. Colin Morris, "A Consistory Court in the Middle Ages," pp. 150–59.

27. Lander, "Church Courts and the Reformation," p. 228.

the plague never left London. Social disruptions due to epidemic are not difficult to imagine. People throughout Europe faced the same social disorders that followed in the wake of plague. A certain Italian notary, Ser Lapo Mazzei, for example, wrote to his friend, the merchant Francesco Datini, of a severe plague in Florence in 1400: "The shops scarce open their doors, the judges have left their benches; the Priors' Palace is empty; no man is seen in the courts. The dead are not mourned, and the only comfort is by the cross." [28]

During early Tudor years, moreover, London faced a new epidemic unique to England: the sweating sickness.[29] It first appeared in the autumn of 1485 and presumably was carried into London by Henry VII's army after the triumph of Bosworth field. Within a few days after the initial outbreak of this sweating fever in London, two successive mayors and six aldermen died. A second outbreak of sweating sickness appeared at the end of Henry VII's reign in 1508; this remarkable coincidence of disaster and royal succession led Polydore Vergil to see in the first two "sweats" a cosmic symbol for Henry's reign, "that Henry should only reign by the sweat of his brow, which was certainly to be the case." [30] Three more outbreaks of sweating sickness touched England (and London), in 1517, 1528 (when it spread to the continent for the first and only time), and 1551. The sickness then disappeared as mysteriously as it had appeared.[31]

The initial drop in litigation during a plague year perhaps was due as much to general social disruptions as to decline in population. But continued depressed figures in litigation for a year or two following a plague outbreak probably reflect a drop in total population. The awful plague of 1500, which had followed an equally awful plague in 1499, no doubt brought a flutter to the hearts of millenarians, but it also lodged itself ineradicably in the minds of Londoners as having been particularly terrible and devastating—even by normal standards of a disease-ridden age. Robert Fabyan, a contemporary London chroni-

28. Quoted from Iris Origo, *The Merchant of Prato* (London, 1960), p. 326.

29. For a recent assessment of the sweating sickness, see R. S. Gottfried, "Population, Plague, and the Sweating Sickness: Demographic Movements in Late Fifteenth-Century England," *Journal of British Studies* 17 (1977), 12–37.

30. Denys Hay, ed., *The Anglica Historia of Polydore Vergil A.D. 1485–1537*, Camden Society 74 (1950), p. 9.

31. For the dates of plagues and epidemics, I have relied especially on Charles Creighton, *A History of Epidemics in Britain*, 2 vols., 2nd ed. (New York, 1965), 1:230–31, 237–48, 287–94.

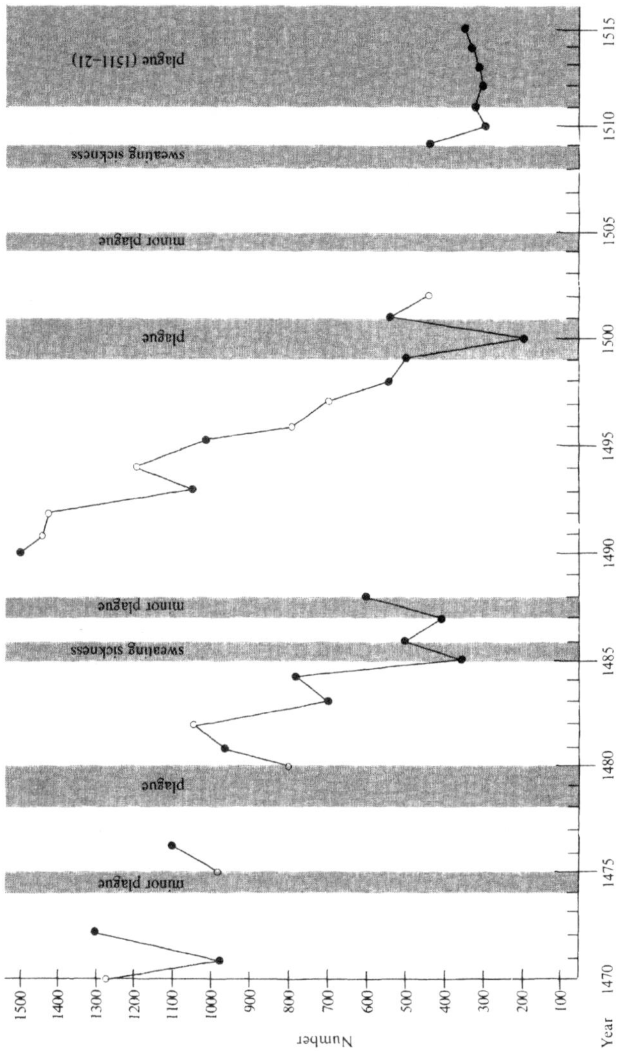

FIGURE 2

Number of Defendants Charged in the London Commissary Court, 1470–1516

cler, set the London death toll in 1500 alone at 20,000.[32] Even if this figure was an exaggeration, the percentage drop in population was no doubt great—perhaps one-fourth of the population perished.

Plague was not alone as a cause for decreased commissary court litigation. There began during the late 1490s a marked drift away from London church courts by London litigants. During non-plague years of the 1470s, 1480s, and early 1490s, suits introduced into commissary court generally numbered over a thousand. But during non-plague years in the late 1490s numbers of cases began to fall; during the non-plague years of 1509 and 1510—two years preceding another epidemic—numbers of suits introduced yearly into commissary court had already fallen to around four hundred. A drift away from London consistory and commissary courts was in process. For a generation of Londoners before the Reformation, church courts—the concrete, physical expression of abstract ecclesiastical authority and justice—were seen with new, ever increasingly critical eyes. Londoners before the Reformation already had called into question, rightly or wrongly, the competence of ecclesiastical justice.

32. Robert Fabyan, *The New Chronicles of England and France,* ed. Henry Ellis (London, 1811), p. 287. This has been republished as the *Great Chronicle of London,* ed. A. H. Thomas and I. D. Thornley (London, 1938), in which see p. 294 for the plague of 1500 (no mortality figures are given in this edition).

Explanation of Figure 2

Because of the peculiar beginning and terminal dates of the court book covering the years 1511–1516, I have computed these years from July to July. Thus the figure for 1511 represents July 1511 to July 1512, and so on. All earlier figures are for the calendar year.

● indicates that records are available for the full year.

o indicates that the annual total is an estimate based on records for only part of the year, as follows. 1470: 1337, based on 8-month total of 893. 1475: 976, based on 6-month total of 488. 1480: 823, based on 11-month total of 754. 1482: 1046, based on 9-month total of 785. 1491: 1461, based on 9-month total of 1171. 1492: 1454, based on 6-month total of 727. 1494: 1236, based on 8½-month total of 964. 1496: 793, based on 5-month total of 331. 1497: 722, based on 6½ month total of 392. 1502: 442, based on 6-month total of 221.

II

An Ecclesiastical Legal System

When I speak of an ecclesiastical legal system, I mean more than mere written rules or canon law. I mean also the behavior and the attitudes of those who administer the rules as well as the behavior and attitudes of those for whom these rules are designed.[1] Thus, when approaching church courts in pre-Reformation London, it is necessary to go beyond canon law, beyond the courtroom, into the streets of London—indeed into the minds and actions, as far as possible, of Londoners themselves. The noisy fishwife, whose malicious gossip surfaced in court as a legal charge by the "public voice" against a neighbor, was as much a part of the legal system as career-minded judges and lawyers who gave legal shape to these rumors, or as an abstract "rule of law" which forbade such defamatory language in the first place. Attitudes of Londoners towards their courts of correction are an integral part of the ecclesiastical legal system. People's expectations of justice and the courtroom reality of it were not in pre-Reformation London the same; there was—and is—a tension between the two. This tension will become apparent in my evidence below and is important for my thesis to explain why Londoners largely abandoned their church courts during the three or four decades preceding the English Reformation. But now, to comprehend a "legal system," we must briefly go through each element of procedure, from initial personal conflicts in the streets of London to resolution of these conflicts in the courts.

1. London and Londoners

London was not much different from other urban areas that today we call "pre-industrial cities." This label is commonly pasted on any urbanized unit, past or present, which is not as small as a rural village yet which has not been touched by modern technology and industrialization. Such pre-industrial cities have many similar characteristics.[2]

1. Cf. Ross, *Towards a Realistic Jurisprudence*, pp. 147–48; and Sigmund Freud, *Civilization and Its Discontents*, trans. James Strachy (New York, 1963), p. 75.
2. For the pre-industrial city in general, with a summary of the scholarly works on such cities world-wide, see Gideon Sjoberg, *The Preindustrial City: Past and Present* (New York, 1960).

Today if one is to sense the texture of medieval London life, one could better do so in, say, the din of North African bazaars than in modern London or large English market towns.

Pre-Reformation London, like other medieval cities, was girded by a wall, although urban dwellings had long since spilled outside its walls. The primary market areas around St. Paul's Cathedral and along Cheapside were probably congested, crowded, and noisy by day. Vendors hawked their wares from carts, water-bearers brought to the city skins and jugs of water slung over the backs of oxen, numerous shops and stalls opened directly onto the street, geese from the countryside were driven through the streets to be slaughtered. Men, women, children, and innumerable beasts were all caught up in the jostling and shouting. Houses, inns, and shops huddled tightly together, each with a sign in front to identify the building: the Cock, the Two Nuns, the Cardinal's Hat, the King's Head, in a paisley print of images and color.

Yet London, like other medieval cities, had a "rural spaciousness." After all, it contained only forty to seventy thousand souls. There were planted fields, kitchen gardens, and tree-filled courtyards, from which Lewis Mumford somewhat romantically heard the songs of birds and smelled the garlands of flowers. Mumford, turning a fish-eye to smelly, modern, industrial cities, eloquently eulogized the earthy barnyard smells and enclosed blocks of housing of a medieval city; to him the medieval religious spirit had brought to the city the quiet sense of a cloister—the medieval city offered Mumford only rest and repose.[3] He was no doubt partially correct.

A medieval city, in fact, had a split personality. It was at once uniquely, turbulently urban and comfortably rural. Populations were comprised of old city-dwellers and a large, steady infusion of country folk. Country values were never totally lost in cities. It has become a commonplace among urban historians that the medieval city could not sustain its own population; and it has been estimated that in any one city as many as one-third of the population had been born and bred in country villages.[4] In pre-Reformation London, rapid recurrence of

3. Lewis Mumford, *The City in History* (New York, 1961), pp. 369–71. Population estimates for medieval London are notoriously difficult; see J. D. Mackie, *The Early Tudors* (Oxford, 1957), p. 41. Mackie guessed London's population to be about 75,000 under Henry VII.

4. L. K. Little, "The Size and Governance of Medieval Communities," *Studia Gratiana* 15 (1972), 386–87. For an excellent earlier estimate of the medieval city's inability to reproduce itself see J. E. T. Rogers, *A History of Agriculture and Prices in England, 1259–1793*, 7 vols. (Oxford, 1866–1902), 4:102.

plagues and epidemics ensured a high replacement rate of native city-dwellers with country folk.

Many country folk who drifted into London, however, were as unwanted by city fathers as they were desperate for survival. They often represented that scourge of all European towns and cities: vagabondage. The problem of vagabonds had no real solution; it strained the city fathers' ideals of charity, baffled them as to why there were so many aimless wanderers, and angered them that these vagabonds contributed to the crime, pandering, and prostitution in the city. Minutes of meetings of London's mayor and aldermen contain a constant refrain of the need to rid the city of vagabonds. In 1473 Edward IV issued a proclamation (reissued two years later by the mayor and aldermen of London) against those who

> beyng strong and mighty of body . . . wander a bought from town to town as vagabondes sowyng sedicious langages whereby the comon people many tymes be put in grete fere and Jeobardy of their lyves and losses of their goodes and many other gret inconveniences folowen by occasion of the same as murdres roberes riots and other myschifes to the gret disturbaunce of the people. . . .

In a futile gesture, London officials ordered them to return to work in the fields or to their normal business under pain of imprisonment.[5]

We cannot, nor could the city fathers, estimate how many vagabonds drifted into London each year. Nuisances caused by vagabonds probably made their numbers seem greater than they really were. But the crime, the prostitution, and the ceaseless begging were real enough and kept civic and church courts busy. Thus in 1518 civic authorities made an attempt to identify and license only legitimate beggars: the old, the blind, and the lame. Aldermen were required to certify legitimate beggars in their wards by giving them metal tokens which were to be pinned on the beggars' cloaks. Because these tokens were issued by the city, we know from civic records approximately how many "legitimate" beggars there were. Most aldermen only approximated numbers of beggars in their wards and asked for tokens in round figures of twenty, thirty, or forty. An alderman himself decided what constituted a legitimate beggar; we know nothing of the actual selection process or what became of the tokens after they were issued. Alderman Thomas Baldry of Cordwainer Ward—a quiet ward within the city walls—asked only for one token for his ward; but Alderman Thomas Semer of Fleet Ward (or Farringdon Without) asked for 200 tokens for the many beg-

5. Journals, vol. 8, fols. 52v–53r, and 121r.

gars who crowded about the west gate of the city.[6] The total number of tokens applied for was 751, which was only an estimate and probably an overestimate. Thus, in 1518, about 700 people were licensed to beg in London. There were, in other words, as many licensed beggars in London as there were liveried merchants; Sylvia Thrupp set the number of London merchants also at about 700.[7] Beggars, however, were much more conspicuous than merchants. It must be remembered that the twenty-five London wards occupied little more than one square mile of land. The legitimate, tokened beggars would seem, at least today, like a throng. Numbers of beggars and vagabonds appeared to contemporaries as great, although these unfortunates perhaps comprised only a small percentage of London's population.

Vagabonds, beggars, and a resident urban underworld of prostitutes, thieves, and confidence men made up the bottom, amorphous, and perhaps the most crime-prone stratum of London's social structure. London's west end, Thomas Semer's Fleet Ward, especially provided an inordinate number of criminal complaints to church courts. During one typical year, 1493, there were 1,061 cases in the commissary court; 86 came from St. Bride's and St. Sepulcre's parishes in Fleet Ward; 2% of the parishes (2 from 100) in London provided about 8% of complaints to the court.[8]

Above this continually shifting underworld, people became increasingly defined both by themselves and by conventions of medieval urban society. As people took on legitimate definitions or places in society they became increasingly "respectable"—at least it was assumed that wealth and social position brought moral superiority. Londoners classified themselves in two ways: by legal status (citizen or noncitizen), and by craft membership or occupation.[9] At the top of London society was the merchant class, which Sylvia Thrupp has so superbly analyzed.[10] Thrupp rightly has argued that probably only this oligarchy of merchants in pre-Reformation London can be called a "class" with a class outlook on public affairs, that is, a consciousness of their status in marriage arrangements and ties of friendship.[11] Mer-

6. Letterbook N, fol. 76v: a list of each alderman's name and the numbers of tokens requested. For Aldermen Baldry and Semer and their wards see A. B. Beaven, *The Aldermen of the City of London, temp. Henry III–1908*, I (London, 1908), 115, 155.
7. Sylvia Thrupp, *The Merchant Class of Medieval London* (Ann Arbor, 1962), p. 43.
8. Acta correct., vol. 5, fols. 71r–180r.
9. Thrupp, *The Merchant Class*, p. 2; see also chapter 1 for a good summary of London and its community.
10. Ibid., especially pp. 14–27.
11. Ibid., p. 32; see also Peter Laslett, *The World We Have Lost*, 2nd ed. (New York, 1973), chap. 2, "A One Class Society," pp. 23–54.

chants dominated city, ward, and parish affairs, taking their "natural" place at the head of society. Thus, they are especially visible in surviving records.

Between the merchants on top and the beggars on the bottom were innumerable gradations of people, subtle distinctions within professions and hierarchies among the crafts and religious corporations. London was physically small, and the rich and the poor, the merchant and the pimp, seem in retrospect to mingle with and jostle each other as in a William Hogarth print. This seeming lack of neighborhoods is really an illusion. A medieval city like London had fairly well defined neighborhoods based on ethnic and occupational groups. Ethnic groups like the Lombards, the Spanish, and the German merchants of the Hanse had their own streets or quarters; and crafts like the shoemakers, the butchers, the goldsmiths, and the tanners also had their own streets. These were natural groupings of people of like interests.

Londoners then had many competing loyalties, to family, to craft, to "class," to ethnic group. Londoners also were organized two other ways which cut across economic and ethnic ties. A person belonged to one of London's one hundred parishes and he belonged to one of twenty-five political wards.

A parish was the center of religious life. Here daily masses were said; each Sunday, processions through the parish marked the beginning of divine services; and from the pulpit came news, lessons in salvation, moral exhortations, and royal proclamations and propaganda. Parish business, apart from divine services, was in the hands of parishioners, specifically the two lay churchwardens, who presumably were the more well-to-do members of the parish.[12] Churchwardens each served two-year terms, with a new man elected by parishioners yearly.[13] These two men governed parish properties, took in chantry monies out of which they paid chantry priests, arranged for and paid out of parish funds for the repairs and upkeep on the parish church, and were responsible for most parish litigation.

The important point to grasp is how much parishioners governed their own parishes through their elected representatives. What was a rector responsible for? Very little. Apart from divine services, for which invariably stipendiary priests and chaplains were employed, London

12. Cf. Thrupp, *The Merchant Class,* p. 25.

13. All but a few London parishes elected a new churchwarden each year for a two-year term. Only two exceptions have been found in twenty-five extant churchwarden account books: St. Mary Magdalene, Milkstreet, had two seemingly permanent churchwardens (Guild. Lib., MS 2596/1) and St. Michael, Cornhill, had three different churchwardens each year (Guild. Lib., MS 4071/1).

rectors had few responsibilities in their parishes. Day-to-day business of the parish, the parish property, the parish festivals, the parish monies, and reporting parish criminals to the church courts were the responsibilities of parishioners and their representatives.[14]

A Londoner also belonged to a political ward; however, he had much less say here than in parish affairs. The chief officer in a ward was the alderman, who was chosen for life by other London aldermen from a list of names submitted by the citizens of the ward—except Portsoken Ward, in which by ancient agreement the alderman was always the prior of Christ Church.[15] Portsoken Ward is special in my research because only there have pre-Reformation ward records survived.[16] (Portsoken Ward encompassed the east London suburbs immediately beyond the city wall; it was lightly populated and the entire ward was coterminous with only one parish, St. Botolph Aldgate.)

Below the tightly controlled oligarchy of aldermen were many other men on whom the aldermen relied and who really administered and policed their respective wards. There were members of the "common council," who by London ordinance were to be "the wisest and most wealthy persons" of the ward. Numbers of councilmen ranged from four to sixteen according to the population of a ward.[17] Portsoken Ward had only four council members, and they seem to have had permanent appointments to office. The council, among other duties, supervised the constables who were responsible for the police of the ward. Portsoken Ward, for example, had four constables. Service as constable seems to have been a practical prerequisite to selection on the common council. Lesser officers—scavengers, rakers, and bedels—were largely responsible for the physical upkeep of the ward, although they too had "police" powers. Scavengers, who had overall responsibility for the upkeep of the streets, and rakers, who actually swept the streets, were required by their oaths of office to report wrongdoers to the constable.[18] The bedel—only one in Portsoken Ward—was most

14. Cf. Peter Heath, *The English Parish Clergy on the Eve of the Reformation* (London, 1969), pp. 68–69.

15. Beaven, *The Aldermen of London*, 1:179. The priory of Christ Church, or Holy Trinity, had been founded in 1108 by Matilda, wife of Henry I, with a grant of the soke of Aldgate. To this was added the soke of the Cnihtengild, which was surrendered by the English Cnihtengild in 1125. The priors ultimately became the aldermen of Portsoken Ward, and remained so until the sixteenth-century dissolution of the monasteries.

16. See below, pp. 33–35.

17. H. T. Riley, ed., *Liber albus: The White Book of The City of London* (London, 1861), p. 36.

18. Ibid., pp. 34 (including n. 1), 221, 272.

overtly the "policeman on the beat." He took an oath that, among other things, he

> shall suffer no man accused of robbery or of evil covin, or huckster of ale, or woman keeping a brothel, or other woman commonly reputed of bad and evil life, to dwell in the same ward, but . . . shall forthwith shew the names of such unto the alderman.[19]

Constables, scavengers, rakers, and bedels were elected yearly at the meeting of the ward, the wardmoot, by the alderman "and the reputable men of the ward." [20]

Londoners, therefore, belonged to several social, economic, political, and religious groups, each of which bore some responsibility for the behavior of its members. These responsibilities often overlapped from one group to another. Just as loyalties to parish and ward overlapped, so did secular justice overlap ecclesiastical justice. It should not at all be surprising if churchwardens were also constables and members of common councils. We may be sure of one thing: parish churchwardens and ward officers wished to discipline the same types of wrongdoers. A prostitute or pimp was charged in church courts for "moral" crimes; but this same prostitute or pimp was also a social menace to the wards and to the city and was charged in city courts for civic crimes. Hence civic courts—temporal jurisdiction—cannot be considered apart from church courts—ecclesiastical jurisdiction. In theory there were clear lines which separated temporal from spiritual jurisdictions; in practice these lines were blurred, especially in the reporting and prosecution of criminal cases.

2. Reporting Suspects

The detection and reporting of wrongdoers to London's church courts was a problem that concerned only the criminal law. Civil suits all had by definition a named claimant who brought a defendant to court. Thus, this section will be restricted to describing the detection and reporting procedures of the criminal law, or more precisely in canonical vocabulary, of "office" cases (as opposed to "instance" cases, or civil suits). Office cases usually were heard in the commissary courts; instance cases usually in the consistory.

A brief review of office procedures is important if we are to understand what routinely took place in the commissary court. Prosecutions

19. Ibid., pp. 272–73.
20. Ibid., pp. 32–33.

from the office (*ex officio*) of the bishop originally had grown out of the uniquely canon law procedure of "inquisition." In an inquisition a court proceeded against a suspect (one with bad fame, *mala fama*) with no accuser other than the public voice (*publica vox*) or public rumor. The charge was a public charge rather than a private one. In other words, no one was certain that a suspect had committed a crime, but most members of a community, especially important persons, believed that the suspect was guilty of wrongdoing. This rumor was called a *diffamatio*—the same word that was used for "defamation"—and the defendant a *diffamatus*. An inquisition was a useful tool of the courts to get at the root of evil rumors, either to confirm the public voice or to clear a suspect and restore him to good fame (*bona fama*). A defendant, therefore was charged "from the office" of the bishop or judge; the "office" prosecuted the "public" charge. The judge could hold an inquisition and call witnesses from the community or he could order the defendant to purge himself with compurgators.[21]

What we really want to know is who, in fact, brought a suspect to the attention of the office. What can we learn from the standard court book formulas? Court books after 1502 contain wording that is much more precise, more self-consciously legal, than earlier volumes.[22] In almost all reported cases after 1502 a defendant was noted as having been referred to the court by his public fame ("notatur officio fama publica referente"). Yet this does not tell us who the accusers were. Canonists made a further distinction in *ex officio* cases between procedures *ex officio mero* and *ex officio promoto*—cases that are heard on their own merit, and those that are heard through the promotion of another. In either case, someone reports a suspect to the court. But a record of a prosecution *mero* need not contain the name of an accuser (e.g., a complaint by churchwardens against a notorious prostitute), while the record of a prosecution *promoto* will contain the name of an accuser and the case proceeds like a civil suit, x against y (e.g., a defamation suit).[23] This means that in many office cases (notably *ex officio mero*) we do not know the accuser unless the scribe casually mentions one—for example, that a constable apprehended a prostitute. Yet in many other office cases (notably *ex officio promoto*) the accuser is

21. See Paul Fournier, *Les officialités au Moyen Age* (Paris, 1880), pp. 262–75; also Oughton, *Ordo judiciorum*, pp. 31–33, and R. Naz, "Inquisition," *D.D.C.*, 5:1418–26. I have found only one office case in the consistory court book: a judge ordered an "inquisition" against an incontinent priest. See Lib. assign., fol. 203r.

22. See Appendix B, pp. 155–60, for samples of wording.

23. Cf. Oughton, *Ordo judiciorum*, pp. 31–33.

named as if it were a civil suit. In rare cases, the office actually brought charges on its own (for example, in a contempt of court charge); in those few cases, the judge assigned a court officer, usually a proctor in the court, as promoter to prosecute.[24]

Prosecutions *ex officio promoto* closely resemble civil actions and thus we know who detected and reported the suspects. Such actions over defamation, marriage, tithes, testaments, breach of faith, and the like made up between forty and fifty percent of commissary court litigation.

What then of the remaining fifty to sixty percent of defendants who yearly were brought to court to be tried *ex officio mero*? Who reported them to court? These men and women were accused of what may be lumped into a category called sexual offenses: prostitution, adultery, fornication, and pimping (see Appendix A, Tables 2-5). There were also stray parish scolds and dabblers in white magic who were charged in court without named accusers; but their numbers are negligible. We must look closely at London's sexual offenders because they alone taxed London's puny investigative, policing powers.

There were civic and religious procedures in London designed specifically to bring into the open suspected criminals. "Indicting juries" in the wards yearly drew up "wardmoot presentments" or lists of wrongdoers. And periodically the bishop of London or his official conducted visitations of London, collecting among other things indictments of suspected criminals. Both procedures were similar: prominent men from ward or parish reported to the proper authorities those neighbors who were suspected of moral failings; that is, political and religious groups were responsible for their own self-discipline. Preindustrial London was not unlike a village where most people knew of each other's activities. Gossip circulated, rumors spread, and those suspected of sexual offenses were readily reported to ward and parish authorities. Private squabbles, malicious gossip, and legitimate charges alike found their way to ward and parish officials, where the accusations were shaped and hardened by legal rules into specific charges.

Our best evidence for wardmoot presentments comes from Portsoken Ward, where there has survived a remarkable series of presentments for fifteen different years between 1465 and 1482 and for 1507. No other wardmoot presentments survive for pre-Reformation London. The Portsoken wardmoot, like other wardmoots, met yearly on 21

24. E.g., Acta correct., vol. 8, fols. 175v, 224v: "dominus assignavit Magistro [Hugo] Emlyn [procuratori curie de arcubus] in promotorem officii."

December, St. Thomas the Apostle's Day.[25] All householders and hired servants in the ward met together "for the correction of defaults, the removal of nuisances, and the promotion of well-being of such ward." [26] In order to expedite the inquiry constables of the ward made a list of twelve "reputable" men to act as an indicting jury, subject to the alderman's approval. Constables themselves may have changed yearly, but in Portsoken Ward at least they managed to choose many of the same men to serve on the jury year after year. Certain jurymen undoubtedly were the most well-to-do in the ward and took their place at the head of their community. Others held the lesser offices of scavenger and raker. Richard Sasword, a raker or streetsweeper in 1479, was empaneled on the jury almost every year from 1471 to 1481. William Segeram, raker from 1474 to 1478 and again in 1480, was on the jury from 1476 through 1482. Who better would know the nuisances of the ward than the man who walked every one of its streets? And a certain Richard Wellys was on the jury the same year that he was a scavenger.[27]

Indictments, or presentments, of this jury were prepared in two sections: the first listed indictments against wrongdoers, and the second against places, such as faulty chimneys that were susceptible to fire or dangerous cellar doors. The indicting jury of Portsoken Ward—and probably other wards as well—indicted virtually only sexual offenders. Of thirty-two people who were presented in 1471, for example, twenty-nine were accused prostitutes or pimps; one was a nuisance beggar and pickpocket, a second slandered his neighbors, and the third, Wat Whyte, was indicted "for kepyng of gees & dokes & for makyng of a diche in the kyngis hie way." And so it was the following year, 1472: twenty-four persons were presented, all sexual offenders but two—a beggar, and the same Wat Whyte for his ducks and geese.[28] Year after year the types of indictments remained the same, and year after year

25. For the date of wardmoots see Letterbook N, fol. 48v (28 September 1517): "Item yt ys agreed that every Alderman in his Warard [*sic*] yerly Upon Seynt Tomas Day in ther Court of Wardemote shall swere suche persons as shalbe Chosen of the Comen Councell accordyng to the olde custume." According to the *Liber albus*, the book of customs of London, wardmoots in the early fifteenth century met "twice at least, or oftener, in the year" (pp. 32–33).

26. *Liber albus*, p. 32. Cf. Port. Ward Present., membrane 3: the indicting jury "presentyn and Indyte these noyaunces and Defautes syngly expressyd by us found within the said Ward."

27. Port. Ward Present., membrane 11. In 1471, this same Richard Wellys and his wife were indicted by the ward for harboring suspicious and "misruled" people (membrane 6).

28. Ibid., membranes 6 and 7.

through the late fifteenth century many of the same suspects were indicted, apparently to little avail.

Wardmoot indictments were turned over to the mayor's court for prosecution. It would have been easy to prepare another copy of the indictments for the bishop's court of correction, but this was not done. Few of the suspects indicted by Portsoken Ward were charged also in commissary court during the same year. There was no direct reporting procedure from civic ward officers to church authorities. A few suspects, however, were charged for the same offenses in both civic and church courts; presumably they were tried and punished only by one of the courts. Katherine Martyn, for example, was charged as a prostitute in the London commissary court after she had been indicted by the wardmoot (the scribe noted in her case: "erat indictata a wardo"). Katherine was only charged in commissary court, and no action was taken against her. Joan Hoges was charged in commissary court both for prostitution and for adultery with the prior of Christchurch (St. Katherine's), but no action was taken against her: "fuit indictata in Wardo quo habitat per duodecim Legales viros Juratos." Joan Blond, tapster at the sign of "Le Bell" in Warwick Lane, also had been indicted by the wardmoot inquest ("indictata est in Le Warmoth quest") before she faced the same charge in commissary court; but she, unlike the others, had to face trial (and was acquitted).[29] Throughout the commissary court books, scribes often noted that a named prostitute or pimp "was indicted" (*indictata est*) but did not say by whom; this was the language of the wardmoot inquests where such indictments arose. It was natural that many prostitutes and pimps, who had been charged by their wards, ultimately appeared in London commissary court. Their indictments were proof of their ill "public fame," and thus, anybody could report them to the commissary court. (Charges against a suspect in wardmoot, however, were not always the same as those in commissary court: Christine Downs was indicted as a "strumpet" in Portsoken wardmoot, but was charged the same year in the commissary court only as a defamer; and John Younge, indicted as a beggar, was charged in church court as a defamer.)[30] Wardmoot inquests and church courts, therefore, had some connection. The connection, however, was not a direct reporting procedure but rather exposure to public fame by wards of certain notorious wrongdoers.

Church authorities, like ward officials, had a procedure for detecting and reporting suspects. This was the visitation of the parishes by the

29. Acta correct., vol. 1, fol. 7r; vol. 4, fol. 38r; vol. 5, fol. 60r.
30. Port. Ward Present., membrane 7; and Acta correct., vol. 1, fols. 149v, 175r.

bishop or his official. Parishioners were well organized to report the sins of their neighbors to church authorities. Unfortunately the earliest surviving episcopal visitation book for the city of London dates from 1561, and archidiaconal visitation books are extant only from 1662.[31] These records, nevertheless, are useful in showing procedures of visitation. At the time of the extant episcopal visitation books, and probably in pre-Reformation London also, a visitation of the city was completed in four days; a bishop or his representative sat on successive days in four different London parish churches roughly representing four quarters of the city. From the parishes of each quarter came the respective churchwardens to report on all parish properties and defects: the parish fabric, the administration of the sacraments, the behavior and morality of the incumbent priest, and the morality of parishioners. The findings or *comperta* of the visitors were then used as a basis of prosecution in church courts against malefactors, lay and cleric.

The excellent volumes of pre-Reformation Lincoln visitations, edited by A. H. Thompson, amply demonstrate the responsibility placed on parish churchwardens—not the incumbent clergy—for the moral governance of parishes.[32] Churchwardens were parish pooh-bahs on whose shoulders rested much responsibility for reporting wrongdoers for correction. It was they who drew up the visitation presentments to give to the visitors, who then turned the findings into *ex officio* court charges. In 1524, for example, the churchwardens of St. Margaret Pattens in London paid 6d "for makyng of a bill to present to the Offishall at the visitacion kept at Seint Mari at Hill." [33] Being the most prominent men in the parish, churchwardens probably were familiar with reports of wrongdoers in the wards.

We can be certain that visitations took place in pre-Reformation London, but we do not know how often—whether every third year (required of the bishop to visit his cathedral chapter) [34] or haphazardly

31. A copy of the visitation articles of an undated fifteenth-century episcopal visitation in London may be found in Richard Arnold (d. 1521), *The Customs of London,* ed. Francis Douce (London, 1811), pp. 273–76. The earliest London visitation record is Guild. Lib., MS 9537/2 for 1561. There is an earlier visitation book, dated 1554, for the counties of Essex and Hereford (MS 9537/1).

32. A. H. Thompson, ed., *Visitations in the Diocese of Lincoln, 1517–1531,* Lincoln Record Society 33, 35, and 37 (Lincoln, 1940–47).

33. Guild. Lib., MS 4570/1, fol. 90v; see also the churchwarden accounts from St. Botolph Aldersgate for 1507 (Guild. Lib., MS 1454, roll 27): "Also paid unto Carkyk for making off a Bill for the vysytaccion off the Bissop of London."

34. Guild. Lib., Registers Bonner and Thirlby, part I, MS 9531/12, fol. 63v. The composition between bishop and dean and chapter is dated 18 June 1450; why it appears in Bonner's register in the 1540s is a mystery; the document is from the episcopate of Thomas Kempe (1448–1489).

every ten years or so (as was the case in Lincoln diocese).[35] Commissary court records do not show where most charges originated, whether from visitation or from another source. But in one instance a scribe noted that Richard Forster, the chief apparitor, summoned two people to court, and that they were to answer to specific charges which had been asserted in a certain document ("responsum certis articulis in quadam cedula contentis eis et eorum cuilibet ex officio mero obiiciendis"), which suggests that this document (*cedula*) may have been a visitation presentment in which no named accusers were necessary.[36] And at arbitrary times in the commissary court books there was charged a group of defendants from the same parish; the charges seem to have been entered together, perhaps from a bill made up by churchwardens at visitation.[37]

The church court itself had no officer empowered to ferret out wrongdoers. There were summoners attached to the court, however, who presumably took upon themselves the additional duty of reporting wrongdoers to the court.[38] It was this function especially of summoners that brought them popular scorn. Brian Woodcock guessed that most criminal charges in Canterbury diocesan courts probably had originiated with apparitors who collected village gossip and rumors of ill fame. He supported his supposition with the researches of W. H. Hale on the commissary court records of London—the same records on which my study is based. Hale supposedly found that most criminal charges originated with summoners' inquisitions. But, in fact, Hale found no such thing.[39] Evidence of the summoner's role as an active policeman in London is skimpy. Once, a summoner reported to

35. See Thompson, ed., *Visitations*. Note especially the eleven-year lapse between the visitations of William Atwater (1519) and John Longland (1530), a crucial period in the development of anticlerical attitudes in rural England.

36. Acta correct., vol. 8, fol. 258r.

37. For example, see Acta correct., vol. 4, fols. 90v–91r (in pencil, 80v–81v), in which all defendants but one were from All Hallows the Greater. They all had the same summoner, but this was probably for convenience of delivery of citations.

38. A rare commission to an apparitor, John Medewall, may be found in Lambeth Palace Library, Reg. Morton, vol. 1, fols. 10r–v (dated 29 January 1487). Medewall was an apparitor for the dean of Arches, and he was empowered only to sequester goods in testamentary matters, to cite persons before the court in office and instance cases, and to cite executors to prove testaments. That summoners had "police" powers may be confirmed in the 1603 canons which declared that "they [apparitors] shall not take upon them the office of promotors or informers for the court" (Edmund Gibson, ed., *Codex juris ecclesiastici Anglicani* [London, 1713], pp. 1038–39, canon 138). I am currently preparing an article on London summoners.

39. Woodcock, *Medieval Ecclesiastical Courts*, pp. 49, 69; he relies on Hale's *Criminal Precedents*, pp. lvii–lviii. Woodcock claimed that based on "his survey of the early Act books of the London diocesan court," Hale had "found" that the apparitors

the court that he saw a certain man working on a feast day. Another time, a summoner reported a woman to the court for a sexual offense, based on what he had heard at the wardmoot inquest; the defendant successfully purged herself of the crime, and the judge, in a veiled warning to the summoner, warned that no one accuse her further of this crime under pain of excommunication. And a third time, the summoner William James contributed this evidence in court about a prostitute: a certain William Daventry had confessed in court to fornication with a prostitute named Alice; the summoner James added some information about Alice that he heard (in jest?) from the diocesan registrar Richard Spencer: "master Spencer told me his boyes to Jape the same Alice at home in his house."[40] Summoners undoubtedly reported others to court, but there is no evidence. Surviving evidence for *ex officio mero* cases suggests, in fact, that there was never a shortage of people to report criminals.

The parish clergy sometimes reported wrongdoers. On one occasion, a rector charged John Wode as an adulterer and father of Alice Mery's child; his charge was exhibited in court in a document ("prout in scedula per Rectorem ibidem exhibita").[41] Probably there was only one charge on the document, because no other charges from that parish were entered in the court book at the same time.

At least one case was referred to the London commissary court from another jurisdiction. A certain Joan Bray from Croyden confessed to fornication with a London priest, Richard Glover. The Croyden official then referred the priest's case to the London commissary.[42]

Occasionally throughout the period under investigation sexual offenders were caught (the normal phrase is *deprehensi erant*) by ward constables. These suspects, it was usually noted, were taken to one of the sheriff's prisons.[43] We do not know exactly how these suspects were charged in a church court after being held in a secular prison. It may be that constables as a matter of course turned over to church courts those accused of "spiritual" crimes, or it may be that incarceration of a

were responsible for most charges in court through their inquisitorial activities. Hale, in fact, was merely "inclined to believe" that most cases before the Reformation came to the courts through inquisitions (reports of ill fame) of apparitors; his inclination to belief was not supported by any more than the evil reputation of summoners.

40. Acta correct., vol. 6, fols. 100r, 106r.

41. Ibid., vol. 11, fol. 148r.

42. Ibid., vol. 11, fol. 27r.

43. For a good account of London prisons, see Gamini Salgado, *The Elizabethan Underworld* (London, 1977), pp. 163–182.

suspect brought him ill public fame and hence made him fair game for anyone to report to church authorities.

Where the court record notes that suspects were caught by the constable, this probably meant, in reality, that one neighbor saw or suspected another neighbor of an immoral act and roused the constables to investigate. Thus, scribes noted more precisely in a few cases that certain fornicators were captured by the constable and others ("capti fuerunt per constabularium et alios").[44] From one particular defamation suit we can see how the process worked: a woman had lost some laundered clothes from her washline and accused her neighbors of theft; the neighbors then countercharged against the woman with a defamation suit alleging that the defendant had said "they are fals londyns & sche went to a soyth sayer to knowe yf they hadd take away clothes & sche saide that they schuld [i.e., do] have them & therupon sche caused the constable to serch ther house." [45]

Some defendants were caught in embarrassing sexual circumstances by witnesses, other than constables, who reported the offenders to court. Certain men, for instance, had peered through the window of Joan Deyse's house and saw Joan in her bed in the kitchen (!) with a certain unnamed man; the men immediately notified "le wache" (civic officers on night-watch), who then apprehended the fornicators. Another man, who committed adultery with his servant, was caught by his own wife ("deprehensus erat per uxorem suam propriam"). A certain Margaret Lothrupp was caught by her fiancé in the act of adultery over a latrine with Thomas Taylor. One alleged adulterer was caught mysteriously under the bed of his lover by two men, John Martin and Richard Verte. One woman was charged in court for fornication because allegedly "she toke her gowne tayle and put over her hede." This public invitation seems to have been a sure sign of a fornicator; however, she was never summoned to court. And John Basley reported to the court his married male servant, who had enticed his female servant to "Grenewych" where the two servants committed adultery.[46]

In most cases in which a couple was apprehended in the sexual act, scribes did not say who had caught the suspects. But in those cases where scribes noted an accuser, this same accuser was known to the suspect; in other words, neighbors were reporting on neighbors. There were few strangers singled out for prosecution because of their flagrant

44. See *inter alia*, ibid., vol. 1, fol. 13v; vol. 4, fols. 10r, 12r, 57r; vol. 5, fol. 75r; vol. 8, fols. 88r, 235r; vol. 9, fol. 94v; vol. 11, fols. 108v, 109r, 230v.

45. Ibid., vol. 11, fol. 158r.

46. Ibid., vol. 1, fol. 84v; vol. 5, fols. 30r, 108r; vol. 4, fol. 59r; vol. 11, fol. 13r.

wrongdoing. Most charges seem to have emanated from those living together in small groups: parishes, guilds, wards, crafts. And their crimes were usually detected in familiar neighborhood locations. Suspects were caught nude in bed, hiding under the bed, at the house of a third party, on a parish street at night, or outside a notorious brothel. In all cases the fame or reputation of a suspect was in question. Those who already knew the suspect were the ones who complained about his reputation.

Fame, ill fame, good fame, *diffamatus, diffamatio*: these were key words which underpinned much of the detection and reporting of criminals in London church courts. Canon law had decreed that a person could be accused by ill fame alone; and a person's ill fame—largely a creation of gossip, rumors, and the good and ill will of his neighbors—took on the garb of a prosecutor. Only a court could test a suspect's fame, and, if innocent, restore him to good fame. A Londoner turned instinctively to the church courts to establish his good fame, to accuse another of defamation, or to expose a neighbor's bad fame.

3. Trials

Much of the shouting and name-calling of open, rowdy, noisy London, the fishwife shrieks, the whispered rumors, the mindless and conspiratorial gossip, ended in the church courts as specific charges. These charges were heard before an ecclesiastical judge to whom canon law procedures had allotted great discretion in weighing evidence and delivering sentences. "No form of procedure," Gabriel LeBras wrote, "has ever given a greater importance to the *officium iudicis*, and in no other has the search for the truth been more effectively kept free from the shackles of formalism." Yet as John Noonan has pointed out, the search for truth in church courts was often put aside in order to fit legal facts into legal categories;[47] real life often had to be distorted to satisfy the demands of abstract legal rules. In the higher consistory court, judgments appear to have been rendered generally according to rules of law, and litigants rarely appeared in court. In the lower commissary court, however, judgments appear to have been more ambiguously personal. Judges had a dual nature in London that depended on the

47. Gabriel LeBras, "Canon Law," in *The Legacy of the Middle Ages*, ed. C. G. Crump and E. F. Jacob (Oxford, 1926), p. 358. See also Fournier, *Les officialités*, pp. 129–208. But for actual cases in the application of marriage laws see John T. Noonan, Jr., *The Power to Dissolve: Lawyers and Marriages in the Courts of the Roman Curia* (Cambridge, Mass., 1972), pp. ix–xix, and *passim*.

court in which they worked: in consistory they saw primarily rules before them; in commissary, primarily persons.

Cases brought before the London consistory were usually instance (civil) cases which went through the full or plenary processes of the law. The elaborate procedures whereby claims were made, witnesses called, depositions taken in private, and sentences rendered on the basis of the written depositions have already been described in Chapter I. The general rule which governed proofs in the plenary procedure was that a claimant bore the burden of proof (*onus probandi incumbit ei qui dicit*). The channels of justice in consistory were well worn, and if one can judge from the lone surviving London consistory court book, procedures never varied. Proctors trundled through court sessions for their clients, and advocates argued the merits of cases before judges in closed sessions. Justice in the consistory court was thorough, sophisticated, and more expensive than the lower court.

London's lower court, the commissary court, heard primarily office (criminal) cases, although some civil cases were heard also. Justice in the commissary court was summary, quick, and relatively inexpensive. The proceedings took the form of canonical purgation, that is, the long-used medieval system of oath-helpers. Proofs depended on social relationships rather than scrutiny of evidence. A defendant, when charged in court, was first obliged to swear an oath of his innocence. This oath then became the central issue in the trial, and compurgators or oath-helpers—a defendant's neighbors—were obliged to swear whether or not they believed the defendant's oath (a scribe's note from one case: "[Judex] compurgatores suos jurari fecit de credulitate").[48]

To modern eyes, justice through oath-helpers appears bizarre and irrational. But justice can be had in many ways, and for thousands of Londoners who had been caught up in canonical purgation, the commissary court provided a certain social justice. Innocence and guilt were arrived at through the personal interplay of neighbors who were willing to act as compurgators. Court decisions also depended on how far a plaintiff was willing to prosecute a case: if a plaintiff objected to a defendant's compurgators, he could force his suit to the higher consistory court and find sophisticated justice; but there he bore the burden of proof, and failure of a suit meant that he also bore court costs. In reality, much of the judicial process took place out of court in the gossip of neighbors, in a defendant's gathering of friends as compurgators, and in a plaintiff's weighing of the costs and risks of forcing his suit to a higher court.

48. Acta correct., vol. 11, fol. 139r.

Whether or not the sophisticated plenary procedure of the consistory court was, in fact, more accurate as a gauge of truth and was more just than the crude, social, summary justice of the commissary court is by no means an easy question to answer. The ends of justice are perhaps as easily obtained when neighbors are allowed merely to vent their feelings in an official, legal way as they are through the conviction and punishment of wrongdoers.

Not all suits in London church courts were prosecuted to the bitter end. Canonists had long taught that the preferable ends of justice are peace and concord between litigants; this could be reached, they said, through outside arbitration and concord as well as through court trial. Henry of Susa, the great Hostiensis, for example, taught that a judge ought to induce litigants to concord and to reconcile them when possible: otherwise he risks giving an unjust decision.[49] This was a common theme of canonists and was repeated by the fifteenth-century English legist, William Lyndwood. In a gloss on a Stephen Langton statute that encouraged out-of-court compositions, Lyndwood argued that a judge could even interpose himself, as arbiter, to encourage mutual concord among suitors. Lyndwood echoed Hostiensis by repeating the familiar tagline that a judge first and foremost ought to lead contending parties to an amicable peace: "Judex primo et ante omnia debet partes inducere ad concordiam si possit."[50] Arbitration among litigants and final concord, of course, must be agreed upon by both parties; the agree-

49. Hostiensis, *Lectura in quinque libros Decretalium* (Venice, 1581), 2.4.1, # 19, fol. 20v: "Primo debet iudex partes inducere ad concordiam & componere inter ipsas si potest, alioquin iniuste pronunciabit."

50. William Lyndwood, *Provinciale* 1.16 (Oxford, 1679), p. 72, gloss "exigant": "Nam utroque casu, ut hic apparet, non debent impediri, nec ab eis aliquid debet per judicem vel ejus ministros ea occasione exigi." It has been argued that compromise is a common solution to legal disputes in pre-industrial societies. (Cf. R. C. van Caenegem, *Royal Writs in England*, Selden Society 77 [London, 1959], p. 42; repeated by Jane Sayers, *Papal Judges Delegate*, p. 239.) The reasons given are varied: execution of court decisions are difficult in "primitive law"; rights are more easily compromised to preserve personal relationships in pre-industrial societies than in industrial societies, where rights are aggressively pursued at the expense of personal relationships. But, Barbara Yngvesson warns, this dichotomy between primitives and moderns is too sharp, too oversimplified; self-interest exists among primitives and compromise among moderns (Barbara Yngvesson, "Law in Preindustrial Societies," in *Social System and Legal Process: Theory, Comparative Perspectives, and Special Studies*, ed. Harry M. Johnson [San Francisco, 1978], pp. 145–46; and Pospíšil, *Anthropology of Law*, p. 341). It is of little value to see church courts or legal systems as pre-industrial (primitive) and industrial (modern); the elements of a legal system are the same for primitives and moderns alike. Rather we want to see how Londoners solved their disputes. Compromise was only one of many solutions to conflict.

ment was binding in both spiritual and temporal courts; that is, the suit could not be pursued further in another court. Thus, Richard Lye was charged in commissary court for having defamed William Shawdford; Lye allegedly had called Shawdford a cutpurse and claimed that Shawdford specifically had stolen his purse and was still holding it. As a theft case, this also belonged to the secular courts. Both litigants agreed to accept the arbitration of their parish priest in all actions, spiritual and temporal ("tam spirituales quam temporales"), and the case was dismissed.[51]

Although many cases in commissary court were sent to arbiters for a peaceful solution, most were tried by canonical purgation. A procedural change available in defamation and marriage suits after the turn of the sixteenth century was the exception to this rule.[52] Save for a few people who readily confessed the charges against them, defendants swore oaths of their innocence and then were required to return again to court with compurgators. The crucial oath was that of the accused who swore to his own innocence—not merely to his fame or to his credibility. How effective was this oath depended on the strength of the defendant's fear of perjury. Either most charges were groundless and defendants innocent or there were many defendants who had little trepidation at committing perjury, for in overwhelming numbers and in all types of cases defendants successfully purged themselves.

When canonists adopted the easy method of prosecution by public rumor, they made it possible, if not inevitable, that the pettiest disputes would find their way to court. An antidote to this avalanche of petty charges was the quick, summary procedure of canonical purgation. Purgation was not concerned with proofs but with fame—that same public fame that acted as a prosecutor. Hence, it was relatively easy to be charged in court by bad fame and relatively easy to be acquitted by the compurgation of one's friends and restored to good fame. If a suitor then objected to the compurgation, the case was sent through the full, plenary procedures of the consistory; in this way the lower commissary court acted as a screening board for serious disputes destined for the higher courts.

Canonical purgation, as a legal procedure, varied widely according to a judge's discretion. A judge alone ordered the number of compurgators or dismissed cases without use of compurgators by an un-

51. Acta correct., vol. 8, fol. 51v; cf. fol. 84r in same vol.: a letter from the sheriff to the bishop's court stating that in an action in the sheriff's court, the contending parties accepted arbiters in all matters temporal and spiritual.

52. See below, pp. 68–72, 119–20.

known method that in retrospect seems arbitrary. He seems to have had no guidelines to follow except his own instinctive judgment concerning the probable guilt or innocence of a defendant. Thus, a judge often simply dismissed a case without any reason given in the court record. On occasion, a scribe noted the reason: the judge did not think the article, or charge, was true ("dimittitur quia dominus [i.e., iudex] sic vult et articulus non continet veritatem"); or he felt that a defendant had been charged out of malice ("quia ex malicia presentatus" or "ex malicia detectus"); or he saw that the defendants were old and poor ("et quia vidit eos senes et pauperes ipsos ex gratia dimisit").[53]

Other defendants were also charged in court but never faced trial. The poor—those whose total possessions were worth less than 40s—had a special standing in London church courts because they rarely had to answer charges against them or to face purgation. They summarily were dismissed *in forma pauperis* without further trial. Questions of guilt or innocence were not raised. A relatively common type of court book entry in its entirety is this: "Agnes Colte communis meretrix. dimittitur in forma pauperis." [54] Paupers and other *miserabiles personae* in theory had always enjoyed the special protection of church authorities. Compassion for the poor, however, probably was not so much the motivation for the insulation of paupers from church courts as was their inability to pay their own court fees. In the commissary court, all defendants, innocent or guilty, had to pay a dismissal fee (*feodum dimissionis*) for the scribe and summoner.[55] If court officers prosecuted paupers, they did so at their own expense.

Also among those defendants dismissed outright by a judge were men and women who were dismissed at the request (*ad instanciam*) of another. The outside party might be a proctor/lawyer, a curate, a friend, a spouse, an alderman, or some person with influence at court. Presumably the interceder vouched for the defendant's innocence or posted surety for good behavior or settled with the opposing party out of court. Elizabeth Crow, for example, was dismissed from court without further trial at the request of her alderman, Sir Thomas Wyndowt of Cripplegate Ward; and Joan Bernarde, accused of prostitution, pimping, and adultery with the cook of the papal collector in England

53. For "malicious" presentments, see, e.g., Acta correct., vol. 5, fols. 134v, 163v, 166v; for simple, untrue charges, see, e.g., vol. 9, fols. 65r, 97r; for dismissal of the "old and poor" couple, see vol. 11, fol. 304r.

54. For Agnes Colte, see Acta correct., vol. 4, fol. 5v; another example is on the same folio: "Johanna Jamys alias Norton communis meretrix et etiam pronuba inter sororam suam et alios homines suspectos. dimittitur in forma pauperis."

55. See below, pp. 54–55.

was dismissed at the request of Dr. William Haryngton, a London advocate.[56] Having influential friends at court who could "fix" a case was implied in this statement made by Margaret Valentine, a notorious prostitute, charged with adultery with John March, a ward bedel: "I woll plese a bedill, a shargaunt, & a woman, & a Sumner for they woll bere me owte a genyst all curtes [i.e., courts]." [57]

Also summarily dismissed without trial were defendants who were under the jurisdiction of another court for the same charge; a defendant introduced to the court a *preventio* and his case was dismissed. Thus, Isabella Down, charged with fornication with the pardoner of Westminster, was dismissed from court after she showed her *preventio* from the archbishop's peculiars court at St. Mary-le-Bow:

> Isabella Down fornicavit cum uno [blank] pardoner de Westminster of hir own confecion that he hath lay with hir diverse neightes. Isabella comparuit xxi die Julij [1480] et allegat [*sic*] preventionem apud Bowe et die lune proximo introducet prevencionem. Illo die fuit cont. ad diem Jovis. illo die introduxit preventionem.[58]

As sometimes happened, cases were dismissed for lack of a plaintiff. In cases *ex officio promoto*, the court pursued a case on its own only until a defendant denied the charge; that is, the court required a plaintiff to substantiate the public rumor. In which case, a plaintiff was required to step forward to prosecute his charge. Presumably this meant a willingness by a plaintiff to appear in court to certify his charge or witness the defendant's compurgation. But by court time, tempers often had cooled or a plaintiff was unwilling to pursue his charge; the case was then dismissed (*dimittitur quia pars non prosequitur*).

During any one year, about half of all cases in commissary court were not concluded in court. Most of the time cases disappear from court records in mid-proceedings and generally we do not know why cases were dropped. But sometimes prosecutions came to a halt be-

56. Acta correct., vol. 8, fol. 188r–v; vol. 9, fol. 61v; for Wyndowte see Beaven, *The Aldermen of London,* 1:130. The Bernarde case took place in 1502; the papal collector then was Adrian De Castello, bishop of Hereford, who was not in England; the sub-collector was Polydore Vergil, who arrived in England in 1502 (*Letters and Papers, Foreign and Domestic, Henry VIII,* 1,2:1392–93; Vergil, *Anglica historia,* pp. 132–33).

57. Acta correct., vol. 4, fol. 38r. See also fol. 138v in same volume for charges against John March, the bedel, on the same adultery charge. Margaret successfully purged herself and was dismissed from court; March's case was only noted in the court book and no further action was taken.

58. Ibid., vol. 3, fol. 13r.

cause defendants did not appear in court. The weapons of the court to compel courtroom appearances were restricted to minor and major excommunication. For his first non-appearance in court a defendant suffered minor excommunication and was suspended from entering church (*suspensus ab ingressu*), which presumably denied him the Eucharist.[59] The second consecutive non-appearance brought major excommunication and the threat of secular intervention. If a plaintiff insisted on forcing a defendant to court, he and the court applied to the bishop to "signify" the contumacious defendant to Chancery; Chancery then issued a writ of *de excommunicato capiendo* to the sheriff, who was supposed to imprison the culprit in order to force him to court. How many London excommunicates were actually signified in Chancery is a moot question. Only thirty-three such significavits survive in the Public Record Office from all jurisdictions in the entire diocese of London between 1470 and 1516.[60] Unless a plaintiff was willing to pursue a defendant with the help and expense of sheriffs, then probably nothing was done to the defendant; he remained suspended from church or excommunicated. Many cases in commissary court books end only with suspension or excommunication. In the case of Thomas Strode, an adulterer, the court scribe specifically noted that the excommunication was not sent forward ("excommunicatio non fuit processa"); that is, no further action seems to have been taken on the excommunication. But a scribe on another occasion noted that this same court signified in Chancery for the sheriff to capture a contumacious defendant, Dominic Lumby.[61] Defendants perhaps could avoid prosecution but only at the risk of remaining in a state of excommunication; many chose to remain excommunicated. We may, I think, accept Rosalind Hill's judgment when she wrote that excommunication by the late Middle Ages had "degenerated from a tremendous sanction into a minor inconvenience."[62]

Many defendants suffered suspension or excommunication at some time during their trials and were subsequently absolved for a fee (9d for suspension; a further 9d for excommunication). Such large num-

59. F. Donald Logan, *Excommunication and the Secular Arm in England* (Toronto, 1968), p. 14.
60. P.R.O., C 85/125–6; cf. Logan, *Excommunication and the Secular Arm*, especially pp. 67–68.
61. Acta correct., vol. 1, fol. 95v; vol. 11, fol. 79v. Lumby's significavit has not survived in Chancery records.
62. Rosalind Hill, "The Theory and Practice of Excommunication in Medieval England," *History* 42 (1957), 11.

bers of suspensions and excommunications probably were the result not so much of defiance of court authorities as of the peculiar medieval indifference for time and dates. Occasionally, scribes themselves listed a day of the week for a court appearance that did not correspond to the calendar date which they also gave. It is no wonder that litigants themselves often appeared in court a day or two before or after their scheduled court day.

If a case proceeded along its scheduled course and compurgation was ordered, then a judge's discretion over the number of compurgators was important. No particular offense required a set number of compurgators, and numbers of compurgators ranged from one to twelve. But serious crimes (e.g., smothering a child) in general required more compurgators than minor ones. William Lyndwood allowed that purgation could be either by a defendant's own oath or with the help of compurgators.[63] Thus, many defendants were ordered to purge themselves only by their own oaths, *cum propria manu,* and were released.

The number of compurgators' oaths that a judge ordered included a defendant's own oath. When a parish priest's bad fame, for example, had been confirmed in an inquisition, he was ordered to purge himself with twelve men, six curates and five honest parishioners—that is, eleven men and the defendant. Another priest was ordered to purge himself with six "hands," "viz. iii presbiteris et ii laicis," that is, five men and the defendant.[64]

Judges were lenient in accepting fewer compurgators than were ordered. The casualness toward strict fulfillment of purgation pervades the correction books. A suspected pimp, for example, was taken from her house by constables and placed in the sheriff's prison; when the suspect appeared in court, she was ordered to purge herself with six hands; she successfully purged with three (four, counting her own) and was dismissed.[65] Richard Glover, a London priest, was charged in London commissary court after Joan Bray confessed to sexual inter-

63. Lyndwood, *Provinciale,* 5.14, p. 312, gloss on "purgationem": "Purgatio Canonica est super objecto crimine, proprio Juramento, vel si oporteat, Juramento compurgatorum de ipso crimine diffamati innocentiae ostensio."

64. Acta correct., vol. 8, fols. 89r, 250r.

65. Ibid., vol. 11, fol. 230v: the woman, Paronella Appys, was accused of pimping for the wives of her neighbors and certain men of Holborn. She "extracta fuit de domo sua per constabularios ibidem." She was ordered to purge with six hands, but successfully purged with Margaret Longhorn, Agnes Harryson, and Katherine Brose; she was then dismissed from court *ex gratia.*

course with him; Glover was ordered to purge with five clerks, but successfully purged himself with only two others. Another defendant was caught nude under the bed of a woman by two neighbors, charged with adultery, and ordered to purge with three hands; he purged with his own hand, *cum propria manu*, and was dismissed.[66] Such cases took place at all times under all judges.

Failure to purge oneself was not automatically followed by a guilty verdict; occasionally a second purgation was allowed. Thus Joan Whith was charged as a sorceress, failed her first purgation when her oath-helpers refused to swear for her, and succeeded in a second attempt with a new set of oath-helpers:

> Johanna Whith sortilega et maledixit cuidam Rosemande infirme. . . . Mulier comparuit xvi die Marcii [1471], negavit articulum; die Mercurii proximo purgare se se 4. illo die mulier comparuit cum Katerina Warwyk, Agnete Porter, et Elena Hawkyn que recusaverunt iurare et ideo defecit in purgatione et continuatur ad diem Sabati. illo die comparuerunt Agnes Pollard, Alicia Craswell, Margarita Croxiston, et aliis; et dimittitur.[67]

In retrospect, defendants seem to have been rushed through the compurgation process with undue speed. During the busy years of the early 1480s, in fact, many defendants merely appeared in court with their neighbors and were dismissed by the judge without the compurgators' oaths (*comparuit cum vicinibus et dimittitur*). In 1483 there were 86 such dismissals among 195 completed cases, and in 1484 there were 61 among 320 completed cases. Throughout the years similar dismissals occurred without the necessary oaths (e.g., *produxit numerum compurgatorum et gratis dimittitur absque iuramento*).[68] Judges alone decided how stringent compurgation should be; and because of lenient judges or burdensome case loads, successful compurgation in London was not difficult at all.

Compurgation is essentially a system of justice appropriate to rural villages, where a villager's intimate knowledge of the affairs of his neighbors makes a compurgator a knowledgeable witness. One need only look at the cases in a recently published Lincoln court book for the years 1514 to 1520 to discover how few compurgations were successful or even attempted. From over 160 defendants in Lincoln rural villages, only eight denied the charges against them and were ordered

66. Ibid., vol. 11, fol. 27r; vol. 4, fol. 144r.
67. Ibid., vol. 2, fol. 53v.
68. See, for example, ibid., vol. 11, fols. 182r, 184v, 207r, 248r.

canonical purgation; of these eight, only two were successful.[69] Few, if any, villagers were willing to risk perjury charges—or the judgment of God—for falsely swearing before a court to save a neighbor. In Lincoln most defendants confessed their crimes. Defendants could find little refuge in their villages where they were well known and already subject to bad fame.

London, I have argued, was little more than an urbanized village; but it was still *urban*, with a large floating population and a constant influx of strangers. In urban London tongues wagged more capriciously and compurgators were easier to find—some perhaps even were paid. In the small Lincoln sample that we possess, most defendants ultimately confessed and were punished, but in a much larger London group of cases most defendants were acquitted and set free. Compurgation worked in a vastly different way in an urban setting than it did in the tightly knit rural villages for which it was designed. A villager's loyalty to his village and his interdependency with his neighbors were the foundations on which a successful compurgation system rested, but such foundations were largely eroded in a city. In London a man had overlapping loyalties and friends from without his parish or ward or craft. What survived of rural ways in London was the garrulous gossip of the village.

4. Sanctions

Charging people in court was largely the responsibility of neighbors, but in an acutal trial and sentencing the judge played the paramount role. He alone set the conditions for the trial and allowed out-of-court settlements; he often urged quarreling parties to an amicable peace. Those defendants whose cases did not end amicably were also at the mercy of a judge's discretion. A judge set the conditions of court sanctions; he decided if a defendant ought to be punished and the severity of that punishment.

We have seen that paupers, with few exceptions, were free from the corrective processes of church courts in London. Additional cases exist

69. Margaret Bowker, ed., *An Episcopal Court Book for the Diocese of Lincoln, 1514–1520*, Lincoln Record Society 61 (Lincoln, 1963): attempted compurgations on pp. 6, 112, 122, 130, 136, 139, 140; successful compurgations on p. 112 (Laurence Cuff) and p. 136 (George Bell). This is a record of the bishop's Audience court, a summary court. About half the cases in the court book came to the court by way of episcopal visitation, in which churchwardens reported wrongdoers to the visitors (see Bowker's introduction, p. xi).

in commissary court books in which a defendant's influence at court allowed him to escape punishment. In 1509 a certain doctor of law, Thomas Borrowe, for example, was caught in adultery with one Juliana. Only Juliana was punished; she was ordered to leave her parish (the same as Borrowe's) within three days and not to consort with him. Borrowe escaped (formal) punishment, perhaps because the judge had tried to protect a colleague.[70] When Margaret Auger was charged in court for adultery, her accomplice was noted as being a clerk from the church of St. Paul's; the clerk was not charged in court and his name was badly scratched out by the court scribe, perhaps in an attempt to protect him from the prying eyes of other clerks.[71]

Those who confessed or were convicted in the commissary court faced canonical correction, or penance. It was thought that penance should serve both personal and public needs: penance must bring the sinner himself to a state of grace and keep him there, and it must act as a deterrent for others by publicly showing the criminal in a foolish, degrading way. Penance also must be "decent," that is, men of rank ought not to be humiliated by penance so as to preclude them from acting authoritatively. A judge, therefore, must take into account the social status of the guilty party. Above all, a guilty party should be made to detest his crime and thus willingly submit himself to penance.[72]

Normal methods of punishment or sanctions in London's commissary court were public penance and pecuniary penance. To William Lyndwood, public penance meant penance performed "in the presence of the church without solemnity." [73] Thus, public penance became a cosmic—comic—drama of sin and redemption acted openly with all London as a stage. Almost invariably public penance in London involved a convicted person, now officially contrite, leading his parish procession on Sunday, looking foolish in only a smock, and

70. Acta correct., vol. 10, fol. 37v. I have been unable to find further information on Borrowe.

71. Ibid., vol. 5, fol. 64r.

72. E. Jombart, "Pénitence," *D.D.C.*, 6:1318–20; Rosalind Hill, "Public Penance: Some Problems of a Thirteenth Century Bishop (O. Sutton)," *History* 36 (1951), 213–26; H. Gee and W. J. Hardy, eds., *Documents Illustrative of English Church History (A.D. 314–1700)* (London, 1896), p. 163 (from the answer of the Ordinaries in 1532): "but when open penance may sometime work in certain persons more hurt than good, it is commendable and allowable in that case to punish by the purse and preserve the fame of the party; foreseeing alway [*sic*] the money be converted *in usus pios et eleemonsynam.*"

73. Lyndwood, *Provinciale* 5.16, p. 339, gloss on "Solemni Poenitentia": "Sed proprie dicitur publica illa, quae sit in facie Ecclesiae sine solennitate."

carrying a lighted candle; this then was repeated for two or three Sundays. The entire drama was played out weekly in a hundred London parishes.

Although penance was usually standard, a judge could make it more or less severe. A person guilty of defamation, for example, usually was required in addition to public penance to offer a public apology to the defamed party; restitution was a condition of penance. But in one case, a confessed defamer was only admonished without further penance not to use such words again.[74] Penance had personal and social ends, and judges had to weigh in their own minds how justice could best be served. On occasion, punishment was simply cancelled because the wrongdoer was a pauper (*dimittitur quia valde pauper*), and in one case because the guilty party was pregnant—which ironically was the public proof of her crime ("dominus quia vidit eam gravidam et impregnatam eandem dimisit cum monicione").[75] Twice in 1516 judge Thomas Benett saw fit to cancel penance because the guilty parties already appeared penitent ("pro eo quod vidit eum penitentem").[76] Imposition of penance was a personal choice of a judge whose decisions seem most often to have been swayed toward leniency by a defendant's personal demeanor.

Public penance, in fact, more often than not was commuted for a money payment, or pecuniary penance. William Lyndwood held that this was allowable insofar as the money went to charitable works and not to the purses of court officers. A guilty party then was given a choice of public penance or money payment, as a court scribe noted in the case of one confessed adulterer: "Dominus iniunxit sibi quod procedat processionem duobus dominicis etc. vel ad solvendum iiis iiiid."[77] How often penance was commuted for a cash payment may be seen in these statistics for two typical years: during 1493, of 70 peo-

74. Acta correct., vol. 11, fol. 178r: John Crokewell defamed William Geffry, clerk of the parish of St. Andrew Eastcheap. Crokewell "comparuit fatens se talia dixisse; ex confessione sua propria et dominus monuit ei quod nulla talia ipse futuro protulisset verba sub pena excommunicationis; et dimittitur."

75. Ibid., vol. 11, fol. 310r; all such entries are too numerous to mention. An interesting sample may be found in vol. 2, fol. 70v (suspects were defect in their purgation "et postea commissarius dimisit eos"); vol. 2, fol. 140v (an accused adulteress had her case dismissed without reason given: "dimittitur causa contra mulierem mandato commissarii"); and vol. 5, fol. 177v (after confessing to fornication and prostitution, the accused appeared in court to receive penance; but when she appeared the scribe only noted this: "comparuit et ex gratia dimittitur et solvit feodum et dimittitur").

76. Ibid., vol. 11, fols. 307r, 313r.

77. Ibid., vol. 8, fol. 288v; Lyndwood, *Provinciale* 1.10, p. 52, gloss on "poena canonica."

ple who faced court punishment, 43 (61½%) paid cash redemption of their penance, and 27 (38½%) performed public penance. Ten years later, during 1502, 62 persons faced court punishment; 38 (61%) satisfied the court with a money payment, and 24 (39%) performed public penance.[78]

Penance and commutation of penance for a fine raises new problems concerning justice. This discussion thus far has suggested that all persons irrespective of social rank or wealth were subject to the same laws. But punishments for those crimes was not, nor could they be, meted out equally. Canonical penance respected social position and was not imposed on men of authority for fear of subverting confidence in their authority; such men were protected by their positions and received preferential treatment. As penance was translated into money, justice still was preferentially meted out according to wealth and position; pecuniary penance, however, demanded more of the wealthy rather than less. Judges, in other words, looked to the person rather than to the crime when they prescribed suitable sanctions.

Court scribes used the verb *composuit* to indicate that a wrongdoer had settled on, or agreed upon, or arranged for, or fixed upon, a sum with a judge for penance. The agreed-upon sum was a matter of personal negotiation between a guilty party and a judge. Indeed, in one case a scribe inadvertently seems to have preserved the bargaining that took place. The wrongdoer settled with (*composuit*) the judge first for 6s (which was crossed out), then for 17s (also crossed out), and finally for 10s. In another case a fine of 40s was ordered, but reduced to 20s if paid before a certain date.[79]

What was the basis by which pecuniary penances were levied? We may safely eliminate the type of offense as the basis. A glance at pecuniary penances of adulterers for a few months in 1489 reveals these figures: 10s, 6s, 6s 8d, 3s 4d, 2s 8d, 2s, 20s, 3s, and 4s.[80] Other offenses at all other times show the same irregularity in levying cash penances. Clearly a pecuniary penance was not a function of the type of offense. Rather we must look to the wealth of the offender for an answer. A poor laborer obviously could not afford the same penance as a rich goldsmith. Thus, payments varied widely from a low of 12d from a self-proclaimed pauper and fornicator, to an incredible £3 6s 8d from an obviously wealthy fornicator.[81]

78. Statistics for 1493 taken from Acta correct., vol. 5, fols. 1r–142v; for 1502 from vol. 9, fols. 2r–99v.

79. Ibid., vol. 5, fol. 166r; vol. 8, fol. 171r.

80. Ibid., vol. 4, fols. 4r, 5r, 6v, 9v, 16r, 21r, 22r, 32r, 36r.

81. Ibid., vol. 4, fol. 191v; vol. 6, fol. 115v.

I do not know how the wealth of wrongdoers was determined. But church authorities in London had tithing lists that measured a man's tithable wealth by the amount he spent on house rents. It would be surprising if church court officers did not instinctively copy this long-used system of assessment as their own method for levying pecuniary penances. (But unlike personal tithes, which went directly to a parish rector, church court pecuniary penances were specifically earmarked for charitable works, *opera charitatis*, or for repair work on St. Paul's.)[82]

Judges showed unpredictable personal discretion when they heard and disposed of cases. Obviously there was much in the personal confrontation between defendant and judge in commissary court which determined the outcome of a case and the sanctions meted out.

Sanctions themselves are a crucial element in a legal system. A court must have a way to enforce its decisions through physical or moral force. Church courts depended on the secular arm for its physical force. An excommunicate could be taken into custody by the sheriff after having been signified in Chancery,[83] and while under excommunication a person could not sue in royal courts. But whom, in fact, would this affect? Presumably not the notorious criminal who lived outside the law anyway. Excommunication probably would affect only the reasonably law-abiding citizen—now temporarily gone wrong—who might have an occasion to sue some matter in a royal court. What effect would this form of secular coercion have on the neighborhood scold, pimp, or prostitute? They were not troublesome enough to be the object of the writ *de excommunicato capiendo*, nor respectable enough to be affected by being barred from the royal courts. In the end the ultimate church court coercive power against neighborhood nuisances, blackguards, prostitutes, and pimps, was the *moral*—metaphysical—force of excommunication.

Yet a legal system without physical coercion—as in most cases in the London church courts—requires widespread popular support and acceptance in order for its moral sanctions to be effective. The effectiveness of church court sanctions, in other words, depended largely on the mental attitude of those for whom the sanctions were intended. Excommunication and other church court sanctions were effective only against those who considered them effective. Any subtle shift in popular attitudes from acceptance of moral sanctions to disdain for or indifference to these sanctions would undermine the legal system.

82. Cf. such notations in vol. 11, fol. 201v; vol. 9, fol. 5v.
83. See above, p. 46.

5. Court Fees

After a case was concluded the costs of justice had to be tallied and assessed. We know nothing of court fees for the consistory, only that they were assessed to the loser of a suit. In the lower commissary court, fees were assessed to the defendant, whether innocent or guilty. He was required to pay a *feodum dimissionis*, a dismissal fee, to the court scribe and summoner. Only legitimate paupers were excused from paying. This court charge varied from 6d to 20d, but most fees were either 12d or 14d. The sum was divided between the court scribe and the summoner. How the fees were divided is not clear. Dismissal fees of 12d and 14d were charged for like offenses from the same parish. The difference of 2d, between 12d and 14d, probably went to the court scribe for any extra work required of him. During January 1490, for example, Lewis Ambrose was charged with adultery; he did not appear in court for two straight sessions and was suspended from entering church. Ambrose then appeared in court, confessed his crime, and paid his court fees; according to marginal notations in the court book the apparitor received 10d and the court scribe 6d. On the same folio of this court book is a similar adultery case that did not include suspension; the summoner again received 10d, but this time the scribe's share was only 4d.[84] The difference in the scribe's share seems to have been for his extra work drawing up a suspension. These were two rare instances when the court scribe specified how fees were divided. Usually we do not know.

Defendants showed surprisingly little resistance to paying court costs, yet it must have rankled those who were innocent of any charges. There were, in fact, very few defendants like the midwife Joan Keryng, who after successful purgation objected to paying her dismissal fees ("non vult solvere feoda"); but even she relented and paid. I have found only two other refusals to pay.[85]

Fees were the main source of income for summoners and scribes who had at their disposal the church court apparatus to force fee payments. In the commissary court a defendant was the one vulnerable

84. Both cases in ibid., vol. 4, fol. 10v: Defendants: Lodowicus Ambrose and Johannes Harvey. The total cost for absolution from suspension was 9d; this was not part of the dismissal fee, but was paid separately.

85. Ibid., vol. 3, fol. 17r. See also vol. 3, fol. 119v: Agnes a Chambur successfully purged herself of a pimping charge, but "illa non vult solvere pro feodo. non comparuit. ideo suspensa" (the last entry in her case); and vol. 4, fol. 255r: Lobius de Movenda "non vult solvere feodum curie ideo suspensus" (he eventually paid).

person from whom court fees could be collected. An accuser in a suit was usually the "public voice," behind which was an actual person who was not liable for his accusation. Court fees could not be collected from a fictional entity like the public voice.

Fees of 12d or 14d were not pittances in pre-Reformation London. The daily wage of a skilled London artisan in the building trades (carpenter, mason, tiler) was only 8d, and an artisan's laborer made only 4d per day. These wages remained unchanged throughout the early sixteenth century despite the "Tudor inflation" that doubled food prices during the 1510s and 1520s.[86] A simple dismissal fee was equivalent to a day and a half's wages for a London artisan or about three days' wages for his laborer. If an apparitor received 4d to 8d—which seems to have been the normal range of fees[87]—then a defendant in the commissary court lost a day's wages to the summoner alone. It is little wonder that summoners were loathed.

6. Judges and the Law

Thus far I have argued that ecclesiastical judges had a paramount role in controlling and shaping a case once it was in the courtroom. It is almost impossible today for us to assess a judge's actual performance, whether he was conscientious or a mere timeserver. What we can determine is the education of an ecclesiastical judge. This is important because judges brought into the courtroom and brought to bear on actual cases the peculiar mores of their profession. Judicial views of London ecclesiastical judges, perhaps, were especially bound to their law school training, because London judges almost invariably came to the bench directly from university. While at Cambridge or Oxford they may have spent some time in the diocesan courts of Lincoln or Ely, but their first judicial post was a London judgeship. Such was the result of a patronage system in which judges were appointed by influential men, rather than recruited from older experienced advocates.[88] It is likely

86. Rogers, *A History of Agriculture and Prices,* 3:616, 618, 620, 621. The same artisan outside London (e.g., Oxford) made 6d/day and his laborer about 3d/day. See also Y. S. Brenner, "The Inflation of Prices in Early Sixteenth Century England," *Economic History Review* 14 (1961–62), 225–39; and E. H. Phelps Brown and Sheila V. Hopkins, "Wage-Rates and Prices: Evidence for Population Pressure in the Sixteenth Century," *Economica,* new series 24 (1957), 289–306.

87. I am preparing an article on apparitors which will include information on their probable incomes.

88. I am preparing an article for publication on the career patterns of London ecclesiastical judges and advocates.

that the notions of law and justice of these young doctors of law were shaped from books alone.

Standard texts in university legal studies, of course, were the collections of canons and their glossators; equally important to law students were general legal treatises of canonists who summarized and commented upon the entire canon law and its legal principles. Young doctors of law were taught by these canonists basic notions about justice, especially the notion that judges alone had certain discretionary powers in court, that they personally could intervene in cases, that like a merciful God they were to lean toward mercy for the penitent sinner.

In England during the late fifteenth century one of the most widely read canonists was Nicholas de Tudeschis, a Sicilian abbot and archbishop of Palermo (from whence he received his more popular name, Panormitanus). The volumes of Panormitanus dominate the surviving legal literature in English libraries. E. F. Jacobs has maintained that "it is abundantly clear that the abbot was a favorite English law book," and that "he was either a set authority or at least recommended reading in the law schools." [89] Indeed, wherever canon law treatises are mentioned in wills of London judges and advocates, the works of Abbot Panormitanus invariably are specified, often alongside William Lyndwood's *Provinciale*. One former London judge, Walter Stone, for example, left "the volumys of Abbott paner upon the decretalles, and the constitucions, provincyall with the legantynes," and another former judge, Henry Mompesson, specified that his nephew Thomas Mompesson "shalhave my hole course of canon with hole Abbote." [90]

Canonical (academic) conceptions of justice have been described by other historians, and I have nothing original to add.[91] A brief summary of the views of the canonists, however, is necessary to understand the social implications of academic principles.

89. E. F. Jacob, "Panormitanus and the Council of Basel," *Proceedings of the Third International Congress of Medieval Canon Law* (Vatican, 1971), p. 206. See also Edmund Craster, *The History of All Souls College Library*, ed. E. F. Jacob (London, 1971), p. 23.

90. P.R.O., Prob. 11/19, fol. 221v (will of Walter Stone); Prob. 11/16, fol. 175r (will of Henry Mompesson). See also C. R. Cheney, "William Lyndwood's Provinciale," *The Jurist* 21 (1961), 429–30, where Professor Cheney surmises that evidence of copies of the *Provinciale* probably would be found in a search of the wills of churchmen and dignitaries.

91. See especially Charles Lefebvre, "Natural Equity and Canonical Equity," *Natural Law Forum* 8 (1963), 122–36; idem, *Les pouvoirs du juge en droit canonique* (Paris, 1938); Walter Ullmann, *The Medieval Idea of Law as Represented by Lucas de Penna* (London, 1946).

Medieval legists, like Panormitanus, all agreed upon one point, that true justice can be found in the immutable law of nature, God's law.[92] They tried to explain this perfect ideal of justice by the word equity. Equity by the late Middle Ages had come to mean many things. It was "justice tempered by sweet mercy," as Hostiensis quoted St. Cyprian; equity should favor mercy (*misericordia*) over the strictness of the law (*rigor legis*). It was a quest for equality or the uniform treatment of particular cases; it was an ideal placed above written, positive law and an ideal to which all positive law yearned; and it was an ideal that should correct written law and fill in gaps where written law is silent.[93]

The problem that the canonists faced was that equity must be brought to bear in men's lives and courts. The barrier between men's courts and the ideal of justice or equity, between the physical and the metaphysical world, somehow had to be pierced. The common ground where natural and positive law met, argued the canonists, was in the mind of the judge—or more precisely in the judge's conscience. By conscience they meant *synderesis* or that habitual (*habitus*) inborn conscience which instinctively recognizes immutable first principles of morality; *synderesis* was thought to be an innate knowledge of natural law. Christopher St. German, an early-sixteenth-century lawyer, defined *synderesis* thus:

> Sinderesis is a naturall power or motive force of the rational soule sette always in the hyghest parte thereof, mouinge and sterrynge it to good, and abhorrynge euyll. And therefore sinderesis neuer synneth nor erryth. . . . Again sinderesis is sometimes called a spark of reason. . . . And this sinderesis our Lorde put in man to the intent that the ordre and connection of thynges shuld be obseruyd.[94]

Through the concept of *synderesis* men could give absoluteness to their laws and avoid—at least academically—the chaos of a relativistic universe. More important for a judge, he was relieved of full responsibility for his decision; his ultimate appeal could be to his conscience, which was bound to immutable principles of natural law. Only through a

92. For an excellent discussion of the idea of justice in natural law by a logical positivist, see especially Alf Ross, *On Law and Justice* (Berkeley, 1959), pp. 268–71.

93. Lefebvre, "Natural Equity and Canonical Equity," pp. 122–36, and *Les pouvoirs du juge*, pp. 164–194.

94. Christopher St. German, *Doctor and Student*, ed. T. F. T. Plucknett and J. L. Barton, Selden Society 91 (London, 1974), p. 81.

judge's conscience, therefore, could men make that crucial contact with natural law and apply principles of equity to everyday laws.[95]

Canonists fully anticipated the difficulties of relying on a judge's conscience for just decisions. They realized the inherent tensions between judicial decisions based on conscience and those based on proofs. Can a judge rule according to his conscience alone even if the proofs of a case point to a contrary decision? Must a judge's conscience be different from, perhaps more refined than, a normal man's conscience? By the thirteenth century, canonists and theologians had worked out answers to these questions that largely favored proofs over conscience as the basis for judicial decisions. Their views reflected a healthy distrust of the metaphysics of conscience, and their arguments for proofs over conscience were repeated time and again by later medieval canonists who added nothing new to the problem.[96]

Tensions between proofs and conscience, however, were not really resolved. Canonists could not ignore a judge's conscience because this was, they believed, a medium to true justice. This tension may be seen in the writings of Panormitanus, who adequately summed up the works of his predecessors. Panormitanus argued that a judge ought to follow his conscience, but that he still should be moved by the proofs before him. In a sensible practical vein, the abbot warned that if a judge issued a sentence against a defendant based on his conscience alone without adequate proofs, then this defendant could appeal to a higher court and win his case for lack of proof against him. By acquitting a defendant, on the other hand, a judge does not act against his conscience, because no one conscientiously can be condemned as a criminal without adequate charges and proofs. Did not Christ, asked Panormitanus rhetorically, absolve a woman whom he knew to be an adulteress because no accuser stepped forward and offered proofs against her? If a judge has a firm conscience in favor of a defendant, he

95. Hostiensis, *Lectura in quinque libros Decretalium* 1.29.40, # 1, fol. 153v, and 1.29.13, #2, fol. 135r; see also Lefebvre, "Natural Equity and Canonical Equity," p. 125; and Thomas Aquinas, *Summa Theologiae* 1a.79.13.

96. For the development of the problem of conscience and proofs see Knut Nörr, *Zur Stellung des Richters im gelehrten Prozess der Frühzeit: Iudex secundum allegata non secundum conscientiam iudicat* (Munich, 1967). See also Max Radin, "Conscience of the Court," *Law Quarterly Review* 48 (1932), 506–20. For a minority view that favored conscience over proofs see Walter Ullmann's study of Lucas of Penna in *The Medieval Idea of Law*, pp. 125–30. But see Norbert Horn, *Aequitas in den Lehren des Baldus* (Cologne, 1968), pp. 105–8, and P. Caron, " 'Aequitas et interpretatio' dans la doctrine canonique aux XIIIe et XIVe siècles," *Proceedings of the Third International Congress of Medieval Canon Law*, pp. 131–41, for more traditional views.

ought not to condemn that person, *regardless of the proofs against him*; innocence should not be punished, and if a judge punishes an innocent person, then he acts against his conscience.[97] Yet a judicial conscience ought to have some controls if justice is to be served. Thus, a judge ought to rule in a case according to evidence and according to a conscience formed or shaped from proofs and the rights of litigants: "debet [iudex] iudicare secundum probata et secundum conscientiam informatam ex attestationibus et aliis iuribus partium." [98] Conscience, thus, was infused with evidence, written law, and proofs; and this same conscience was to soften judgments with mercy. When canonists allowed a judge's conscience in the decision-making process, they encouraged a judge's decision to lean irresistibly toward leniency, toward favoring defendants over their accusers, toward mercy over strict law: these are the social implications of an academic position on true justice.

Equity, although metaphysical, was not a meaningless concept. The canonists—and court judges—thought they were applying principles of universal equity, and hence they made equity a force in the law. The growth in Yorkist-Tudor England of the chancery court (the "court of equity" or the "court of conscience") is the most obvious example of equity as a legal force.[99] Less obvious were the legal norms imparted to ecclesiastical doctors through their study of canon law; these were legal norms that judges brought with them to the courtroom. The scholastic thicket that grew up around equity and conscience was not without fruitful ideas: equity dictated that individual cases ought to be decided on their own merits, and that a judge ought to rule by the ameliorating spirit of the law and not merely by the harsh letter of the law.

The social thrust of conscience and equity, therefore, was to soften the hard edges of law. Mercy always loomed above judicial decisions. Equity could not make the law more strict, but only ameliorate the law with mercy. William Lyndwood, for example, simply stated that a man's conscience was from "knowledge of his own heart" (cognitione suiipsius cordis).[100] And that erudite common lawyer, Christopher St.

97. Panormitanus, *Lectura super Prima Decretalium* (1521), 1.31.1, #8, fol. 107r–v: "Judex an debeat iudicare secundum conscientiam suam an secundum acta."

98. Ibid., "Prohemium," c. "Gregorius," # 18, fols. 2r, 4v–5v.

99. For an old, but still valuable, article on equity and the Chancery court, see Paul Vinogradoff, "Reason and Conscience in Sixteenth Century Jurisprudence," *Law Quarterly Review* 24 (1908), 373–84. His discussion of equity and conscience was based on St. German's *Doctor and Student* (see above, note 94).

100. Lyndwood, *Provinciale* 1.4, p. 27, gloss on "conscientia."

German, writing in the late 1520s on the nature of equity and conscience, summed up equity thus: "Equytye is a rightwysenes that consideryth al the pertyculer cyrcumstaunces of the dede / the whiche also is temperyed with the swetnes of mercy."[101] Thus, the ancient aphorism of St. Cyprian that "equity is justice tempered by sweet mercy" remained central to the definition of a difficult word.

Canon law theory meshed remarkably well with actual courtroom practices in London's consistory and commissary courts; but while the consistory court leaned intellectually toward strict proofs for justice, the commissary court was largely a court of conscience. In the commissary court the judge was as important as the litigants and their compurgators in controlling the course of summary cases; justice here always seems arbitrary and formless, constantly reshaping itself with each case, with each new, unique judge-defendant confrontation. From all indications in the surviving court books, judges did much to shape and to control commissary court cases—and as a rule they acted leniently toward defendants. Were the merciful actions of these judges indicative of sound university training in canonical equity? Or is a consistent pattern of leniency in London simply indicative of hurried responses by many judges to crowded court calendars? Or were London judges more lenient because Londoners themselves were perceived to be lenient and casual in the enforcement of norms, and judges, therefore, responded to peculiar, urban "community norms"? When we seek motivations for a judge's actions, we ultimately are led back to the same area explored by the canonists: the unfathomable depths of a judge's mind. There we may go no further. Why, in May and June of 1516, did Thomas Benett, a young judge with less than eight months' experience on the bench, dismiss the penance of each of two confessed adulterers because each appeared penitent to him ("pro eo quod vidit eum penitentem")?[102] Whatever Thomas Benett's motivations—perhaps he had two pleasant spring days and felt charitable—mercy and leniency were necessary ingredients in the intellectual mixture of an ecclesiastical judge's notion of justice. And mercy and leniency were the rule in London's commissary court.

101. St. German, *Doctor and Student*, p. 95. Charles Ogilvie, *The King's Government and the Common Law* (Oxford, 1958), pp. 93–94, where St. German is placed in an Aristotelian tradition via Jean Gerson.

102. Acta correct., vol. 11, fols. 307r, 313r. I have found little on Benett's career. He apparently received his doctor's degree by 1511, the year he joined Doctors' Commons (George Squibb, *Doctors' Commons: A History of the College of Advocates and Doctors of Law* [Oxford, 1977], p. 131).

7. Conclusion

Justice in London took place on two levels: in the streets among neighbors, and in the courtroom between judge and defendant. In the streets, people's expectations (that normative values be enforced) ought to have been satisfied; in the courts, justice (that the guilty be punished and the innocent acquitted) ought to have been meted out. Ideally these two goals, popular expectations and justice, should coincide. In fact, there seems to have been no conflict between the norms that Londoners thought ought to be enforced and the norms that London church courts tried to enforce.

Rather, the tension between people's expectations and the realities of the courtroom seems to have arisen over the failure to convict and punish those who violated–or were thought to have violated–the norms. Year after year, in great numbers, accused persons were reported to the commissary court and charged with wrongdoing; year after year most of these same men and women were acquitted in one way or another and restored to "good fame." So long as respectable members of the community were satisfied with merely exposing wrongdoers and did not demand strict justice from the courts, the two levels of justice coexisted in relative harmony. During the late fifteenth century, people were not deterred from reporting their neighbors to court by the fact that most accused persons were easily acquitted through a method of compurgation, designed for village life, that did not work in urban London. The moral and social ends–and expectations–of these accusers seem to have been served merely by reporting suspects to court; they had put on public display their own standards of morality. Actual conviction and punishment of wrongdoers seem to have been of secondary importance. In any case, those who were accused suffered from having to pay a dismissal fee.

Such harmony between people's expectations and courtroom reality depended largely upon the attitudes of lay people. Around the turn of the sixteenth century, I believe, there was a new climate of reform and of civic apprehension–in fact, a climate of changing expectations. Respectable members of society seemingly became less concerned with putting their own moral correctness on display and more concerned with punishing the moral depravity of their wayward neighbors. If in fact such a shift in attitudes and expectations among important people took place–the evidence will always be circumstantial–then it was a subtle shift that drove men and women in large numbers from the arms of lenient ecclesiastical authorities to those of tougher secular authorities.

It is not readily apparent how Londoners viewed ecclesiastical justice. That they saw ecclesiastical justice as a visible, coherent system seems unlikely. Before the eyes of Londoners were fellow neighbors who misbehaved or who reported wrongdoers, and court officers who handled cases. A "system" of ecclesiastical justice was, as yet, perhaps too abstract, too impersonal, to catch the eye or capture the imagination of all but the most thoughtful—or religiously radical—Londoners. For the modern historian to impose a precise systematic structure on ecclesiastical justice distorts the realities of how Londoners actually behaved beyond what we know from the court record. But a system there was, no matter how fuzzy its contours. There were rules of behavior which had been authoritatively established; there was a court system of compulsion to enforce those rules; and there were Londoners, some of whom chafed at the rules and were not deterred by sanctions, some of whom accepted the rules as valid norms and insisted on their enforcement.

We now must look to the empirical behavior and attitudes of litigants and judges to comprehend the legal system. And we must analyze patterns of behavior in the types of suits heard in commissary court in order to understand why Londoners of the generation before the Reformation drifted away from that ecclesiastical legal system.

III

Defamation

For, as I have read in volumes' old,
A false lying tongue is hard to withhold;
a slanderous tongue, a tongue of a scold,
Worketh more mischief than can be told;
. . . .
Malicious tongues, though they have no bones,
Are sharper than swords, sturdier than stones.
. . . .
More venomous and much more virulent
Than any poisoned toad or any serpent.

—John Skelton,
"Against Venomous Tongues" [1]
(c. 1520)

In the garrulous, noisy London of John Skelton, defamation was a common crime, so common that it could be the subject of Skelton's anger in a way that is unthinkable for a modern poet. Today, defamation has been divided into two closely defined categories, libel (written defamation) and slander (spoken defamation). In modern London slander suits are virtually nonexistent, and libel suits are few and celebrated. In Yorkist-Tudor London, however, defamation suits made up about one-third of church court business. During one year, 1472, as many as 405 defamation suits were charged in London's commissary court alone. And during the sixteenth century so many defamation suits were charged in the common law courts that these courts were forced to take steps to discourage such litigation.[2]

In canon law, the crime of defamation sprang naturally from a sys-

1. Philip Henderson, ed., *The Complete Poems of John Skelton,* 3rd ed. (London, 1959), p. 248.
2. W. S. Holdsworth, "Defamation in the 16th and 17th Centuries," *Law Quarterly Review* 40 (1924), 304. Modern judicial statistics may be found in *Civil Judicial Statistics* and *Criminal Judicial Statistics* (London, 1970).

tem of criminal detection in which a suspect could be charged by the public voice solely on his bad reputaton or *mala fama*. A person's *bona fama* or good reputation among his neighbors, therefore, was important for him to maintain. But words such as public voice and *fama* are nebulous and irritatingly imprecise. William Lyndwood, for instance, tried to understand and to distinguish in the public voice a difference between public rumor and public fame. Quoting Hostiensis, he stated that rumor is a particular assertion from an uncertain source and is founded only on suspicion; a rumor against a person, he said, in itself does not prove bad fame. Public fame, on the other hand, is public acclamation against a wrongdoer by his neighbors.[3]

The public voice—whether rumor or fame—is a fiction and was as unhelpful for the courts as it is for the historian in locating the real source of criminal charges. Rumor and fame orginate with and are carried by specific people, not a public voice. In practice, loose words by any single person could form the basis of a courtroom charge by public voice. It was important, therefore, for people to clear their names of malicious gossip which might indict them by *fama* of a crime; their remedy was to charge defamation against those who publicly repeated imputations of wrongdoing. Thus, defamation suits proliferated.

The interpretation of the crime of defamation in medieval English church courts was based on a constitution of the Council of Oxford (1222). This constitution made it actionable in church courts to "maliciously impute a crime to any person who is not of ill fame among good and serious men." A specific crime had to have been imputed to a plaintiff, although words were actionable when a crime was only implied rather than specifically charged. The defamatory words have to have been spoken maliciously; thus, a defendant's intent was necessarily considered by a judge in his ruling. A plaintiff also must have suffered some sort of harm and been put to canonical purgation as a result of the defamatory words. (In practice, as we shall see, the London commissary court held that words which were spoken maliciously and did personal injury were actionable as defamation even though no specific crime had been imputed.) Those who were guilty of defamation faced public or pecuniary penance, but no money damages were allowed to a plaintiff.[4]

3. Lyndwood, *Provinciale* 2.6, pp. 113–14, gloss on "diffamati": "*Rumor* est particularis assertio, ex incerto authore [*sic*] & sola suspicione proveniens; & minus probat quam Fama. Nam *Fama* est communis viciniae acclamatio; *Rumor* vero cum pauci aliquid dicunt, non tamen publice."

4. Richard Helmholz, "Canonical Defamation in Medieval England," *American Journal of Legal History* 15 (1971), 225–68. The crucial sentence in the Oxford constitution is

The need to show malice was central to a definition of defamation: that is, according to the Oxford constitution, the words had to have been spoken "for the sake of hatred, profit, or favor" (gratia, odii, lucri, vel favoris). William Lyndwood went so far as to argue that if malice could be shown, even the truth was defamatory; he supposed that a person who spoke the truth against another, but who spoke publicly and maliciously and not in the normal course of legal procedure, was subject to punishment for defamation. His teaching reflected more the moral theology of the sin of defamation than strict legal doctrine. There is, Lyndwood implied, a moral and social as well as a legal value in keeping the peace; any malicious words ought to be actionable.[5] In fact, judged by the many court cases of defamation, it appears that the recourse to defamation suits functioned as a peaceful, legal outlet for the pent-up, explosive emotions of people in close-living social groups.

Lyndwood's rule about the truth being defamatory was not the practice of London's church courts. Here, the truth spoken openly in the streets, without the formality of a court charge, was not considered actionable as defamation. Joan Stokis, for example, was charged with publicly defaming Alice Taylor as an adulteress; when Joan appeared in court to answer for her defamation, she "proved" Alice's crime and was dismissed:

> Johanna Stokis communis diffamatrix vicinorum et presertim diffamavit Aliciam Taylor sic dicendo de eadem quod viveret in adulterio cum Edwardo Pratte. xii° die Februarii comparuit dicta Johanna et probavit crimen et ideo dimittitur.[6]

Questions of malice and the public nature of Joan Stokis's words seem not to have arisen in court; only the truth of her words mattered. We do not know how she proved her words.

But what if a person *falsely* charged another of a crime in court through the normal accusatorial process? Was a false court charge proof that a defendant had been defamed? Lyndwood did not address himself to this question. The courts in practice seem to have held that

this: "Excommunicamus omnes illos qui gratia odii, lucri, vel favoris, vel alia quacunque de causa malitiose crimen imponunt aliqui, cum infamatus non sit apud bonos et graves, ut sic saltem ei purgatio indicatur vel alio modo gravetur" (see F. M. Powicke and C. R. Cheney, eds., *Councils and Synods* [Oxford, 1964], 2,1:107).

5. Lyndwood, *Provinciale* 5.17, p. 346, gloss on "malitiose": "Et ex hoc quod dicit *Malitiose*, apparet quod sive dicat verum sive non, tenetur hac poena si possit constare quod ex malitia hoc dixit."

6. Acta correct., vol. 4, fol. 33v.

malice must be shown, even in a false charge in court. This protected those accusers, like churchwardens, who innocently charged another, honestly believing that person to have been guilty of a crime. Thus, only in rare instances did defendants countercharge suits of defamation after they themselves had been charged falsely in court with specific crimes; their suits were unsuccessful.[7]

A crime which was imputed to a person could be one that was cognizable in either temporal or spiritual courts. The potential for conflict between the two courts over defamation suits seems obvious. Because defamatory words imputed a crime, they could act as a criminal charge in court; that is, in order to test the truth of defamatory words—the truth was a proper defense for defendants—plaintiffs were often tried in court for their imputed crimes. This means that church courts, in order to test the truth of a defamatory word like thief, might try the plaintiff as a thief. Through the fifteenth and early years of the sixteenth centuries, a handful of defamations for the temporal crime of theft were heard in London church courts, and on rare occasions plaintiffs were put to purgation to prove they were not thieves. For example, consider the case of *Richard Barret vs. William Whyte* (1493), in which Barret, the plaintiff, had to face purgation over the crime of theft which Whyte defamatorily imputed to him:

> Willielmus Whyte gravis diffamator vicinorum et presertim diffamavit Ricardum Barret et Agnetem eius uxorem dicendo quod idem Ricardus anglice furtive asportaret vi argenta cocliaria et quinque par [*sic*] linthiamina et ceteras res et jocalia. iii octobris comparuerunt partes et dictus Willielmus Whyt fatebatur se [dicisse] Ricardum barret asportasse dicta Jocalia; et dominus assignavit Ricardo Barret ad purgandum se in crastino desuper vi^{ta} manu et dicto Willielmo Whyte ad contradicendum si sua putaverit interesse. comparuit Ricardus Barret et purgavit se Ricardo Raynolde, Nicholo Clyff, Thomas [*sic*] Sutton, Johanne Bekingham, Johanne Benet, Thomas [*sic*] Playter. viii octobris dominus iniunxit dicto Whyte penitentiam publicam [quod] Dominica proxima precederet processionem in camsia [*sic*] et toga et nudis pedibus, etc.[8]

Such cases were never stopped by the temporal courts through writs of prohibition.

Actual conflicts between courts are perhaps illusory. Plaintiffs may not really have been tried for theft in the normal sense of the word, but

7. See ibid., vol. 5, fol. 129v (*Christine Olyver vs. Joan Matlock*); and vol. 2, fol. 274v (*Henry and Joan May vs. Elizabeth Browne*).
8. Ibid., vol. 5, fol. 138v.

may only have requested that they themselves be put to canonical purgation. This in effect justified their suits by the Oxford constitution (that is, to show harm done them by having been put to purgation) and denied defendants a defense that their defamatory words were true.

During the late fifteenth and early sixteenth centuries the royal courts were developing a rule that writs of prohibition could be issued to halt church court defamation suits that had imputed crimes cognizable only in temporal courts. The exact date of this common law rule, which encroached on church courts, is unknown. William Holdsworth correctly placed the new rule at "the beginning of the 16th century," but suggested, incorrectly, that the new common law practice dates from the mid-1530s—when parliament and the law courts had begun a full-scale plunder of church authority.[9] More recently, John Baker traced such actions for defamation for temporal crimes to the period between 1508, "when the first action for calling a man a thief was entered in the King's Bench," and 1517, when "the action was fully established."[10] With the aid of the London commissary court books, a more precise date for the new common law rule may be suggested: November or December 1512. In early November 1512, the defamatory word thief was used as the basis of a defamation suit in the London commissary court just as it had been for decades. But by 10 December 1512, questions of theft were equivocally noted as belonging to temporal courts. In a defamation suit on that date Margery Wetherby charged that Elizabeth Smyth had called her a "fals errant hore and theiff." Elizabeth Smyth denied that she had imputed a sexual crime to Margery, but acknowledged that she called her a thief; she asserted that she would prove the charge of theft in the temporal courts.[11] This is the first, albeit ambiguous, signal of a new policy. Shortly thereafter, also in December 1512, a charge was made in court over the defamatory words "fals errant pykpurse"; no citation was sent out to the defendant to appear in court. And in February 1513, Leonard Johnson

9. Holdsworth, "Defamation in the 16th and 17th Centuries," p. 304; William Holdsworth, *History of the English Law* (Boston, 1927), 4:411 and n. 2. For the development of this rule see Helmholz, "Canonical Defamation," p. 260, n. 26.

10. John H. Baker, introduction to *The Reports of Sir John Spelman*, Selden Society 94 (London, 1978), pp. 237–38.

11. Acta correct., vol. 11, fol. 89r: "Elizabeth Smyth notatur officio quod est communis vicinorum suorum diffamatrix et precipue cuiusdam Margerie Wetherby quam vocavit fals errant hore and theiff etc. et nonnulla alia verba diffamatoria eidem publice imposuit etc. x Decembris comparuit et negavit imposicionem criminis fornicationis et fatebatur se vocasse eandem fals theiff et hoc asseruit probare et actionem inde attemptare in curia temporali."

brought a defamation action against Henrica Peterson for the words "fals horeson"; Henrica Peterson also had uttered other defamatory words which were crossed out by the scribe: "& thou didst . . . a wey . . . the kynges money." Two words in the phrase are no longer legible, but the gist of these defamatory words seems to be theft of some sort. In any case, the defamatory words imputed a crime over which church courts had no cognizance, and the judge dismissed the defendant, Henrica Peterson, because "this case does not concern an ecclesiastical court" (dominus in presencia dicti Leonardi dimisit dictam Henricam prout quod causa ista non concernit forum ecclesiasticum).[12]

Case evidence for a new common law rule is ambiguous and inconclusive. More persuasive is an analysis of the types of defamatory words charged in commissary court after December 1512. After that date defamations for the temporal crimes of theft and murder were no longer charged in London's commissary court as they had been earlier (see below, p. 78). Hence, in a defamation suit in 1514, the words "thou arte a bawde" were allowed in court, but the words "thou arte a false thef" were deliberately crossed off the court record.[13] A new rule had come into being further separating temporal from spiritual jurisdiction.

1. Procedure

Defamation suits in commissary court may be divided into two broad categories, each with a particular trial procedure available to litigants. During the late fifteenth century canonical purgation was the normal method of trial, with only a few notable exceptions. But shortly after the turn of the sixteenth century, new trial procedures were made available to litigants, who now were allowed to use witnesses to prove facts rather than compurgators to confirm oaths. A few isolated experiments in which witnesses were used in court may be found during the 1490s,[14] but the numbers of cases using the new procedure increased in tempo during the first two decades of the sixteenth century. With a new procedure, the complexion of defamation suits changed significantly. Acquittal rates fell from around 40% of all cases to around 16%; and conviction rates rose from between 2 and 3% of all cases to between 12 and 14%. A summary of more extensive findings (see Appendix A, Table 1) graphically demonstrates the change:

12. Ibid., vol. 11, fols. 89v, 91r.
13. Ibid., vol. 11, fol. 195v.
14. E.g., ibid., vol. 4, fol. 267r (*wife of John Moody vs. Alice Nicholson*).

	1484	1502	1512	1513
Number of defamation suits	171	160	129	110
Cases with witnesses	0	0	29 (22%)	32 (29%)
Acquittals	78 (46%)	77 (48%)	21 (16%)	18 (16%)
Confession of charge	0	11 (7%)	18 (14%)	13 (12%)

Who was largely responsible for bringing about this procedural change that favored plaintiffs, the court or the litigants? The commissary court itself clung to methods of compurgation and seemed little inclined to press for the truth of a case. In 1490, for example, the court record states that Margaret Edwardby had defamed Margery White publicly while in court on another case by calling her "thefe and brothell"; yet the judge ordered the defendant Edwardby to purge herself with two others although witnesses certainly must have been in court at the time who had heard the defamatory words (entire entry: "Margareta Edwardby [deleted: communis diffamatrix] publice in curia diffamavit Margeriam White sic vocando eandem in anglice thefe & brothell. xii° die Julii [1490] Dominus Commissarius assignavit dictam Margeriam ad purgandum se se 3ª [manu] die veneris proximo futuro").[15] In 1493 a similar defamation took place, this time "in the presence of an officer [of the court]" (in presencia officarii); and again the judge ordered compurgation rather than call the court officer to testify.[16]

Changing patterns in commissary court litigation, in fact, seem at all times to have been due to changing patterns in the attitudes of litigants rather than to new policies handed down by the court. Thus, a few defamation cases during the judgeships of Richard Blodywell (1492–1496) and John Perrot (1496–1501) in which witnesses were called to give evidence rather than compurgators to confirm oaths are too isolated to represent a new court policy. If rational evaluation of the facts in defamation suits was to be used in the commissary court, the initiative had to come from plaintiffs who were dissatisfied with defendants' easy acquittals through compurgation, but who chose not to risk the expense of consistory court trials. In 1496, for example, Eleanor Hull charged that Alice Hayward had defamed her in front of two named witnesses. This is the first time in extant commissary court records that named witnesses to a crime were noted; the plaintiff, Eleanor Hull, no doubt included their names in her court charge. Judge Perrot ordered Eleanor to prove her charges (seemingly at

15. Ibid., vol. 4, fol. 123r.
16. Ibid., vol. 5, fol. 142v.

Eleanor's insistence; Perrot normally ordered compurgation). One of Eleanor's witnesses, William Olaver, appeared in court to testify that he had heard the defamatory words. Olaver's testimony apparently induced Alice Hayward to confess, and she duly received penance. The case was not proved against her, nor ought it to have been; according to canonical rules, two witnesses were needed to prove a proposition.

> Alicia Hayward notatur quod est communis diffamatrix vicinorum suorum et presertim diffamavit Elianoram Hull dicendo quod habet alium virum superstitem et hec verba protulit in presencia M. Olaver et Willielmi lake. xxv Februarii comparuit et negavit; tunc dominus assignavit prefate Elianori ad probandum isto die a septimana viz. die Sabbati proximo. quo die comparuit Olaver et testificat huiusmodi verba in presencia Alicie Hayward confitens se ita dixisse et quod huiusmodi verba audivit a seipsa. tunc dominus assignavit sibi ad recipiendum penitenciam pro confessione die mercurii.[17]

Between 1503, when one court book ends, and 1509, when court records again resume, this new trial procedure had come into much wider use in the commissary court. Canonical purgation was still the standard practice, but plaintiffs could try, if they desired, to prove their charges with witnesses. The burden of proof then shifted from the defendant to the plaintiff, presumably at the request of plaintiffs. The result was a modified plenary procedure: witnesses were summoned and examined, but *viva voce* in open court rather than by secret written depositions as in consistory court; and defendants were expected to interrogate witnesses in court ("ad ministrandum interrogatoriam").[18] Litigants could conduct their own cases in this simplified procedure without the expensive use of proctors and advocates. During the early sixteenth century, however, proctors increasingly were used in commissary court to help litigants with a more technical procedure. Plaintiffs benefited most from the new procedure; acquittal rates fell and conviction rates rose.

This new procedure was not without its difficulties for an inexperienced layman or laywoman. Agnes Harvey, for example, charged Margaret Tutill with defamation and tried to prove her case by pro-

17. Ibid., vol. 7, fol. 12v. Two other isolated cases in which witnesses for the plaintiffs were called rather than compurgators for defendants may be found in vol. 7, fols. 22r–23v (*John Elliott vs. Joan Matlock, et al.*); and vol. 8, fol. 1v (Richard Spencer, the registrar of Canterbury and London, called witnesses to prove he was defamed).
18. This phrase is from the case of *Elizabeth Haerysby vs. Thomas and Alice Lacy*, in ibid., vol. 11, fol. 69v.

ducing a certain Agnes Stokes as a witness. Canon law had long required at least two witnesses to prove a proposition, and the judge ordered the plaintiff "to produce more witnesses" (ad producendum plures testes). On the following court day, the defendant Margaret was dismissed because the plaintiff Agnes failed to prosecute her case.[19] A proctor perhaps could have advised Agnes to arrange for the proper number of witnesses before beginning a lawsuit. A proctor also would have helped the wife of William Hare in her suit against Sybil Nichol. Sybil allegedly had called Hare's wife "a common hore and wors than a hore." William Hare prosecuted his wife's case and brought two men, Philipott Socii and Robert Pledury, to court as witnesses to the defamation; but these men told the judge that they did not understand either English or Latin ("responderunt quod non intelligunt anglica neque latina"). Hare perhaps lived in a neighborhood of foreign merchants or workmen. In the meantime Sybil purged herself of the general charge that she was a common defamer. The special charge that she had defamed Hare's wife had yet to be proved. So Hare on the following court day introduced two new witnesses, William Bukkett and Roland Fruley; but they, like the previous witnesses when faced with testifying before the court, could only respond lamely that they did not understand English or Latin either. Sybil Nichol was dismissed.[20]

As far as plaintiffs were concerned, the new procedure which placed the burden of proof on them was a mixed blessing. A defamation had to be a public utterance, and so plaintiffs now could call witnesses who had heard the words spoken publicly. But they also faced the problem of witnesses with faulty memories or untrustworthy appearance, or even—in the case of Mrs. Hare—witnesses who claimed not to understand English. Plaintiffs who chose to prosecute with witnesses now were subject to pay court expenses if their suits failed; this, of course, was normal practice in the consistory with its plenary procedure. Thus, when Anne Loxar failed to prosecute a case which she was obliged to prove with witnesses, she was charged the expenses of the commissary court:

> Dictus Simon Andrew notatur officio quod diffamavit prefatam Annam Loxar quam vocavit communem meretricem etc. dicto xix die decembris [1511] comparuit dictus Simon et negavit in presencia partis, habentis ad probandum die mercurii post festum epiphanie domini proximum. quo die

19. Ibid., vol. 11, fol. 61r.
20. Ibid., vol. 11, fol. 85r.

comparuit dictus Simon et peciit dimitti una cum expensis ratione non prosecutionis cause etc., quem dominus dimisit una cum expensis et decrevit partem principalem citandum fore.[21]

2. Numbers and Dispositions of Cases

Because London's commissary court books are so complete on a day-to-day and year-to-year basis (except where records for certain years are missing) it is possible to quantify cases and their dispositions. Numerical data has the comfortable appearance of concrete evidence; but my statistical Table 1 (see Appendix A, p. 142) on the disposition of defamation suits must be prefaced with a cautionary note. By pouring all defamation suits, or any other types of suit, into the same hopper, the specific realities of any one case become distorted. The commissary court records are like badly shattered mirrors in which each piece of glass—or scribal entry—reflects its own unique, peculiar reality. A defamation suit in which the parish nuisance was brought to account for his scurrilous tongue is not the same as a suit in which insults and defamatory words were exchanged between two parties in a heated argument, which in turn is not the same as the use of a defamation suit to vex a neighbor. Each case, when examined closely, remains unique and defies statistical ordering. My table shows nothing more than patterns in the disposition of legally related suits. Nevertheless, these patterns are important as clues to the ebb and flow of attitudes of litigants towards the court.

The number of defamation suits, compared to the total number of suits introduced into commissary court, was always high; the annual figures fall between 20% and 30%. After about 1509, the percentage rose even higher, to between 36% and 45%. This substantial rise in the percentage of defamation suits was not due to an increase in the number of such suits; rather, unlike other church court litigation, the number of defamation suits did not radically decrease. The number of defamation suits fell only slightly, and their percentage of the whole increased.

After the temporal courts embraced a new policy of prohibiting church courts from hearing defamation suits for temporal crimes, they undoubtedly took away from London church courts some defamation suits. But such suits at any time in London were rare; most litigation in

21. Ibid., vol. 11, fol. 30v. The preceding case on this folio is a charge of defamation against Anne Loxar by Simon Andrew. The case ultimately went to arbiters. Other cases in which the plaintiff was charged the court expenses may be found in vol. 11, fol. 4v (two cases).

London's commissary court were for spiritual, not temporal, crimes. At this early date in the sixteenth century there is no indication that Holdsworth is correct in stating that "as usually happened when the Common Law Courts and the Ecclesiastical Courts came into conflict, the Common Law Courts soon deprived the Ecclesiastical Courts of the greater part of their jurisdiction." [22] The drift of litigants to the temporal courts, as we shall see in succeeding chapters, was more subtle and complex than a conflict of jurisdictions. In any case, only a small portion of defamation suits in London church courts had ever impinged on temporal jurisdiction, and only a few of these suits were lost to temporal courts, despite the expanding jurisdiction of temporal courts over defamation.[23]

Not all suits which were reported to commissary were disposed of in a tidy manner. Often about half of the cases were not resolved in court at all. These defendants either were not actually summoned to court, or they refused to come to court, or their cases disappear from the court record in mid-proceedings with no further explanation. There were in general eight different ways in which cases were disposed:

(1) No citation issued. About 10% of the defamation suits were charges which had been registered in court but no citations were sent out to defendants. During years when court case loads were extraordinarily heavy, such as the early 1490s, numbers of cases in which no action was even begun against defendants rose accordingly. During those years as many as one-fourth of the defendants in defamation suits were not cited to court. We can never be sure why no citations were sent to certain defendants; perhaps the court was overburdened, or perhaps the registrar screened out charges which seemed to him to be a waste of time.

(2) Acquittal. Percentages of acquittals during the fifteenth century were generally between 40% and 50%. Such defendants were acquitted by successful compurgation, by purgation only on their own oaths of innocence, or by simple dismissals from court because their cases were not prosecuted. The year 1485, the year of the sweating sickness and the Tudor usurpation of the throne, is an odd exception: fewer defendants were acquitted outright and proportionately more settled out of court. Perhaps during time of social stress, trivial disputes over name-calling are more easily and amicably settled than during calm times. After about 1509 the percentage of acquittals fell significantly, from

22. Holdsworth, "Defamation in the 16th and 17th Centuries," p. 304.

23. See Baker, introduction to *The Reports of Sir John Spelman*, p. 242, for numbers of defamation actions in the king's courts: between 1508 and 1530, there were only four or five such actions per year, mostly for theft.

40–50% to around 16%; defendants obviously had much more difficulty freeing themselves from persistent plaintiffs armed with a new trial procedure.

(3) Case dropped. Many cases each year were never concluded in court. They simply disappear from court records in mid-proceedings. But the treatment of the accused amounted to an acquittal, because no defendant was punished and no court arbiters solved the dispute to the satisfaction of both parties. Perhaps the litigants reached an amicable agreement on their own out of court, or perhaps plaintiffs failed to prosecute their cases, which were then silently ignored by scribes. Often about one-third of defamation suits were "not concluded."

(4) Outside agreement. A few litigants settled formally out of court by certifying to the court that concord was reached by the parties on their own, or by accepting the arbitration of court-appointed arbiters. Except for that exceptional year 1485, percentages of outside agreements in defamation suits were betweeen 5% and 15%.

(5) Guilty verdict. Very few defendants confessed their guilt or were found guilty by the court. Before 1509, numbers of guilty persons ranged from none in 1484 (of 171 charged) to twenty in 1493 (of 211 charged). After about 1509, however, plaintiffs had slightly better success in forcing acknowledgments of guilt: consistently about 12% of defamation suits resulted in guilty verdicts accompanied by public or pecuniary penance. Clearly, the new trial procedure gave plaintiffs more leverage against accused defamers, although less than half of the successful plaintiffs made use of it. Probably the mere threat that witnesses could be produced encouraged some defamers to confess their guilt.

(6) Contumacy. Ten to twenty people each year were excommunicated (either suspended from church or placed under major excommunication) for failure to appear in court to answer for defamation charges. We have no record that these people were ever absolved from excommunication, and we can never be sure if church authorities appealed to the secular arm to force contumacious defendants to court; only one "significavit" to Chancery survives from many that may have been issued on those who were excommunicated by the commissary court.[24] A handful of people each year probably were placed outside the bonds of the church and remained at large in open defiance of the church's jurisdiction.

(7) Sent to consistory. During the late fifteenth century difficult defa-

24. See P.R.O., Significations of Excommunication, C 85/125, "Margaret Droper," and Margaret's case in Acta correct., vol. 10, fol. 46v.

mation suits were sent from the commissary court to the consistory court for solution. But after the turn of the sixteenth century, when new trial procedures became widely available in the commissary court, appeals to the consistory court completely dried up. This is one of many indications of declining legal business in the consistory court in the early sixteenth century.

(8) Other dispositions. An occasional suit was disposed of through ways not listed above: a defendant moved out of the jurisdiction, or he died, or his case was halted by an inhibition from the court of Arches, or he could not be found in order to be summoned. The numbers of such cases were numerically insignificant.

3. The Litigants

Who were the litigants whose defamatory name-calling fills so many folios of commissary court records? Court scribes recorded the names of plaintiffs as well as defendants in defamation suits, with the exception of cases in which plaintiffs were unnamed neighbors (*vicini*). Consequently we are overwhelmed with names. By the late fifteenth century a man's name no longer necessarily described his occupation; unless a title or occupation is appended to a name, we cannot be sure of a litigant's place in society.[25] In rare instances, the familiar name of a court officer flashes from court book folios: John Barthorne, a proctor of the court of Arches, appeared in court as a plaintiff against Christine Sergeant, who had defamed him as an adulterer; and Dr. Thomas Jane, official-principal of London's consistory, brought charges against Agnes Curiaunce for saying "maister Jan iapes [=fornicates] with our dame Raf Tilburns wiff."[26] But in general the names of litigants reveal little about their social status.

One important fact which we can discern from these names, however, is the sex of plaintiffs and defendants. Thus, in the fifteenth century there were as many female plaintiffs in defamation suits as male; and unknown complainants, known only as "neighbors," initiated as many as one-third of the prosecutions. Charges by neighbors may have originated in visitation or in wardmoot inquests. After the turn of the sixteenth century numbers of male plaintiffs declined substantially, and neighbors provided only occasional complaints to the court. In

25. Cf. F. R. H. DuBoulay, *An Age of Ambition: English Society in the Late Middle Ages* (London, 1970), pp. 57–8.

26. Acta correct., vol. 3, fol. 79v; vol. 4, fol. 137r. I have been unable to identify a Sir Ralph Tilburn. Christine Sergeant failed to appear in court and was suspended from church. No citation was sent to Agnes Curiaunce.

other words, the commissary court was resorted to less and less by men, including churchwardens, but continued to find plaintiffs among women. The prohibition on the imputation of secular crimes made no difference to this trend; as many women as men imputed such crimes before the temporal courts assumed the cases in 1512. The commissary court in the early sixteenth century, therefore, was becoming a women's court. What this signifies is difficult to say. It may be just one more signal of the declining social standing of London church courts; that is, in a consciously male-dominated society, the drift away from church courts by males meant for sixteenth-century Londoners that the commissary court perhaps was no longer a court worthy of serious consideration.

Defendants in defamation suits, those who allegedly had imputed crimes to others, were also most often women; in some years the ratio of women to men was as high as three to one. Because few defendants were convicted of defamation, we cannot say whether or not these many court charges were justified. Women, it seems, suffered under the cliché that they inherently were more maliciously garrulous and defamatory in speech than men. "Sometimes women were put in great blame," said John Skelton in a rhymed couplet, "men said they could not their tongues atame." [27] By any measurement, more women than men faced court trial for defamation:

	1472	1486	1493	1512	1513
Known Defendants					
Male	107	31	73	28	43
Female	234	96	106	86	61
Man and Wife	50	15	27	13	5
Known Plaintiffs					
Male	145	57	64	54	41
Female	147	54	62	66	60
Man and Wife	8	2	6	2	2
"Neighbors"	105	31	79	7	7

4. Defamatory Words

Defamatory words, in order to be actionable in court, generally had to impute falsely a crime to another. Some words were held actionable if they did (legal) harm to another without the imputation of a crime. Often, at least before December 1512, the defamatory words took the shape of a common triad of crimes: whore, thief, and bawd (pimp). The words slipped easily off the tongue, and in many cases, no doubt,

27. John Skelton, "Against Venomous Tongues," *The Complete Poems*, p. 248.

no more harm was meant than a nasty insult. But a crime had been imputed to another, and the injured party looked to the courts for legal recourse. The recourse in most cases proved ineffective for the parties who were insulted, but at least they had cleared their own names and had acted in an official way to expose a defamer—and the defamer, after his purgation and acquittal, was charged the expenses of the court (the dismissal fee).

The imputed crime itself was central to a defamation suit, but the commissary court was lenient in interpreting what constituted a crime. Words which did personal injury by disparaging another were actionable. Hence, in 1508, it was charged that a certain Michael Mawnford disparaged (*vilipendit*) the curate of St. Bartholomew's Aldgate; he told the curate to "leve thy prechyng for it is nott worthe a Fartte, necnon multa alia verba conviciosa ac inhonesta sibi publice imposuit." [28] The court allowed action on these words, as if they were defamation. Mawnford seems to have harmed the curate by insulting his professional abilities, thereby undermining the curate's authority over his congregation. Mawnford did penance for his words.

Some defamatory words imputed crimes directly: "lowler and heretyk," "prestis hore," "monkis hore," "traytor." Some were indirect slurs in which a crime was only vaguely implied: John and Agnes Lawdwyne, for example, were required to purge themselves of defamation of their neighbors for having said "there byn a cokkolde betwixt seint Dunstanys Church and the Condite in Fletstrete";[29] these words were imprecise but the implied charge of adultery against an unspecified neighbor constituted a general charge of defamation of one's neighbors; a special charge would have named the neighbor. In the case of *Sir Thomas Bundy vs. Roger Clay and Alice Pyhell*, no crime was imputed to Sir Thomas although he suffered harm from open talk about his romance with a certain Anne Love. Allegedly Clay and Pyhell had circulated gossip about Bundy which brought about his indictment by the wardmoot inquest—probably as a suspected fornicator. Clay allegedly had said, "Anne Love lened uppon Sir Thomas shulder in the chirche and knaked nuttes susspecyously," and then went on to describe how Anne and Thomas met "suspecyously in tavernes." The court record then alleges that honest parishioners reported their suspicions to the "aldermans deputy"—presumably at the wardmoot inquest. The defamatory words may not have imputed a crime, but Sir Thomas still had suffered harm and had been presented—perhaps

28. Acta correct., vol. 10, fol. 11v.

29. Ibid., vol. 9, fol. 10v; both successfully purged themselves with four neighbors.

falsely—to the wardmoot inquest. This case was sent to the consistory court for resolution.[30]

Year after year, defamers who were charged in commissary court usually had imputed sexual crimes to their neighbors. Although scribes before about 1490 rarely recorded the exact defamatory words used in suits, these words where extant are usually sexual in nature. From the 1490s onward, court scribes became more precise in the wording of defamation suits, just as the court was becoming more self-consciously precise in trial procedures; and from this time, the defamatory words in a plaintiff's charge were recorded verbatim in English to provide a sharply defined basis for litigation. Extremely common were the words "hore," "horeson," "Walsche hore," "Lumbardis hore," "prestis hore," and the like. After December 1512, when defamations for theft and murder and other crimes within the sphere of temporal courts no longer were taken to London church courts, the percentage of sexually related defamations increased. The sample years recorded below are typical of the predominance of defamations of sexual crimes:

	1493	1502–3 (18 mos.)	1512	1513
Type of Crime Imputed				
Sexual	89	47	97	89
Nonsexual	27	21	10	4
Both ("whore, thief, bawd")	27	39	13	0

Defamations for nonsexual crimes, which were under the jurisdiction of temporal courts, were for theft and murder. But defamations for theft imputed theft of small items only and, thus, perhaps of little interest to the king's courts: "a smoke [smock]," "iiii togas," "unam togam and a pese of cloth Cornysse," "ii towells, i sherte, a napykne and a payer of childeres hosyn" (presumably imputing that unusually common crime of robbing a washline), or "mete of my Lordes of Seint James and spice and ffiggis and reysysns."[31] And defamations for murder usually imputed to a woman the crime of infanticide, a crime which was regularly tried in church courts (see below, Chapter V). The mortality rate among swaddled infants was high, which no doubt raised suspicions that some infants were deliberatly smothered. Cruel defamatory words were often directed toward a mother who had lost her child, and intimated "that sche schuld [=did] sley her owen childe."[32]

30. Ibid., vol. 5, fols. 162v–163r.

31. Ibid., vol. 3, fols. 76v, 73r, 96v, 157r; vol. 5, fol. 103v.

32. Ibid., vol. 2, fols. 66v, 127v.

Imputation of nonsexual crimes was not always for crimes under the temporal courts' jurisdiction. To say that a person was a "fals liar" or a perjurer was to accuse him of a crime actionable in church courts; the same was true of actionable words like "heretyke," "leper," and "wych, seying that it were almes she wer burned at a stake." [33] Some insults did personal harm without imputing a crime cognizable in either temporal or spiritual courts. During the wars with Scotland in 1513, for example, London church courts held that to be called a Scot was defamation: in September, 1513, the rector of St. Anthony's, Thomas Leche, defamed Thomas Melmerby of his parish whom he publicly and maliciously called a Scot ("publice et malitiose vocavit scotum"). The curate Leche was ordered to perform penance by publicly asking for Melmerby's forgiveness and to pay the expenses of the court.[34] One month later, a similar defamation case was admitted to the commissary court, in which John Andrew defamed Robert Gray, saying "Robert Gray haith a brother in Scotlande and his a scott his self"; this quarrel ended in an amicable concord.[35] And as late as 1515, when England and Scotland were still officially at war although open hostilities were at a minimum, to be called a Scot was still considered defamation: Henry Whyt had to give a public apology to Thomas Coldeale for having said of Coldeale, "thou was born in Scotland on the bakke syde of Barwyke." [36]

The vast majority of defamatory words imputed that a person was a fornicator, adulterer, prostitute, or pimp. And it was no accident that over half the cases in the commissary court were for sexual misconduct: fornication, adultery, prostitution, and pimping. Defamatory words which imputed sexual crimes to others and actual charges of sexual misconduct were, among other things, vocal expressions from all ranks of society of a preoccupation with norms of sexual behavior.

Some defamations for sexual crimes undoubtedly were the result of angry swearing. Swear words are learned young in life and are easily spoken in anger. To call a woman a "rottyn hore," in other words, need not always indicate a particular concern for the evils of prostitution; such words were common, mindless epithets. But these harsh words were, nevertheless, predominantly sexual expressions. Londoners swore by using sexual slurs: "hore, rottyn hore, thow arte with childe with piggis," or "go home and kepe prestes from thy wyves arse," or

33. Ibid., vol. 3, fols. 7v, 47r; vol. 2, fol. 7v.
34. Ibid., vol. 11, fol. 132r.
35. Ibid., vol. 11, fol. 137v.
36. Ibid., vol. 11, fol. 233v.

"sche beryth feyre [fire] in her ars for every man to lyte his candyll att."[37]

Judged by London's commissary court records, pre-Reformation Londoners were greatly concerned with sexual norms and sexual misbehavior. Sexual offenses and defamations of sexual offenses represented most of yearly commissary court business. London's commissary court, therefore, was largely a court of sexual behavior, and it is to sexual behavior that we must now turn.

37. Ibid., vol. 5, fol. 91v; vol. 11, fol. 301v; vol. 3, fol. 264r. There is a fascinating literary tradition–legends concerning Virgil–about the lighting of fire "at a person." Virgil, as revenge for having been tricked and left dangling naked in mid-air in a basket, orders the woman responsible (usually Nero's daughter) to stand naked in the public square where each citizen lights his torch "at her person." I am indebted to Luke Wenger for this citation: see John W. Spargo, *Virgil The Necromancer: Studies in Virgilian Legends* (Cambridge, Mass., 1934), pp. 136–7, 198–206.

IV

Sexual Crimes

London's commissary court, along with other London courts and the confessional, was a place where sexual mores were enforced. Venereal offenses dominate court records. If actual sexual crimes were not charged to defendants, then defendants were tried for defaming others of sexual crimes. Large numbers of defamation suits and sexual misconduct suits were intimately related: the former were a defense against gossip and the latter were often a result of that same gossip; and both together make up much of the warp and weft of the sexual moral fabric as we know it in pre-Reformation London. Below are numbers and percentages of sexual and defamation suits during typical years from 1471 to 1514:

	1471	1484	1493	1502	1514
Total suits	980	764	1,061	547	328
Sexual offenses	587 (60%)	507 (66%)	681 (64%)	332 (61%)	143 (44%)
Defamation suits	227 (23%)	171 (22%)	211 (20%)	160 (29%)	149 (45%)
Combined total	814 (83%)	678 (88%)	892 (84%)	492 (90%)	292 (89%)

Sexual morality was a theme much discussed by medieval theologians and legists and consequently much studied by modern historians.[1] When we search beyond the writings of theologians and legists, however, we do not find extensive evidence of *popular* attitudes concerning sexual behavior. Rather we find what people were taught. Where documentation exists, not surprisingly, we find a condemnation

1. See John T. Noonan, Jr., *Contraception; A History of its Treatment by the Catholic Theologians and Canonists* (Cambridge, Mass., 1966), esp. pp. 193–99, 293, 312. For other, less sympathetic, treatments of medieval sexual ethics, see Derrick Sherwin Bailey, *The Man-Woman Relation in Christian Thought* (London, 1959), pp. 234–35, and W. G. Cole, *Sex in Christianity and Psychoanalysis* (New York, 1955). An older but still useful survey of attempts to control sexual behavior in England is Geoffrey May, *Social Control of Sexual Expression* (New York, 1931). A Freudian psychologist, G. R. Taylor, has attempted (unsuccessfully) to find consistency in medieval sexual mores and practices: see *Sex in History*, 2nd ed. (London, 1951). A recent and very good analysis of continental penitential literature is Thomas Tentler, *Sin and Confession on the Eve of the Reformation* (Princeton, N. J., 1977), esp. pp. 162–232 ("Sex and the Married Penitent").

of illicit sex outside marriage as defined by theologians. Thus, the minds of the London mayor and aldermen, when they issued a proclamation against "the stynking and horrible Synne of Lechery" in 1483,[2] were not far from that of the urbane Humanist, John Colet, who in the late 1490s preached to his Oxford audience to "keep under and extinquish the fire of lust." Colet urged his listeners to seek the spiritual reality of God and to reject the lowest human sense, touch or "carnal defilement." When he wrote his lecture, Colet had before him Ficino's *De voluptate*, which contained a neo-Platonic hierarchical ordering of the senses from the lowest, "touch," to the highest, spiritual communion with God.[3] Colet's views on sex, nevertheless, as well as the aldermen's horror of lechery, were an integral part of a traditional theologian's position of distrust of the flesh.[4] The opinions of lay and church authorities toward coitus, however, were not necessarily the same as the attitudes which governed the lives of the lay masses.

What then were Yorkist-Tudor Englishmen taught concerning sex? J. W. Blench, in his study of English sermon literature between 1450 and 1600, has found that the predominant theme of pre-Reformation English preachers was the *memento mori* lament of Everyman: death is imminent, and people must not foolishly place their trust in earthly vanities. These were comforting words in an age of incessant plague. Preachers did not neglect to upbraid their congregations for their moral failings, but sexual wrongdoing was only one of many sins denounced from the pulpit; others were dishonesty, blasphemy, and all of the seven deadly sins.[5] John T. Noonan has found little evidence from either pulpit or confessional that the doctrine of coitus only for procreative purposes was widely disseminated; he argues, however, that doctrinal condemnations for "unnatural sexual acts" probably had a wider audience.[6] And Thomas Tentler in his study of the litera-

2. R. R. Sharpe, *Calendar of Letter-Books of the City of London: Letter-Book L* (London, 1912), p. 206.
3. John Colet, *An Exposition of St. Paul's First Epistle to the Corinthians*, trans. and ed. J. H. Lupton (London, 1874), pp. 47–48. Cf. Bailey, *Man-Woman Relation*, p. 165.
4. See Cole, *Sex in Christianity*, p. 5, who views Western "dualism," or the separation of the spiritual and material realms, as originating not in Christianity but in late Hellenistic culture.
5. J. W. Blench, *Preaching in England in the Late Fifteenth and Sixteenth Centuries: A Study of English Sermons, 1450–c. 1600* (Oxford, 1964), pp. 228–63. See also G. R. Owst, *The Destructorium Viciorum of Alexander Carpenter* (London, 1952); the *Destructorium* was an extremely popular work of the fifteenth and sixteenth centuries which contained all the themes of popular preaching and in which sexual themes played only a small part.
6. Noonan, *Contraception*, p. 274.

ture of sacramental confession has argued that although the medieval church "was inordinately concerned" with sexual sins and "irrational physical pleasure" (as opposed to "rational self-control"), confessors "were told to be cautious" not to offend parishioners by presumptuously prying into their sexual lives.[7] It does not seem likely that English men and women were unduly subjected to warnings against sexual misconduct, although they perhaps were well acquainted with rules concerning marriage. Hence, Chaucer's audience heard from the righteous Parson a canonically correct sermon on the seven deadly sins. Under the sin of lechery they were told the legitimate functions of marriage:

> Thanne shal men understonde that for thre thynges a man and his wyf flesshly mowen assemble. The firste is in entente of engendrure of children to the service of God; for certes that is the cause final of matrimoyne. Another cause is to yelden everich of hem to oother the dette of hire bodies. . . . The thridde is for to eschewe leccherye and vileynye. The ferthe is for sothe deedly synne. ("Parsons Tale," ll. 938–39)

The first two reasons are meritorious; the third is venial sin; and the fourth, "oonly for amorous love and for noon of the foreseyde causes," is mortal sin.[8]

The high incidence of defamations for sexual crimes and of sexual crimes themselves is perhaps itself testimony to persistent teaching from pulpit and confessional about sins of the flesh. Nevertheless, the evidence allows us to say only that sexual crime was an important topic among pre-Reformation Londoners, and at least some Christian sense of sexual morality was current in popular belief. With few exceptions, cases that reached the courts were restricted to what Thomas Aquinas termed "natural lust": adultery, fornication, and prostitution.[9] Only rarely were people charged with crimes "against nature," notably sodomy.

In the minds of Londoners, then, a practical distinction seems to have existed between ordinary sins of lust and the more serious sins against nature. Unnatural sexual acts were rarely prosecuted or used as offensive words in defamation. Only one person was ever accused of

7. Tentler, *Sin and Confession*, pp. 165–66, 223.

8. Cf. S. Wenzel, "The Source for the 'Remedia' of the Parsons Tale," *Traditio* 27 (1971), 433–53, for the ultimate source of the Parson's sermon: an anonymous treatise on virtues which Wenzel calls *Postquam.* But "the traditional pessimistic view of women and marriage that appears in *Postquam* is considerably toned down" in Chaucer (p. 451).

9. *Summa Theologiae* 2a2ae.154.12.

sodomy (homosexuality) from over 21,000 defendants between 1470 and 1516: William Smyth had "publicly preached" that he had committed a sodomitic crime with Thomas Tunley; this case was dropped by the court before a decision was rendered:

> Willielmus Smyth commorans apud le Wernakyll publice predicavit [quod] c[ommisit] crimen sodomiticum cum magistro Thoma Tunley. vir citatus ad 9 diem Maii [1471]. quia [non] comparuit suspensus. citatus ad 24 diem Maii [deleted by scribe: per litteras. quia non comparuit, excommunicatus].[10]

And homosexuality was the implied crime in only one defamation suit: Agnes Andrew defamed Margaret Myler (not her husband, strangely), saying that Margaret's husband was a "woman" and that he grabbed priests between their legs; the case was sent to arbiters and dismissed from court.[11] Two other cases must be mentioned in order to complete the list of "unnatural" sexual behavior: in 1476, two priests on separate occasions allegedly exposed their genitals ("secreta sua") in public.[12]

The lack of criminal charges against sodomites in the London commissary court does not mean, of course, that there was no sodomy. We can never know for sure from the silence of the records. Perhaps such acts were considered serious enough to be handled in a higher church court or by the bishop personally. Perhaps secular courts had already assumed these prosecutions; hence, in 1533 parliament made a felony "the detestable and abhomynable vice of buggery committed with mankynde or beaste" and denied benefit of clergy to those committing the crime.[13] However, a lack of defamations for sodomy does, I believe, argue for a probable low incidence of sodomy.

1. Adultery

Adultery and fornication may be classified as crimes by nonprofessionals, in contrast to the professions of pimping and prostitution. In

10. Acta correct., vol. 1, fol. 4r.
11. Ibid., vol. 2, fol. 132v.
12. Ibid., vol. 3, fols. 132v, 253r.
13. 25 Henry VIII, c. 6; also 28 Henry VIII, c. 6, 31 Henry VIII, c. 7, and 32 Henry VIII, c. 3. The sudden appearance of this statute is odd. Lehmberg in *Reformation Parliament*, p. 185, argues unconvincingly that the statute "may have been aimed at the Church, especially at the impending visit of monasteries"; that is, benefit of clergy was denied in the statute to monkish offenders. See also Elton, *Reform and Renewal*, p. 148, who ties in the buggery statute to discussions over sanctuary. I suspect that the statute merely gave legal sanction to an already common practice, i.e., trying unnatural sexual offenses in secular courts.

London there was constant gossip on the streets about unfaithful wives and husbands. Much of this gossip ended in defamation suits, much in charges of adultery and fornication. Of the common sexual crimes charged in London, adultery was most often charged.

Churchmen generally considered adultery a more serious crime than fornication. Adultery, said Thomas Aquinas, is illicit intercourse with a married woman. It is a more serious crime than fornication because it is an act that hurts a third party, the husband; and apart from the sexual crime involved, the offending man commits the added injustice of appropriating another man's rights.[14] William Lyndwood, too, considered adultery a graver sin than fornication; he argued that it violated marriage vows—which fornication did not—and assumed that it should be more harshly punished. Nevertheless, Lyndwood placed both carnal sins together in the category of *crimina mediocria*, neither the gravest nor the least serious among sins.[15] Sexual crimes, when refracted through a scholastic, legal mind, are stripped of their salacious and polluting qualities; sins become ordered, codified, and sensibly placed in perspective against a backdrop of more serious wrongs.

By the fifteenth century, court-ordered penance for adultery and fornication had long since been separated from the sacrament of penance. We do not know what private penance was ordered from the confessional for adultery or fornication. By the fifteenth century, Lyndwood reminds us, private penance was at the discretion of the priest ("Hodie tamen omnia ista sunt in arbitrio Sacerdotis"), and the older penitentials seem no longer to have been strictly observed.[16] We do know that in London court-ordered penance was usually commuted for a fine based on the offender's wealth rather than the seriousness of the crime. Thus, although adultery was thought to be worse than fornication, the two crimes were treated alike in the courts; neither crime was held by the court to be so serious that a simple fine would not suffice as punishment.

In an early-sixteenth-century manual on the law of marriage, William Haryngton argued for an older, harsher judgment against adulterers. The offending woman, wrote Haryngton, ought to be beaten with rods and sent to a nunnery for two years. Open crimes required open punishments "with the moost ignomynye & shame"; secret sinners ought to be punished by secret penance extending for no less than

14. *Summa Theologiae* 1a2ae.73.7, 2a2ae.154.8.
15. Lyndwood, *Provinciale* 1.11, p. 58, gloss on "adulterium": "et proprie dicitur adulterium, ubi celebrati conjugii jura violantur"; also 5.14, p. 314, gloss on "adulterio."
16. Ibid., 5.14, p. 314, gloss on "adulterio." See also Tentler, *Sin and Confession*, pp. 16–17.

seven years.[17] Haryngton was a London-based doctor of canon law and an advocate in the court of Arches; and he himself became judge of the London commissary court, *sede vacante*, in 1523. Unfortunately his court book has been lost during the last century, and we have no way of knowing if he applied his strict standards on the sacrament of penance in court.[18] We know that his predecessors on the bench were not unduly harsh in meting out punishments for adultery—whatever their personal penitential views might have been.

Adultery was charged against a great many people of different social classes in the London commissary court. Goldsmiths and armorers, innkeepers and paupers, were all charged. Even John Warde, the alderman from Bishopsgate Ward, was forced to purge himself in court for an alleged act of adultery with Katherine Butler.[19] Foreigners were also charged: Francis Wynsor, a "Spanyard" (with a very English name), for example, was charged with both adultery and bigamy; because he had urgent business for the king in Spain, Wynsor was allowed to purge himself of both crimes by his own oath and his case was dismissed from court.[20] In most cases a defendant is merely a name in the records with no title attached, but the occasional appearance of a merchant or a man of prominence suggests that the court was indiscriminate in accepting charges against anybody.

The corespondent of a defendant in an adultery or fornication case also was often prosecuted by the court, although the court record does not list the corespondent as defendant. Often the court record states that both parties purged themselves—although only one had been charged. Throughout the records both men and women seem to have been charged and purged at an equal rate. Figures from three typcial years will suffice:

	1472	1490	1512
Men face purgation alone	111	183	17
Women face purgation alone	116	160	15
Both face purgation	55	92	12

In about 40% of the cases, defendants successfully purged themselves; their purgation usually had the corollary effect of cancelling charges against their corespondents.

17. William Haryngton, *The Commendacions of Matrymony* (London, 1528), no page numbers.
18. For Haryngton as a commissary judge see Hale, *Precedents*, p. 96.
19. Acta correct., vol. 6, fol. 102v (1495).
20. Ibid., vol. 11, fol. 156r; see also fol. 161r, in which Wynsor is charged with defamation (ending in concord), and fol. 169r, in which Wynsor's corespondent in adultery is charged and her case dropped ("vacat").

If no corespondent could be named, a charge was usually dropped; that is, the defendant was not even summoned to court. On two occasions in 1471, for example, suspects were summoned to court only to be dismissed because no corespondent could be named: William Huper was charged as an adulterer "with various women" (cum diversis mulieribus) and Gady Kilmont as an adulteress with a "cordner" (unnamed).[21]

London's commissary court was not merely a court of penalties; it attempted on occasion to right a wrong. In two instances, adulterers who had left their corespondents with child were ordered by the court to pay sums of money to the women, presumably for the expenses of childbearing. The sums of money paid to the women, 30s by one man and £4 by another, were not paid in lieu of court punishment; additional sums were paid to the court as pecuniary penance for commutation of punishments.[22]

The frequency of adulterers charged in commissary court and the dispositions of their cases may be divided into three chronological groups (see Table 2, p. 144). The first group (1471–1493 on the table) is marked by large numbers of adultery cases which flooded the court during the late fifteenth century. In 1493, for example, 33% (348 defendants) of all court cases (1,061 defendants) included charges of adultery. Very few, at most 8%, of those charged were convicted. Suspects were not even summoned to court in about one-fifth to one-third of the complaints reported to the court; either these charges perhaps were clearly groundless or the court was too busy to handle them.

The second group (1497–1498 on the table) contains adultery charges only from the rural-suburban parishes in the deaneries of Middlesex and Barking. A lower percentage of adultery cases made up the court calendar from these deaneries than from London. Conviction rates for adultery in the villages, however, were somewhat higher than in the city. I have argued earlier from Lincoln diocesan evidence that a compurgation system was more effective in villages than in a city (see above, pp. 48–49); based on evidence from the suburban villages surrounding London, the argument appears to be valid.

During the early sixteenth century (the third group, 1502–1514, but especially after c. 1509), numbers of adultery suspects were far fewer than in previous years. This simply may reflect those years of endemic plague, which perhaps dampened the ardor of many lovers for bodily contact. Widespread disease probably was the reason why earlier, in 1485, the year of the sweating sickness, numbers of suspected adul-

21. Ibid., vol. 1, fols. 132r, 161r.
22. Ibid., vol. 4, fol. 64r; vol. 7, fol. 30v.

terers also fell drastically from previous years. But the early decades of the sixteenth century were different from 1485; they are characterized by a tougher prosecuting spirit by plaintiffs—a spirit which we have already seen in the new trial procedures used in defamation suits. After the turn of the sixteenth century, suspected adulterers were convicted at a higher rate than in earlier years; often about 20% of those charged for adultery were convicted, compared to about 6% in the late fifteenth century. Procedural changes in defamation suits probably discouraged much loose talk and name-calling which in earlier years had been the basis for criminal charges of adultery and fornication. People were perhaps more sure of their allegations before they impugned another's good fame. Hence, fewer persons were falsely charged, but a greater percentage of suspects had court summonses sent out to them, and more of them were convicted.

2. Fornication

In practice fornication was treated by the courts no differently from adultery. Fornication simply meant coitus between an unmarried man and an unmarried woman, or as Lyndwood states, "solutus cum soluta." [23] A handful of couples, however, who had exchanged marriage vows but whose marriages had not yet been solemnized, were charged in court as fornicators; guilty couples were ordered to solemnize their marriages, and some were even ordered to perform penance for their fornication. A good example of a couple caught in that twilight zone between having exchanged marriage vows and having the marriage solemnized is the case of Robert Ap[ ]lly and Elizabeth Asbery:

> Robertus Ap[blank]lly notatur officio super crimine fornicationis cum Elizabeth Asbery. citatus ad comparendum die lune proximo xxviii° Julii [1511]. comparuit dictus Robertus et negat etc., tamen fatebatur familiaritatem et allegat matrimonium cum eadem, quem dominus monuit ad solemnizari faciendum matrimonium cum eadem citra festum sancti Michaelis [29 September] proximum sub pena Juris.[24]

Couples who were married but had not solemnized their marriages in church were involved in five of nineteen guilty pleas for fornication in 1512, two of ten in 1513, and one of eleven in 1514.

23. On sexual crimes, see Lyndwood, *Provinciale* 5.14, p. 314, gloss on "adulterio"; and 2.2, p. 96, gloss on "Fornicatione."
24. Acta correct., vol. 11, fol. 8r. See also vol. 11, fol. 25r: "Johannes Hall notatur officio quod contraxit matrimonium cum Margareta Dudding [parochiae] sancti gregorii et quam impregnavit et modo recusavit subire solempnisacionem matrimonii eiusdem cum eadem. . . ."

Like defendants in adultery cases, alleged fornicators were from varied social strata. John Aperis, a goldsmith, was charged in court as a fornicator (and successfully purged), as was the Lombard "Gabriel de Worsis"; two merchants, William Haberdyn and Hew Goodwy, both purged themselves of fornication charges in 1493.[25] On separate occasions two men were charged for fornicating with an illegitimate and quite mysterious daughter of Edward IV named Grace. In February, 1490, a certain William Leche was charged as a fornicator with Grace ("cum Gracia que erat filia Regis Edwardi"); Leche was allowed to purge himself easily by his own oath. Four years later, in December 1494, a certain Robert, chaplain to the "Lord of Lylle," was charged for fornicating with a certain Amy Tailor "and even with Mistress Grace, daughter of King Edward" (necnon cum M. Grace filia Regis Edwardi); Robert was not summoned to court.[26] Who exactly Grace was and what was her social standing are baffling and perhaps unanswerable questions; she apparently did not find the respectability of another of Edward's illegitimate daughters, Elizabeth (by Lady Elizabeth Lucy), who, as wife of Sir Thomas Lumby, married into an estimable family.[27]

A constant stream of suspected incontinent priests faced canonical purgation. Many priests in London, and no doubt in the entire church, were unsuited for a celibate life. Natural sexual urges wormed into and undermined clerical ideals of chastity. This was as true for a lowly London stipendiary priest in the fifteenth century as it had been for a Desert Father in the fourth century. London, like any urban center, offered an alluring wealth of opportunity for sexual promiscuity which was found in few other places in medieval society. The city attracted rowdy priests like John Huntington, who in front of the churchwardens and other parishioners went to a tavern with a known prostitute and offensively barked, "thow hore, goo fet me drinke and come and sitt down by me and let se whoo will say against it." [28] Or, it was reported of the curate Sir Geoffrey that "after he had shryvyn yong women at Ester in the vestry and asayled them, thenne he wolde commen with theme and kysse and put his handis under theyr clothis and comen with theme to haue poynted with them, where he and they

25. Ibid., vol. 1, fol. 104v; vol. 5, fols. 44v, 80r, 83v.

26. Ibid., vol. 4, fol. 18v; vol. 6, fol. 88v.

27. See Charles Ross, *Edward IV* (Berkeley, 1974), p. 316, n. 2. Ross states that Grace "may have been brought up in the household of the dowager queen Elizabeth Woodville, and was present at her death in 1492 (B. M., Arundel MS 26, ff. 29v–30r)." Until her appearance in the London commissary court books, this was "the only known reference to her."

28. Acta correct., vol. 5, fol. 78r (82r in pencil).

myght mete to do syne with theme and specially with Johan the servaunt of Agnes Nele." [29]

Popular charges and insinuations of fornication dogged the steps of priests. "Prestes hore" was a popular epithet and was used indiscriminately on the streets of London in anger or in jest. The slightest indiscretion by a priest brought catcalls and court charges of incontinence. In one case, Joan Dawson charged Katherine White in court for defamation, saying that Katherine had repeated some false gossip which she attributed to Joan: "Joanna Dawson shulde sey that the parson off Seint Mari Somerset schulde have a mayde in his chambur." [30] Such malicious gossip often found its way to court as a criminal charge against an innocent parson. Yet, enough priests confessed to fornication to fuel popularly held beliefs of clerical incontinence.

London ecclesiastical authorities were joined by civic authorities in the prosecution of lecherous priests. As early as 1383, the mayor and aldermen had taken upon themselves to punish these offenders. Guilty priests found no sanctuary either in benefit of clergy or in the church courts' supposedly exclusive jurisdiction over fornication and adultery.[31] Throughout the margins of the "Journals" (the minutes of the aldermen's court and the court of the common council) are crude drawings of a "tun" or a barrel set upright; these invariably mark scribal entries which noted that fornicators, usually priests, were condemned to the Tun in Cornhill (that is, a small jail shaped like a barrel set on end).[32] London civic authorities in 1383—then caught up in an earlier wave of purifying zeal—had assumed their jurisdiction over sexual morality, they claimed, because of the ease with which guilty priests were freed by church courts after only payment of small fines.[33] Indeed, this was the case in Yorkist-Tudor London as well. In 1502, for

29. Ibid., vol. 5, fol. 157v (162v in pencil). This same priest had faced earlier charges; see fols. 106v, 153r.
30. Ibid., vol. 3, fol. 87v.
31. Secular authorities, of course, recognized benefit of clergy in only a few crimes cognizable in temporal courts, but church authorities vainly assumed this privilege for their own clergy in ecclesiastical crimes as well. See L. C. Gabel, *Benefit of Clergy in England in the Later Middle Ages*, Smith College Studies in History 14 (Northampton, Mass., 1928). For jurisdiction of the church courts over sexual crimes, see E. B. Graves, "Circumspecte agatis," *English Historical Review* 43 (1928), 1–20. See also C. R. Cheney, "The Punishment of Felonous Clerks," *English Historical Review* 51 (1936), 215–36.
32. E.g., Journals, vol. 2, fols. 27(b)r, 44v, passim.
33. John Stow, *A Survey of the Cities of London and Westminster and the Borough of Southwark*, ed. C. L. Kingsford, 2 vols. (Oxford, 1908), 1:189; see also 1 Henry VII, c. 4 (1485), which gave prelates the power to imprison incontinent priests.

example, five priests who were convicted of fornication in the commissary court were set free after fine payments of 10s, 8s, 2s, 20d, and 18d;[34] and John Cowper, vicar of St. Leonard's Shoreditch, only paid a fine of 13s 4d for redemption of his penance after he confessed in court to fathering three children by Agnes Colte.[35] The mayor's court, on the contrary, in 1514, ordered the priest Thomas Baker to void the city forever, after he confessed to seven years of adultery with Margaret Hopper and fathering a child by her; Margaret Hopper also was banished from the city.[36] The city fathers invariably were morally more stringent than church authorities in the discipline of incontinent priests.

Among the charges summarized in Table 3 (p. 145) I have included two rape charges which the courts treated as simple fornication. One alleged rapist who had "fornicated" with his victim against her will ("contra voluntatem suam") did have to purge himself with twelve others; this was a more severe requirement than usual. The other suspect, Peter Manyfield, had forced Alice Burke into his room, where he held her for a long time, "committing fornication" (committendo cum eadem crimen fornicacionis); Mayfield then sold her as a prostitute to a German merchant in the Steelyard. Peter Manyfield confessed his crime, but failed subsequently to appear in court to receive punishment; he was, therefore, placed under a sentence of suspension from entering church. No further action was taken against him—at least in the commissary court—presumably because Alice Burke did not press her charges.[37] The first rape charge may not have been a valid one, but the second charge was confessed by the defendant, Manyfield. The superficial facts of Manyfield's case suggest that the complainant simply took her case to the wrong court and received inferior justice.

What is surprising is not that the two suspect rapists were treated so lightly by the court, but that they were tried in a church court at all. For centuries rape had been treated as a felony at common law, and the penalties of the king's courts were much more severe than those of the church courts. The mayor's court was willing to hear rape charges, and on occasion it committed rapists to jail.[38]

Included also in Table 3 are four incest charges which were tried as fornication. Incest, to medieval minds, meant more than its modern

34. Acta correct., vol. 9, fols. 14r, 37v, 79v, 87v, 115r.
35. Ibid., vol. 5, fol. 31v.
36. Repertories, vol. 3, fol. 33v.
37. Acta correct., vol. 4, fol. 13r; vol. 5, fol. 135v.
38. Holdsworth, *History of English Law*, 3:316; Repertories, vol. 3, fol. 150v (14 July 1517).

connotation of carnal coupling between father and daughter; it then also meant fornication between "spiritual relatives," those who were related within several degrees through godparents. Three of the four charges of incest in the commissary court, in fact, were against couples with alleged spiritual affinities; and the fourth charge was against a betrothed couple, between whom an unnamed accuser thought there was an unlawful affinity.[39] None of the couples was convicted.

Disposition of fornication cases, like adultery cases, can be divided into three chronological groups. During the late fifteenth century, many suspected fornicators (about 10% to 15% of all cases) were charged in commissary court. Between 9% and 18% of these suspects were convicted, which was a higher conviction rate than among other sexual offenders. Fornicators, as nonprofessional sexual wrongdoers, perhaps were more susceptible to the pressures of their consciences in court to confess their crimes.

The second group (1497–1498 on the table) contains cases from the deaneries of Middlesex and Barking. Few alleged fornicators were charged: only nine suspects one year, and eight the next—far fewer than suspected adulterers. This is perhaps a case of underreporting of fornicators, or perhaps such suspects were taken to the archdeacon.[40]

After the turn of the sixteenth century (the third group on the table), fewer people were charged in the commissary court with fornication than in the late fifteenth century, but a higher percentage of those who were charged were convicted. Conviction rates rose to between 19% and 33%. By the early sixteenth century cases in commissary court were rarely simple matters, because plaintiffs, when they came to the church court, were generally more tenacious in their prosecutions.

3. Pimping

The final two types of sexual crimes, pimping and prostitution, are by definition crimes by professionals. Pimping (then called bawdry) means that a person traffics in prostitutes, usually for a share of the prostitutes' pay. Scribes used the word *pronuba* to refer indiscriminately to a male or female pimp; but on occasion they also used the

39. Acta correct., vol. 4, fol. 221r–v; vol. 10, fol. 15r; vol. 11, fols. 65v, 92v.

40. Dr. Marjorie McIntosh has corrected an earlier assumption of mine that opportunities for fornication were greater in the city than in rural villages. From her work on the Havering manorial records, she has informed me of all sorts of rural opportunities for fornication: "in barns, in houses while the family was away, in back gardens of village houses, and in the open air, preferably under a hedgerow or rick in case of inclemency."

words *fautor lenocinii* (or one who *fovet lenocinium*) for the same purpose. Court scribes never clearly indicate the difference between a *pronuba* and a *fautor lenocinii*, but it appears that a *pronuba* accepted money for providing a woman and a *fautor lenocinii* provided a place (for payment?) for the illegal act. Alice Wilkynson, the court charged, for example, "encourages lechery" (*fovet lenocinium*) in her house; she confessed that about a year earlier a priest and another woman were left alone in her house for the purpose of fornication. She seems not to have accepted payment from a prostitute but rather rented rooms for what she knew to be illicit relations.[41]

Few pimps were ever convicted by London's commissary court. Hence, little can be said with certainty about the profits of pimping. Payments to pimps seem to have varied greatly: Alexander Elwold allegedly had two prostitutes in his house from whom he received 2s per week; another pimp allegedly received 4s "for his work" (pro labore), which was unspecified; yet another, Alice Whith, allegedly sold Elizabeth Pyssy to "a Spanyard" for the goodly sum of 40s; and in a Middlesex village, a woman allegedly was a pimp for her servant and a man from Flanders, and received 4d per night for four nights.[42]

Only seven pimps were convicted from among 1,030 suspects who were charged in the commissary court during the years listed in Table 4 (p. 146). From surviving information about the few who were convicted, we cannot make a composite picture of a typical pimp. A man, Patrick Hill, confessed that he led a young girl to Waltham Forest and sold her to a Lombard. Two women, Joan Williamson and Joan Radley *alias* Blackface ("blakefase"), confessed to being pimps. We know the position in society of only one confessed pimp: she is Christine, the wife of the jailer of Newgate prison, who supplemented her income by providing Newgate prisoners with harlots.[43] It is perhaps the case that these few people who confessed were part-time pimps, perhaps on the fringes of the criminal underworld; it is doubtful that hardened, professional pimps would break down so easily in the church courts, or indeed would even appear in the church court.

The London commissary court was largely unsuccessful in the prosecution of professional sexual offenders, whether pimps or prostitutes. This inability to attack prostitution and pimping effectively seems to have been the natural result of a compurgation system designed for tightly knit village groups, of a lack of interest and moral commitment

41. Ibid., vol. 11, fol. 293v.
42. Ibid., vol. 1, fol. 111r; vol. 2, fol. 105v; vol. 7, fol. 32r.
43. Ibid., vol. 5, fols. 88v, 110r; vol. 9, fol. 40r.

by the court to appeal to the secular arm to coerce contumacious suspects to court, and of a lack of effective coercive powers of the church court itself. Excommunication may still have been a real threat to an upright member of the community, but it was ignored by prostitutes and pimps.

Civic authorities also prosecuted pimps and prostitutes. They were much more effective in convicting these criminals and more harsh than church courts in meting out punishments. Aldermen, through their constables, were required to rid their wards of all such "strumpettes, mysgyded and idil women daily vagraunt and walkyng about the stretes and lanes of this Citee of London and Suburbes of the same and also repairyng to Tavernes and other private places of the said Citee provokyng many other persones unto the said Synne of lechery" (1483).[44] Wardmoots were required to report prostitutes and pimps to the mayor's court for trial and punishment.[45] First offenders convicted of pimping were condemned to be paraded through the city and set on the pillory; second offenders were again led to the pillory, but afterwards they were taken to the city gates to forsake the city forever. Similar punishment was prescribed for prostitutes and incontinent priests.[46]

Secular punishments and ecclesiastical penance had many parallels. As a penitent was obliged to lead the Sunday procession in humiliating garb, so were prostitutes and pimps required by London ordinance to be led through the city in a sort of mock procession accompanied by minstrels and others beating pans and basins. As incorrigible sinners were excommunicated from the Christian body, so were incorrigible wrongdoers banished from the city of London. Secular punishments at times appear an imitation of church court punishments of penance; perhaps the civic authorities saw in ecclesiastical penance the proper humiliating punishment for sexual offenders. City and church authorities even used the same language in their punishments: both enjoined "penance" upon wrongdoers. The minds of secular and ecclesiastical authorities were not far apart in their perceptions of the world. In 1529, for instance, five convicted pimps faced the mayor's court. They were first upbraided for "not dredyng god ne the shame of the worlde" and for living in sin. The court then declared that "the forsaid persones shall suffire such *penaunce* as here after folowith"—that is, wearing striped hoods, they were to be led throughout the city by minstrels and

44. Sharpe, *Calendar of Letter-Books: Letter-Book L*, p. 206.
45. E.g., Repertories, vol. 2, fol. 92v (91v in pencil).
46. Letterbook K, fol. 179r; Letterbook N, fol. 21r–v.

others who were to beat pots and pans, then stand on the pillory where the proclamation was read, and finally be banished from the city.[47] Such a festive racket acted as the imitative counterpart of the reality of church court sanctions. In earlier centuries this ceremony perhaps served a community function by reinforcing, especially for the youth, community sexual mores.[48] It may be that the din and the clamor of the older carnival-community ritual still was meant to instill proper sexual mores in London youth. It is impossible to say, in fact, if such rituals meant anything at all to Londoners during early Tudor England.

Pimps and prostitutes were punished by the mayor's court with slightly more regularity than by the commissary court. Minutes of meetings of the mayor's court reveal the punishment of one or two pimps every year. People may have taken charges against manifest pimps to their aldermen rather than their churchwardens to ensure that the culprits would not be easily acquitted. This seems to have been the case with Elizabeth Saunders, a girl only thirteen years old, who filed a complaint against a pimp to her alderman, Thomas Semer of Fleet Ward. Elizabeth had been approached five times during a local fair by a carpenter's wife, who finally persuaded the girl that she could find "good service and good wages" with a certain Elizabeth Knyght of St. Sepulcre's parish (in Fleet Ward). The young girl was led to the house of promised employment by an unnamed male companion of the carpenter's wife; but after she entered the house, Elizabeth Knyght locked her and the man in a room where the man raped her. The girl went to her alderman for help and to find justice. Elizabeth Knyght and the carpenter's wife were indicted, convicted, and punished for *pimping*–the only charge which seemed to fit the crime, although no prostitution was involved. The fate of the rapist is unknown.[49] Civic authorities had the muscle to mete out satisfactory punishments; and they, rather than the church courts, were often looked to for just punishment of professional sexual offenders.

During the 1520s especially, civic authorities increased their drive against pimps and prostitutes; in 1520, 1523, and 1526 there were out-

47. Letterbook O, fol. 154r. My emphasis. For other examples of the use of the word "penance" by London civic authorities, see Repertories, vol. 3, fol. 257r–v, and vol. 4, fol. 158v.

48. Natalie Z. Davis, "The Reasons of Misrule: Youth Groups and Charivaris in Sixteenth-Century France," *Past and Present* 50 (1971), 52–54, 56 n. 48. Cf. the recent, interesting work of Peter Burke, *Popular Culture in Early Modern Europe* (London, 1978), repr. New York, 1978, especially pp. 197–204.

49. Repertories, vol. 3, fol. 102r; also Letterbook N, fol. 21r–v.

bursts of reforming zeal in which aldermen were instructed urgently to rid their wards of pimps and harlots. And in 1529 the scribe of the mayor's court duly entered into the court minutes a list of thirteen prostitutes from Portsoken Ward alone who were condemned to the cucking stool to be "washed over the eares." [50] More prostitutes from this small suburban ward were punished in one year than during the thirteen years for all London wards which I have listed on Table 5 (p. 147).[51] The civic drive against purveyors of sex may be related to a sharp drop in the numbers of pimps and prostitutes who were charged in London church courts from around the turn of the sixteenth century: in 1512, for example, only eight persons were charged in court for pimping, far fewer than in previous years, when prosecutions were measured in the hundreds. During the early sixteenth century, resort by Londoners to the commissary court for punishment of professional sexual wrongdoers was clearly in decline. We do not know for certain if this was due to a lack of confidence in the court by accusers, or due to the more stringent defamation procedures which perhaps squelched much loose talk and many potential criminal charges. What does seem certain for the early sixteenth century is that church court prosecutions for pimping and prostitution fell and civic concern afterwards increased.

4. Prostitution

Among sexual criminals, prostitutes were treated by both church and lay authorities with the most ambiguity. Prostitutes (as people) were scorned and segregated from the rest of society; yet prostitution (as social activity) was tolerated and regulated.[52] Support for tolerating prostitution came from the impeccable authority of both Augustine and Thomas Aquinas. Quoting Augustine, Aquinas reasoned thus: prostitution is like "a sewer in a palace. Take away the sewer and you will fill the palace with pollution. . . . Take away prostitutes from the world and you will fill it with sodomy." [53] Prostitution, then, is a me-

50. Repertories, vol. 5, fols. 20(b)r, 29r, 46r–v; vol. 6, fols. 16v, 22r; vol. 7, fol. 91v; vol. 8, fol. 43v. For the history of the cucking stool, see John W. Spargo, *Judicial Folklore in England illustrated by the Cucking-Stool* (Durham, N.C., 1944). This punishment especially was reserved for scolds (pp. 106–124).
51. For Portsoken Ward see above, pp. 33–35.
52. Derrick Sherwin Bailey, *Sexual Offenders and Social Punishment* (Westminster, 1956), p. 51.
53. *De regimine principum ad regem Cypri,* 4.14, in *Opuscula Philosophica* (Rome, 1954). Cf. Bailey, *Man-Woman Relation,* pp. 162–63. For Aquinas's authorship of *De regimine* see I. T. Eschmann, ed., *On Kingship* (Toronto, 1949), pp. ix–xxv.

dium by which normal society is kept morally clean; men with uncontrollable urges to sin can be channelled into a controlled and restricted location, that is, a proper sewer. Aquinas's analogy (via Augustine) is not compelling. It overlooks the nuisance that an open sewer can present, and it ignores the problem of forced prostitution among women in dire economic circumstances. What the analogy does admit, is that in an imperfect world—especially in the medieval world where there was widespread poverty—prostitution is inevitable and the best one can hope for is its control.

Prostitutes proliferated in large medieval European cities. Their ranks were fed and maintained both by chronic poverty, which provided an endless supply of destitute widows, wives, and daughters, and by urban populations overbalanced by males.[54] Among city males, there was an inordinate number of confirmed single men, some by religious vows, others by economic necessity. Perhaps also there were many men with wives still in the country and foreign workmen who were alone far from home—not unlike foreign labor forces in modern European industrial areas.

Like other European cities, London had its regulated brothels. Numbers of London prostitutes unfortunately are impossible to determine. Prostitutes probably were not so plentiful in fifteenth-century London as in, say, Rome or Venice, where, J. R. Hale argues, harlots were counted by the thousands.[55] The primary regulated brothels of London were located across the Thames, in Southwark, nominally just beyond the liberties of the city, but not beyond its actual jurisdiction. They were called the "stews," a word which originally had meant only a public bath but had come to be associated with assignations in the bath house. The "stewside" in Southwark was situated next to the "bear gardens," where bull- and bear-baiting, another illegal but tolerated activity, took place. Although stewside prostitutes were tolerated, they nevertheless were forbidden Christian burial; they were buried in a plot of ground called "single woman's churchyard" apart from the consecrated ground of the parish churchyard.[56]

Stewside London brothels, then, were not in London proper. This meant also that they were outside London diocese and its ecclesiastical

54. J. R. Hale, *Renaissance Europe: The Individual and Society, 1480–1520* (New York, 1973), p. 135.

55. Ibid.

56. Stow, *Survey*, 2:54–55. A note on the word "stew": in the late fifteenth century, "stew" still meant a public bath as well as a brothel; a certain John Auchholt, for instance, was charged as a fornicator with "Anna the washer of the stew [baths] of the Whyt Cok" (Acta correct., vol. 5, fol. 39r).

jurisdiction, which did not extend to the Surry side of the Thames. Southwark was in the diocese of Winchester and its stews were the responsibility of its bishop, who coincidentally had a London palace near the brothels; stewside prostitutes were popularly called "Winchester Geese." [57] Thus did Shakespeare put into the mouth of the duke of Gloucester this chiding rebuke to the bishop of Winchester: "Thou that givest whores indulgences to sin." [58] The stews were regulated by royal constitution as early as the twelfth century; by the fifteenth century there were eighteen brothels on the Southbank, but from 1506 the permitted number was reduced to twelve; they were finally put down officially in 1546 by commandment of Henry VIII, but continued to operate unofficially despite the ban.[59]

Prostitution also flourished in the city of London itself. Although the mayor and aldermen in 1417 forbade stews to be set up in London or its suburbs, by 1428 they could only dictate that no "foreigners" (non-Londoners) were to run the ones which in fact had been established.[60] We do not know the location of these brothels or the extent to which they flourished. Beyond the walls of regulated brothels, unattached prostitutes walked the streets and frequented taverns. Prosecutions of prostitutes were not against women in brothels but were directed at women in the streets, women like Isabella Herne who committed the crime "in the town dyche," and Elizabeth Tomlyns, wife of a Lambeth tailor, who plied her trade in "The George" tavern on Lombard Street.[61]

We have little evidence of the financial rewards of prostitution. There must have been a wide price range. In one case it was alleged that a man spent two nights with a certain Joan, who lived with a notorious pimp named Spanish Nelle; for the first night Joan allegedly received 4d and for the second, "a Ferthing wig and a ferthing worth of singill bere." [62]

Neither temporal nor ecclesiastical courts had much success in prosecuting prostitutes; pitiful police methods and abject poverty ensured a constant supply of willing women on the streets, so that, like Hydra's heads, for every prostitute put out of business several more appeared in her place.

57. May, *Social Control of Sexual Expression,* p. 132.
58. *Henry VI,* pt. 1, act 1, scene 3.
59. Stow, *Survey,* 2:54–55. For the continuation of the stews after the ban, see Salgado, *The Elizabethan Underworld,* p. 51.
60. Journals, vol. 1, fol. 18v; vol. 2, fol. 106v.
61. Acta correct., vol. 5, fol. 100v; Repertories, vol. 5, fol. 52r–v.
62. Acta correct., vol. 6, fol. 21v.

The life pattern of a prostitute named Mariona Wood can be partially reconstructed in order to demonstrate how little civic and ecclesiastical authorities were willing or able to prosecute harlots. Mariona Wood first appears in surviving records in 1479, when she was presented as a harlot by the Portsoken wardmoot. Two years later, in 1481, the same wardmoot presented her again as a harlot.[63] Civic authorities apparently did nothing against Mariona, for her name appears with regularity in commissary court records from February 1482 until the 1490s. She was first charged in commissary court for fornication, but failed to appear in court and was excommunicated. Oddly, this puzzling entry was appended to her case (first appearance): "18 February [1482] she was dismissed by consent of the commissary" (dimittitur de consensu commissarii).[64] Four days later, on 22 February 1482, Mariona again was charged in court, this time with adultery; again she failed to appear and was suspended from entering church (minor excommunication). In September 1482, Mariona Wood was accused of both adultery and prostitution, but the summoner could not find her to deliver the summons; again she was dismissed *de consensu commissarii*.[65] The commissary judge perhaps realized how hopeless it was to bring a hardened, incorrigible prostitute to court. Through the 1480s Mariona Wood was noted periodically in court records, not as a defendant, but as an uncharged corespondent. And through the years she gradually accumulated a list of aliases: by November 1494, she was noted as "longa mariona wode alias Birde alias taler." [66] She was tolerated in her ward and in her parish, first as a prostitute and finally as a pimp. She never left Portsoken Ward or the parish of St. Botolph Aldgate. In 1491 she was charged in court as a pimp as well as a prostitute, and she was accused of the same crimes several times in succeeding years through 1496.[67] Mariona Wood never made an appearance in court. She was excommunicated, of course, but to little avail. Her life as a prostitute and pimp spanned seventeen years of extant civic and ecclesiastical records, and never once was she punished. On occasion, other prostitutes were banished from the city by the mayor and aldermen, but Mariona Wood, through civic indifference or perhaps bribery, was never touched by authorities.

Many other prostitutes were named as corespondents in adultery cases as well, but not charged with a crime. Certain prostitutes (espe-

63. Port. Ward Present., membranes 11 and 13.
64. Acta correct., vol. 3, fol. 103r.
65. Ibid., vol. 3, fols. 114v, 160r.
66. Ibid., vol. 6, fol. 80v.
67. Ibid., vol. 4, fol. 300r; vol. 6, fols. 59v, 79v, 95r, 103r, 175r.

cially of the stews) were so well known to scribes that they simply referred to these women by their "professional" names. Most of these aliases are singularly unimaginative: Little Nan, Little Margery, Little Kate, Long Alice, Great Molle, Johanna Greatbelly, and Pale Besse (presumably to distinguish her from one of her contemporaries, Little Besse Sympson *alias* Black Besse). Others were more alluring: "Pusse le cat," Bouncing Besse, Katherine Sawnders *alias* Flying Kate, and Joan Havyer *alias* puppy *alias* Little Joan.[68]

Some names suggest a cause of the woman's prostitution: an unnamed *meretrix vagabunda* perhaps was forced into harlotry by her poverty. "Johanna with the one hand" and "Bette cum yoldefote [clubfoot]" perhaps were doomed to prostitution by their physical disabilities. Many names indicate that the harlots were foreign-born or at least were from distant parts of the British Isles: French Jane, "Nan a Parys," Spanish Nelle, "Christine that cam from Romayn," Joan Greke, Agnes a York, Anne Ireland, and Agnes Okeley (O'Kelly).[69]

Although prosecutions against prostitutes were usually unsuccessful, the commissary court occasionally did make an effort to protect a girl from sinking into prostitution. Margery Whyte, the cook "in the Spanyards place," for example, was ordered under pain of excommunication by the judge to leave employment at that house because of its evil reputation.[70]

Like pimping suspects, only a few accused prostitutes over the years were convicted in the London commissary court; and like numbers of pimping suspects, numbers of accused prostitutes declined during the early sixteenth century. Only 10 prostitutes confessed guilt from among the 377 women charged during the years noted on Table 5 (p. 147). A rare confession of guilt may be seen in the case of Joan Greke, who was caught openly by the constable:

> Johanna Greke communis meretrix et erat deprehensa cum quodam presbitero in Le Ryoll et constabilarius conduxit eos ad le Cownter [the sheriff's prison] et eciam erat deprehensa in domo cuiusdam Igrane Fusia [?–illegible] cum duobus Lumbardis. x die Januarii [1490] comparuit, negavit articulum, et purgare se 4^{a} die Lune proximo. illo die non comparuit ideo Suspensa. et fatebatur crimen et solvit pro redemptione penitencie ii^{s} et dimittitur.[71]

68. Ibid., vol. 5, fols. 33v, 39r, 52r, 93v, 148r, 149r, 158r; vol. 3, fol. 145r; vol. 6, fols. 31v, 84r.
69. Ibid., vol. 1, fol. 49r; vol. 3, fols. 78v, 96v; vol. 4, fol. 296r; vol. 5, fols. 54r, 80r, 157r; vol. 6, fol. 100r.
70. Ibid., vol. 5, fol. 85r.
71. Ibid., vol. 4, fol. 12r.

It may be that Joan Greke confessed her guilt because she had been caught, presumably in the act of her crime, by a city official. But her confession may simply indicate her lack of professionalism; perhaps she was only an occasional prostitute or new to the field. Many others also had been captured in the act of prostitution by the constable, only to deny the charge, supported by the appropriate number of compurgators. Joan Lynton, for example, was also captured by the constable, apparently as a prostitute, whereupon she was taken to the sheriff's prison and summoned to court (three days before Joan Greke). Her case is typical. She successfully purged herself with four others and was dismissed:

> Johanna Lynton [meretrix] cum quodam viro; et constabilarius deprehendebat eos et conduxit et habuit eos ad le cownter; et eciam dicta Johanna frequentat nimis suspiciose locum vulgariter nuncipatum Stiliard. citata ad vii^{m} diem Januarii [1490]. illo die non comparuit ideo suspensa. xii die Januarii [comparuit] et negavit articulum et in die Jovis proximo purgare se se 4^{a} [manu]. comparuit et purgavit se et solvit feodum.[72]

Cases like this were a potential source of irritation between secular and ecclesiastical authorities; and they point to a need by secular authorities to prosecute prostitutes in their own courts.

5. Conclusion

London church courts expended much energy prosecuting sexual offenders. During the late fifteenth century, cases in commissary court involving sexual wrongdoers averaged about 65% of the total case load. Around the turn of the sixteenth century, numbers and percentages of prosecutions for sexual crimes declined. This decline was due in part to the plague that settled on London from 1511 to 1521, but it also seems to have been a result of more stringent procedures available to litigants in defamation suits. Many charges of sexual misbehavior seem to have originated in street gossip. The tougher legal attitude toward loose defamatory talk perhaps inclined many gossips and name-callers to be more discreet.

Because the commissary court had so little success in convicting professional sexual offenders—pimps and prostitutes—we cannot rule out the possibility that this scarcity of convictions generated a widespread lack of confidence by lay accusers in the church courts' ability to punish these offenders. This may have accounted for the especially steep

72. Ibid., vol. 4, fol. 10r.

decline in numbers of charges in court against pimps and prostitutes during the early sixteenth century. Public confidence is virtually impossible to measure, at least before the era of modern polling techniques. It is a reasonable supposition, nevertheless, that around the turn of the sixteenth century, Londoners showed an increased determination to make their courts punish wrongdoers. This new "legal spirit" in defamation suits has already been demonstrated, and it is at least an implied cause of the higher conviction rates of adulterers and fornicators. The relative paucity of prosecutions against pimps and prostitutes in commissary court illustrates the underside of this new, pre-Reformation, purifying legal spirit; that is, because the commissary court was unsuccessful in convicting professional purveyors of sex, accusers of such criminals ceased to seek justice against them in the commissary court and instead looked to civic authorities who had the will to enforce sexual norms.

William Tyndale, that persistent critic of the established church and spokesman for royal control of the church, understood the real problem with church courts in his day: their inability to convict obvious wrongdoers in quick trials followed by public punishment. If sin were not punished immediately, he said, it would be laughed at, and this would set a bad example for others to follow: "For if an open sinner be found among us, we must immediately amend him, or cast him out of the congregation with defiance and detestation of his sin." Tyndale thus argued for stricter discipline of the laity—the type of swift, summary punishment that should be meted out by the local curate and the "sad [serious] and discreet men of the parish" as "in the early days." Tyndale's historical understanding of "the early days" is baffling, but he is clear in his lament of the present condition of the church: "If in ten parishes round there be not one learned and discreet to help the other, then the devil hath a great swing among us; that the bishops' officers that dwell so far off must abuse us as they do." [73] Tyndale's voice is one of a coming Protestant discipline, of a New Jerusalem on earth, against an older medieval laxity. But it is also a voice that found many London sympathizers who also were looking for stricter moral discipline and—before the Reformation—were looking to secular authorities to provide that discipline.

73. William Tyndale, "The Exposition of the First Epistle of St. John," in *The Works of the English Reformers: William Tyndale and John Frith*, ed. Thomas Russell (London, 1831), 2:480–81.

V

Other Litigation

Alongside the many defamers and sexual offenders (and their compurgators) who filled the commissary court chambers were other men and women seeking justice on less "popular" issues. Some were seeking justice on specific civil issues: quarrels over money, rights, and obligations. Others were charged with rarely prosecuted criminal offenses: heresy, witchcraft, infanticide, and usury—crimes so seldom prosecuted that they were never more than exotic diversions in an otherwise repetitious court calendar.

Disputes over money, inheritances, and marriages are important, tangible issues which materially affect people's lives. Ecclesiastical and secular courts were supposed to settle such disputes or, at least, to reconcile differences. There were, in theory, clear fields of jurisdiction separating church courts from secular courts. But, in fact, this line of separation was more like a shifting frontier. In certain types of litigation one jurisdiction provided an alternative route to justice from the other. We have already seen that the prosecution of professional sexual offenders and incontinent priests in London came to be largely the responsibility of secular authorities. Conversely, during the late Middle Ages complainants seeking recovery of small debts flocked to church courts to take advantage of their liberal contract law. During the sixteenth century this trend was reversed and small debt suits were taken to secular courts. The popularity of a court, in other words, depends largely on whether complainants feel that their suits will be settled in their favor. If complainants were not successful in church courts, then—for certain legal disputes—secular courts were available as alternatives. Creditors, for example, wanted to be repaid money owed them, and they sought out whichever forum was to their advantage.

During the early sixteenth century, as we shall see, many suitors drifted away from ecclesiastical courts and sought justice in certain types of disputes from secular, civic authorities. During these years suitors also demanded that their civic authorities meddle in church affairs to regulate such matters as tithes, oblations, and probates.

Before analyzing specific types of litigation and their disposition during the crucial pre-Reformation years, I should make certain preliminary observations about the disposition of actual suits: plaintiffs and complainants in the commissary court achieved few outright victories against their opponents. Most private disputes were settled out of court, either by court-appointed arbiters or by the contending parties on their own, or were dropped because the plaintiffs lost interest in prosecuting their suits. Few judgments were ever rendered by judges. But the commissary court did provide a time and a place for disputants to bring their quarrels into the sharper focus of a legal framework. The commissary court, thus, rendered a sort of justice; that is, it generally brought disputing parties to a reconciliation. But simple reconciliation and arbitration were perhaps not always what plaintiffs desired.

1. Breach of Faith or Petty Debt

During the late Middle Ages many plaintiffs in England appealed to church courts for recovery of petty debts. The specific court charge was *fidei laesio*—that one party "broke faith" (*fregit fidem*) to another. Breach of faith had long been cognizable in ecclesiastical courts. As early as the thirteenth century, church courts were willing to enforce oral promises or parol contracts.[1] Thus many victims of broken promises that involved financial loss sought recovery of their money in church courts rather than in secular courts, which did not yet recognize oral, unwritten contacts.

After the turn of the sixteenth century complainants in petty debt suits began to abandon church courts. In Canterbury consistory court during the late fifteenth century, for example, the majority of civil suits had been for breach of faith; but after about 1520, numbers of such suits fell rapidly from several hundred cases yearly to only four suits in 1535.[2] The same decline may be seen in Hereford, Lichfield, Chichester, and Exeter after about 1520.[3] A similar pattern of decline took

1. T. F. T. Plucknett, *A Concise History of the Common Law*, 5th ed. (Boston, 1956), pp. 17–18; W. R. Jones, "Relations of the Two Jurisdictions: Conflicts and Cooperation in England during the Thirteenth and Fourteenth Centuries," *Studies in Medieval and Renaissance History* 7 (1970), 80–82, 208.
2. Woodcock, *Medieval Ecclesiastical Courts*, pp. 89, 90–91. Woodcock does not say why there was a decline, but he does rule out, correctly I think, any overt action on the part of secular courts.
3. For a recent assessment of the decline of breach of faith suits in English church courts and the corresponding rise of "assumpsit" in common law courts, see Richard Helmholz, "Assumpsit and *Fidei Laesio*," 406–32, esp. 426–27, where statistics are given for the sixteenth-century decline in breach of faith suits in Canterbury, Hereford, Lichfield, Chichester, and Exeter. See also Houlbrooke, "The Decline of Ecclesiastical Jurisdiction," p. 240, who found no breach of faith suits in Norwich consistory after 1509, when the records begin. He attributes the decline of this type of litigation to common lawyers armed with writs of *praemunire;* such a conspiracy theory does not seem to be valid for London.

place in the London commissary court although London suitors abandoned church courts at an earlier date: from about 1500 in London, breach of faith suits (for petty debt) virtually disappeared from the commissary court.

To whom, then, did London creditors appeal to recover small sums of money owed them? They appealed to the mayor and aldermen of London. As the following mayor's court memorandum clearly implies, civic authorities first met the demands of creditors seeking recovery of debts by appointing weekly *ad hoc* commissions to hear such complaints; but after several years, by 1518, petty debt suits had become so numerous and burdensome that a permanent commission was appointed to hear them:

> [4 November 1518] Memorandum that where two Aldremen and iiii Comeners were lately Chosen & Appoynted to here wekely pety maters under the value of xl^{s} for the grete ease & Comfort of the Citezens which dayly be vexed & Retained to be in Jureys for the same Yt is nowe Agreed that iii of the old Comyssioners shall stond every moneth [*sic*] & iii newe to be Chosen in the stede & place of them that shall so be Removed. And this order to stond & Contynewe monethly duryng the the [*sic*] tyme specified in thact of Comen Counsell therof provided.[4]

This commission was henceforth known as the London court of Requests. The commission expired in 1520 but then was renewed for seven years and ultimately became permanent because the court "is thought to be very good & beneficiall." [5] Unlike the church courts, the court of Requests did not hear complaints of debt over 40s; that is, the king's courts had already set a lower limit of 40s for their debt cases which then also became the upper limit for local courts.[6] Clearly, a new civic court for petty debtors was neither a raid on nor a challenge to ecclesiastical jurisdiction. Rather, creditors before 1518 had already abandoned London church courts; they then turned to secular authorities for help. The mayor's court was forced by plaintiffs to hear suits which it had not solicited.

We must look closely at petty debt suits in the commissary court to discern why this court—and church courts in general—appeared to Londoners to be unsatisfactory. The church courts' willingness to adjudi-

4. Letterbook N, fol. 99r.
5. Ibid., fol. 141v.
6. See John S. Beckerman, "The Forty-Shilling Jurisdictional Limit in Medieval English Personal Actions," in Dafydd Jenkins, ed., *Legal History Studies 1972* (Cardiff, 1975), pp. 110–17. His evidence of pleas of 40s or less in local courts is from the thirteenth and fourteenth centuries.

cate upon oral contracts earlier had made the courts very attractive. Oral contracts were probably the rule in medieval England. Written contracts for the innumerable small business transactions which took place daily were unnecessarily cumbersome. When church courts heard parol contracts they were filling an obvious need in a moneyed, scarcely literate world. How well church courts were able to enforce these same contracts is another matter. Brian Woodcock found from his study of Canterbury consistory records that fifteenth- and early sixteenth-century judges ordered convicted debtors to pay their debts under pain of excommunication—except for one short period (1500–1511) when they only ordered "penance" for breach of faith.[7] It would be surprising if restitution was not made a condition of penance. Theologians and canonists had long argued that penance was not possible without making restitution for a crime or debt.[8]

London court evidence, however, is silent concerning judge-ordered repayment of debts as a condition of court sanctions or of court punishment. Scribes always noted when judges ordered payments on such matters as tithes and probates and when defendants in breach of faith suits *voluntarily* repaid their debts; but their silence as to *court-ordered* repayment of debt seems to suggest that London's commissary court may not have attempted to force guilty parties to make restitution. The hesitancy of scribes to place on record any money payments ordered by a judge may have been connected with the common law's view that church courts could not award money damages. Payment of damages, however, is not the same as restitution. In the end we do not know if repayment or restitution was ever ordered by the court. A typical case is that of Mariona Haws, who "broke faith" to William Bolworth for not paying him a debt of 6s 8d; all that we know of her case is that she was dismissed from the court because she had completed public penance ("dimittitur quia peregit publicam penetenciam pro violatione fidei").[9] But if the debt was not paid then the *violatio* would still exist. One must assume that the courts followed normal canon law precepts and made restitution a part of penance.

More crucial is the question of how successful were plaintiffs in recovering their money. Most plaintiffs seem to have resolved their disputes with debtors out of court. In most cases, a court summons seems to have been enough to bring the two parties to some sort of negotia-

7. Woodcock, *Medieval Ecclesiastical Courts,* pp. 90–91.
8. See Helmholz, "Assumpsit and *Fidei Laesio,*" p. 424, and H. Coing, "English Equity and the *Denunciato Evangelica* of the Canon Law," *Law Quarterly Review* 71 (1955), 236.
9. Acta correct., vol. 2, fol. 137r.

tion. Many suits which were halted in mid-proceedings perhaps were dropped because of some sort of out-of-court settlement which satisfied plaintiffs not to press their suits further. Many other suits went to court-appointed arbiters or were noted by court scribes as having ended in "peace" or "concord." Only rarely was compurgation used as a mode of trial; plaintiffs probably preferred to negotiate for the return of their money.

How successful plaintiffs were in recovering their debts is impossible to say. We do not have records of these negotiations. It seems, however, that many creditors were dissatisfied with negotiated settlements under the aegis of the London church courts. Creditors saw in civic authorities men who were more sympathetic to their plight, men who had the will and coercive powers of sheriffs and constables to force contumacious debtors to appear in court or pay their debts. The mayor and alderman, after all, were themselves businessmen who no doubt had strong views against those who failed to fulfill contracts. In 1521, shortly after its establishment, the court of Requests was given power to imprison guilty parties for nonpayment of debts; in 1529 it was empowered even to imprison contumacious defendants who refused to appear in court.[10] Civic authorities had provided creditors with a potent weapon against their adversaries: imprisonment for petty debt, as Mr. Pickwick discovered in the nineteenth century, could bring ruin and death to debtors and their families.

Debt suits in the commissary court were usually over small amounts, although a few large debts were litigated. Parties disputed debts as small as 4d and as large as £30.[11] Church courts did not restrict themselves to a 40s limit as did the secular courts. In practice, however, suits rarely were litigated in commissary court for large debts of 40s and more; court summonses rarely were sent to such debtors. Rather, plaintiffs probably had only registered complaints against their adversaries in commissary court as parallel actions to other litigation against the same debtors in other courts, whether city courts or consistory. Few debt cases for substantial amounts of money were ever successful for plaintiffs: of the three cases that actually were heard in court involving large amounts of money, one case for recovery of £7 10s resulted only in excommunication of a defendant, another for £5 6s 8d resulted in the defendant's suspension from entering church, and another for £2 3s 9d was successfully compurgated.[12]

10. Journals, vol. 12, fol. 118r; vol. 13, fol. 155r; Letterbook N, fol. 163v.
11. Acta correct., vol. 1, fols. 16r, 152v.
12. Ibid., vol. 5, fol. 68r; vol. 7, fol. 72r; vol. 2, fol. 129v.

The table below contains only breach of faith suits for petty debt. It does not contain a handful of other suits that were sued also as *violatio fidei*, such as recovery of salary by servants, disputes among members of confraternities, and recovery of "mortuary," tithes, and oblations.

	1472	1485	1493	1502	1511	1512 to 1514 (3 years)
Total debt suits	39	26	41	5	3	1
1. *Out-of-court settlement*	*28*	*17*	*13*	*3*	*1*	*1*
Case dropped	25	6	11	2	1	1
Peace, concord	3	11	2	1	0	0
2. Successful compurgation	6	1	1	1	0	0
3. Order to pay debt	1	0	6	1	0	0
4. Suspension or excommunication	3	8	9	0	1	0
5. No summons issued	1	0	10	0	1	0
6. Other	0	0	2	0	0	0

2. Tithes

Church tithe rates had been formulated originally for a rural society. There were three kinds of tithes: praedial (payable on crops), mixed (payable on livestock that was nourished by the land), and personal (payable on salaries, wages, and profits of trade). Only personal tithes were applicable to most urban dwellers; but it had long been an open question in London whether personal tithes were voluntary or mandatory.[13]

Late medieval London tithe rates were founded upon an early-thirteenth-century constitution by Bishop Roger Niger, who had declared that in the general absence of productive fields and farm stock in London, praedial tithes were to be commuted to "offerings" or taxes on urban rents. Unlike their country colleagues, London rectors possessed no glebe lands (cultivatable lands attached to a parish); hence, they had to be supported solely by parishioner contributions. Niger,

13. A more detailed history of this conflict may be found in J. A. F. Thompson's "Tithe Disputes in Later Medieval London," *English Historical Review* 78 (1963), 1–17. Peripheral to London tithe disputes was a confrontation between the Carmelite friars of London and London secular clergy touching payment of lay tithes. For an interesting account that brings to light mid-fifteenth-century London disputes over personal tithes, see F. R. H. DuBoulay's "The Quarrel between the Carmelite Friars and the Secular Clergy of London, 1464–1468," *Journal of Ecclesiastical History* 6 (1955), 156–74.

therefore, ordered that every London renter was to pay his rector a rate of ¼d on every 10s yearly rent, or, if a landlord, on every 10s of assessed property value; this farthing—or more depending on the rent or property value—was to be offered every Sunday of the year, as well as on solemn days, on double feast days, and on feasts of the apostles.[14]

Most fifteenth-century tithe disputes revolved on the problem of determining which feast days were offering days.[15] Londoners looked instinctively to their civic authorities for help in determining a fair number of offering days. Tithe questions invariably were submitted to an arbitration board composed of representatives of the laity (usually aldermen) and of the clergy. In 1457, a composition over tithe rates was reached between the clergy and the city. Civic authorities, at least, adhered to this composition until the Reformation: a farthing (¼d) was to be paid for every 10s yearly rent, and offering days were limited to eighty-two (thirty feast days and fifty-two Sundays); in return for this concession by civic authorities, the clergy agreed to the principle that personal tithes were strictly voluntary. This important concession ensured that tithes would not be levied on salaries, wages, or profits. The composition of 1457 was later confirmed in 1473 by a bull from Pope Nicholas V, which was ordered to be read quarterly in every London parish. But neither composition nor papal bull was able to put an end to the ceaseless wrangling over tithes.[16]

J. A. F. Thompson has rightly shown that the festering sore of tithes in London was a result of rectors demanding more than they had previously agreed upon. When computing tithe assessments it was easier for all concerned to compute the tithe as a yearly assessment rather than eighty-two daily assessments; and rents were more often computed in nobles and marks instead of 10s increments. So, in assessing the tithe, rectors in small, subtle ways were extracting additional tithes by basing rent assessments on a noble (6s 8d) instead of 10s; they demanded 14d per year (that is, for the eighty-two offering days) for every noble paid in rent. This is 3s 6d on the pound or a 17½% tax on yearly rent. The older rate of 20½d per year (for eighty-two offering days) for every 10s rent amounted to 3s 5d on the pound or a 17% tax

14. Thompson, "Tithe Disputes," pp. 2–3. Fields within London parishes were assessed, not by London rental standards, but by an older praedial rate of 10%; thus, the curate of St. Nicholas Fleshmals sued in court for a tithe of 6s 8d (one noble) for a pasture called "brodefeld next the gate," which rented annually for £3 6s 8d (ten nobles) (Acta correct., vol. 11, fol. 232r).
15. Thompson, "Tithe Disputes," pp. 2–3.
16. Ibid., pp. 5–12. See also Richard Arnold's contemporary collection of documents that relate to the tithe issue in *The Customs of London*, pp. 57–73, 78–79.

on yearly rent. The rectors were demanding a small increased amount.

The noble base for tithe assessment used by the clergy seems to have been common in London. Richard Arnold in his *Customs of London* published a tithing list of St. Magnus London Bridge for 1494 which contains names of renters, amounts of rent paid, and tithings due.[17] In all cases, assessments were 14d yearly on the noble. London commissary court records (we have no consistory court records touching tithes) also show that the noble base was widely used for tithe assessments: in 1484 John Whetely was cited for owing £5 8s 6d yearly for tithes on £31 rent assessed for his property (which included rented rooms and shops). This tithe rate is 14d on the noble; Whetely would have been charged 3s 3d less had the tithe rate been assessed on a 10s base according to the composition.[18]

London rectors, therefore, ought to have collected just over 17% of amounts paid annually in rent throughout London, which was a tidy sum indeed. The rector of Richard Arnold's parish of St. Magnus, for instance, expected to collect—but did not necessarily collect—from 131 renters and 16 Bridgestreet shopkeepers a yearly sum of £91 16s 1d—*after* expenses were deducted to pay for the curate who administered the parish for the rector.[19] It is no wonder, then, that parishioners through their aldermen resisted even subtle increases in their tithe rates.

We can never be sure from court records if resistance to tithes by some parishioners was due to a disagreement over assessment rates, a lack of money to pay tithes, a resistance to paying any church dues whatsoever, or simply a belligerent attitude towards all taxes. Tithe suits, after all, were few: there were only between ten and twenty-five tithe suits per year in commissary court. Thomas Collyn, for example, was brought to court in 1502 for paying neither tithes, oblations, the parish clerk's stipend, nor "beam light" (a charge assessed for candles for interior lighting of a parish church); in addition, Collyn was charged for not attending church and not partaking of the sacraments. He acknowledged his lax ways and promised to pay his dues. In the same year, another defendant appeared in court and expressly refused to pay his tithes ("asseruit noluisse solvere decimas").[20] The former case seems to be one of indifference to parish or religious affairs; the latter, a case of open defiance. And in 1499 David Morgan, according

17. Arnold, *The Customs of London,* pp. 224–28.
18. Acta correct., vol. 2, fol. 86r. Whetely's case is muddled by the court's claim that a four-year lapse in payments totalled only £13 10s instead of £21 14s.
19. Arnold, *The Customs of London,* pp. 224–28.
20. Acta correct., vol. 9, fols. 57v, 61r.

to his rector, refused to pay more than 8d on the noble; when Morgan appeared in court he stated that he wished to pay only according to "the custom of the city."

> David Morgan notatur quod subtrahit ecclesie sue parochiali et Rectori eiusdem decimas et oblaciones ratione firme domus habitacionis pro cuius firma Annuatim solvet l^s et recusat solvere Curato suo nomina decimarum et oblacionum ultra viii^d pro qualitate nobili firme sue. citatus ad xix Augusti [1499]. non comparuit ideo suspensus. xii die mensis Octobris comparuit et absolutus est et dicit quod vult solvere secundum consuetudinem Civitatis.[21]

This is a rare case; specific arguments are usually absent from the court record.

In one case the judge did order tithe payment according to city custom; but we do not know if the city custom meant the composition or payment according to the noble standard:

> Johannes Dales notatur officio quod non solvit decimas vicario ibidem. citatus ad diem lune x Decembris [1498]. quo die comparuit et dominus monuit eum [*sic*] quod solvit decimas secundum consuetudinem Civitatis sub pena juris citra Festum Sancti Thome Apostoli.[22]

Actual amounts that many parishioners paid seem to have depended as much on private agreement between a rector and his parishioners as on the city-wide composition. Most tithe suits, in fact, were settled out of court through negotiation and compromise. A parishioner from St. Mary Whitechapel, for example, was charged in court with owing 3s 8d for tithes; he maintained that he owed only 3s, which he offered to pay. The offer apparently was accepted by his rector, who had brought the suit, because this case then was dismissed from court. The rector seems to have accepted whatever he could get and did not press for higher payment.[23] And in 1513 the rector of St. Mary-at-Ax charged William Fryday with nonpayment of tithes for three years on a yearly rent of 8s. The rector asked the court to compel Fryday "to pay 16d [!] on the noble according to the custom of this parish" and 8d for eight offering days ("ad solvendum xvi^d de nobili iuxta consuetudinem illius pariochie et viii^d pro viii diebus offertoriis"). This seems not to have been a clerical error in which "xiv" was inadvertently transposed to "xvi." Fryday, however, was ordered by the court to pay only 3s 4d,

21. Ibid., vol. 8, fol. 214v. Entire entry.
22. Ibid., vol. 8, fol. 154v. Entire entry.
23. Ibid., vol. 9, fol. 55r.

which was considerably less than the local parish rate (which would have been 4s 8d). In fact, Fryday's total payment of 3s 4d was even slightly less than payment on the "noble base" (which would have been 4s 1d) but slightly more than what certain poor renters ought to have paid according to the city composition (which would have been 3s).[24] Compromise and negotiation in the end seem to have determined many actual payments rather than negotiated city settlements or city or parish customs.

Disputes between the clergy and laity in London over tithe rates continued through the early sixteenth century. In February 1529, Robert Carter, a spokesman from the clergy and a protégé of Thomas Wolsey, presented to the mayor and aldermen eighteen articles that included demands for higher tithe and oblation rates. The clergy demanded 100 offering days per year, instead of 82, or an increased sum of 2s 1d per year for every 10s rent (that is, over 20% tax on rents)—or, they said, "by the same rate" of 16¼d on the noble (also slightly more than 20%).[25] This was essentially the same rate as the parish custom of St. Mary-at-Ax in the above case of William Fryday. These extreme demands by the clergy perhaps were only bargaining chips to be used in a new round of arbitrations. Certain demands probably were expected to be turned down in return for smaller concessions by the city.

But Robert Carter, like his patron Wolsey and like the English clergy in 1529, was tottering unawares on the edge of a precipice. London curates were posturing as an aggressive collective power for the last time. Within months after Carter had made his demands on behalf of London curates, his patron Wolsey fell ignominiously from power. Against the English clergy there now rushed a secular tide which, apart from doctrinal considerations, proved to be a "fiscal catastrophe for the English Church."[26] Riding a crest of anticlerical sentiment, London civic officials in 1530 forced the London rectors to confirm the

24. Ibid., vol. 11, fol. 133r. According to the 1457 composition, a renter who paid less than 10s rent per year ought to have been assessed only 1½d per year for every shilling of rent paid. The 8d owed for eight offering days is a mystery; it undoubtedly was part of the local parish custom. For provisions for poor renters see Arnold, *The Customs of London,* p. 72.

25. Letterbook O, fols. 140v–141v. For Carter, see A. B. Emden, *Biographical Register of the University of Oxford to A.D. 1500,* 3 vols. (Oxford, 1957–59), 1:364–65. In 1529 Carter was the rector of St. Martin's Vintry, London, and vicar of All Hallows Barking, London. He had been steward of Wolsey's household and Wolsey's chaplain. Carter survived Wolsey's fall in the summer of 1529 and was a member of the king's committee that drew up a list of heretical books in May, 1530.

26. J. J. Scarisbrick, "Clerical Taxation in England, 1485–1547," *Journal of Ecclesiastical History* 11 (1960), 52.

older composition of 1457. And in 1534, London's mayor and aldermen established by ordinance even *lower* tithe rates in London: tithes were reduced from 3s 5d on the pound (or 17%) to 2s 9d (or slightly less than 14%). This lower rate was enforced by parliamentary statute in 1536 and again in 1546. The 1546 statute even took away from London church courts power to hear tithe disputes, which now were consigned to the mayor's court for settlement.[27]

London laymen long had been accustomed to look to their civic officials for establishment and maintenance of tithe rates; it was probably a painless, even welcome, transition for them to accept the mayor's court as the arbiter of tithe disputes. London curates, on the other hand, could only suffer in silence. The Henrician Reformation brought them fourfold increases in royal taxation and decreased tithe rates during a period of high inflation.[28]

	1471	1485	1493	1502	1513	1514
Total tithe cases	15	23	12	14	14	14
1. *Out-of-court settlement*	*14*	*12*	*6*	*9*	*9*	*7*
Case dropped	13	5	5	4	7	6
Peace, arbitration	1	7	1	5	2	1
2. Successful compurgation	0	5	0	1	1	0
3. Order to pay tithes	0	0	1	0	0	3
4. Suspension or excommunication	0	4	2	1	3	2
5. No summons (settled out of court?)	1	2	3	3	1	2

3. Probate

To a foreigner like Polydore Vergil, England appeared peculiar in probate of wills, because bishops and archdeacons who had cognizance over probate through the courts "appropriate something in the form of a tax and often something very considerable, not without great damage to the heirs"; this custom, he mused, "is not likely to be found among any other people." [29] Probate, in fact, was divided between two jurisdictions: church courts proved that part of a will, the *testamentum*, that bequeathed movable goods and chattels; disposition of land—burgage land in London which unlike most free-hold land elsewhere was devisable—was contained in the "last will" or *ultima voluntas*, and

27. 27 Henry VIII, c. 21; 37 Henry VIII, c. 12. See also Paul L. Hughes and James F. Larkin, eds., *Tudor Royal Proclamations* (New York, 1964), p. 215.
28. Scarisbrick, "Clerical Taxation," pp. 41–54: "Popery may have been superstitious—but it was cheaper" (p. 54).
29. Polydore Vergil, *Anglica historia*, p. 259.

was proved in secular courts.[30] In London this secular probate court was known as the Hustings. Church courts were required to ascertain the wishes of testators and to ensure that these wishes were carried out by executors. Hence, church courts had to oversee inventories of goods of deceased persons, and to ensure that these goods were both properly valued and distributed according to the provisions of the will. For this service church courts collected an administrative fee or tax, which was based roughly on the total value of an inventory or "movables."

Tax rates seem not to have been established by church legislation but rather by what certain courts—notably the court of Arches—thought to be equitable. In the minds of some important laymen probate fees seemed unfixed and always increasing. The commons in 1416 had complained in parliament that church courts were charging as much as 40s to 50s for probate, whereas in the fourteenth century, they claimed, probate fees were only 2s 6d to 5s.[31] William Lyndwood, writing in the 1430s, gives us a more accurate tax rate; he knew of and approved of a rate of probate fees in which about ½% to 3% of an inheritance was collected by church courts.[32] This was not a graduated tax that increased in direct proportion to the worth of an estate; rather, it was an administrative fee. Thus, poorer estates worth from £2 to £20 paid a set fee which we can translate into a rate of between 1% and 3% of the estate; richer estates paid usually less than 1%.

London church courts seem to have used the same probate rates known to Lyndwood. In all cases for which we have sufficient knowledge of an estate's worth and the amount paid for probate of that estate, total probate fees were in accord with Lyndwood's fee scale. There was, however, one small exception in London: Lyndwood's scale allowed for no probate fees to be paid on estates worth less than

30. For the early development of both the *testamentum* and the *ultima voluntas*, see Michael Sheehan, *The Will in Medieval England* (Toronto, 1963), p. 178. Note this statement by Christopher St. German in *Doctor and Student*, p. 71, in which he inexplicably includes the "last will" with the "testament": "Also there is a custom in the cytie of London that fre men there maye by theyr testamente inroulyed byqueth theyr landes—even those that they be seasyed of to whome they wyll exepte to mortmayne. And yf they be cytyzyens and fre men / then they maye also byqueth theyr landes to mortmayne."

31. 4 Henry V, c. 8.

32. The best treatment of the will in the fifteenth century, including a discussion of Lyndwood, is E. F. Jacob's introduction to *Register of Henry Chichele, Archbishop of Canterbury*, Canterbury and York Society, 4 vols. (1937–1947), 2:xxxiv–xxxv. London consistory court wills have been edited for the London Record Society by Ida Darlington, *London Consistory Court Wills, 1492–1547* (London, 1967).

30s, that is, the level of a pauper; in London this minimum level was held to be 40s. Executors of pauper's wills, nevertheless, had to pay a special fee of about 12d for the scribe and apparitor (a minimum fee of 2½% on a pauper's goods).[33]

A small probate tax or administrative fee is not an exorbitant amount to be taken from an estate; perhaps those who were really hurt were heirs of paupers to whom 12d would have meant much. As far as probate courts were concerned, a small fee taken from two or three hundred estates may add up to a handsome sum of money. In 1504, for example, the London commissary court collected £44 3s 5d for the probate of 109 wills; from this amount £5 9d was set aside for scribes' and summoners' fees. An additional 80 wills had not yet been assessed, and another 55 wills were dismissed *in forma pauperis*.[34] London's commissary court perhaps received about £50 to £70 per year in probate fees alone. This money was not destined for the purses of judges, but rather was earmarked for repairs on St. Paul's Cathedral.[35]

Church probate courts also administered intestate estates and estates that executors declined to administer; the latter estates usually were heavily encumbered with debts. For this service the court collected additional fees. When the court itself acted as executor it allocated the remaining goods for court fees, for funeral expenses, for widows' housing, and finally—if any money remained—for creditors. A typical case is that of the estate of Philip More, whose widow renounced the execution of her late husband's will. The inventory of the will showed a value of £5 12s 33d. From this the judge allocated £2 4s to *domino fundi*, presumably More's landlord; 12s for More's funeral; 26s 8d for living quarters for the widow ("pro camera mulieris"); 4s 6d for other expenses ("pro expensis ordinariis"); and 25s 2d for More's creditors ("Et sic remanet inter creditores [ad] distribuendum").[36]

Secular authorities in London always had kept close watch on probate business. The city probate court, the Hustings, already proved that part of a Londoner's will touching land, providing the land was within the city. Civic authorities were approached by heirs and creditors to protect their rights in ecclesiastical probate courts. Thus, in 1518 the mayor and aldermen stepped in to regulate one aspect of local church courts by ordering that probate fees for the bishop and his

33. E. g., for paupers see Acta test., vol. 1, fols. 27r, 28v; vol. 7, fols. 70r, 71v.

34. Figures are taken from Acta test., vol. 2.

35. A typical entry in probate records notes that money was for *operibus Sancti Pauli;* see Acta test., vol. 1, fols., 31r, 32r.

36. Acta test., vol. 3, fol. 52v.

officers be deducted at the same time as inventory and funeral expenses.[37] Presumably this action stopped church probate officers from deducting their fees from the total estate and then dividing the diminished estate among the heirs. Heirs, therefore, after 1518 were protected by the city from a slight loss. Again, in 1521, civic authorities claimed that church court appraisers had often underappraised movable goods of deceased persons. This, they argued, resulted in a loss to creditors and surviving children (now orphans of London and, hence, protected by the city). Thus, the common council ordered that a second appraisal of goods be made by an appraiser from the deceased's craft; this appraiser was to be appointed by the mayor and receive a small fee from the will for his efforts. Executors who made false inventories in church courts were subject to punishment *in secular courts:*

> [Executors and administrators of wills] will cause just inventory on payn of imprisonment of every suche executor or administrator, executors or administrators, so doying to the contrary and farther to suffire Fyne or Fines by the discrecion of the Mayr & aldremen.[38]

What is important to grasp in these two civic regulations is not the specifics of the ordinances, but rather that there were any ordinances at all. Civic authorities, in other words, directly challenged and regulated certain church court actions. The mayor and aldermen of London needed little provocation to interfere with church court probates. They could easily find justification through their centuries-old responsibility for protecting London orphans. (Orphans were defined as underaged children who had lost their fathers but not necessarily their mothers.) Inheritances of orphans were administered by the city's own Court of Orphans, which was not a separate civic institution, but rather an *ad hoc* commission issued to men to administer orphans' legacies.[39] Thus, in the name of London orphans—and creditors—city officials sought to regulate church court probates.

From 1521 London's mayor and aldermen, through their own appraisers, were overseers of the inventory and administration of wills in London church courts. They could prosecute in their own courts those who maladministered wills. Although London church courts continued to prove wills for centuries to come, from at least the 1520s they acted only under the shadow and sufferance of city officials. Whether

37. Journals, vol. 11, fol. 367v.
38. Journals, vol. 12, fol., 117r–v; Letterbook N, fol. 163r–v.
39. Charles H. Carlton, "The Administration of London's Court of Orphans," *The Guildhall Miscellany* 4 (October, 1971), 22–35.

or not this was an improvement in the probate of wills, I cannot say. The mayor and aldermen, nevertheless, had made a significant inroad into ecclesiastical jurisdiction and authority.

	1472	1484	1493	1502	1513	1514
Total Probate Cases	9	12	26	13	13	5
1. *Out-of-court settlement*	*7*	*6*	*7*	*5*	*8*	*2*
Case dropped	6	5	6	4	8	1
Peace, arbitration	1	1	1	1	0	1
2. Successful compurgation	0	1	2	1	2	2
3. Payment of debt (by debtor or executor)	0	1	6	3	1	0
4. Suspension or excommunication	0	2	2	0	1	1
5. No summons (settled out of court?)	2	2	9	3	1	1
6. Sent to consistory	0	0	0	1	0	0

In 1529 parliament included in its broad frontal attack on church finances a statute which reduced probate fees in church courts. The commons insisted on a return to the level of fees charged in Edward III's time, just as an earlier parliament of 1416 had done: fees, they insisted, were again to be from 2s 6d to 5s, and no more. We do not yet have the evidence to say if such low fees ever had been charged in the time of Edward III, but it was enough that the commons in 1529 thought so: they apparently based their opinions on their readings of the parliament rolls of 1416. Edward III's statutes on probate fees mention no figures whatsoever.[40] Thus, in 1529 the commons offered relief to poor heirs by exempting estates from probate fees which were worth less than 100s, rather than 40s as before. Probate fees for middling estates worth between £5 and £40 were only slightly reduced from those previously charged. Wealthy heirs with estates worth over £40 gained most from the statute, for no church court henceforth could charge over 5s, no matter how large the estate. Parliamentary complaints over probate in 1529, according to our best witness, the chronicler Edward Hall (a burgess of Wenlock, Shropshire, who was present at the debates), had revolved around the large fees taken for probate of rich estates.[41] Not surprisingly, the rich benefitted most from subsequent parliamentary statutes touching probate.

Suits over maladministration of wills were heard regularly in London church courts. Executors sought in court to collect debts for testators, and legatees sued for legacies. Like other personal disputes over

40. 21 Henry VIII, c. 5; 4 Henry V, c. 8; 31 Edward III, st. 1, c. 4.

41. Edward Hall, *Hall's Chronicle* (London, 1809), p. 765; Lehmberg confirms Hall's reliability and authority in *Reformation Parliament*, p. 28.

property, testamentary suits usually were settled out of court. Only few plaintiffs used the church courts to dictate an immediate settlement; church courts acted more like referees than final arbiters in order to encourage peaceable settlements.

4. Marriage

Any society's marriage laws have important social consequences that reverberate throughout all social classes. Thus, canon laws of marriage—those laws that held sway throughout Catholic Europe for centuries—have attracted many researchers.[42] The development of medieval marriage laws is now quite well known. By the thirteenth century, canon laws of marriage were fully formulated, at least in the minds of church authorities. A valid marriage was made by mutual consent of a man and a woman (*consensus facit nuptias*). Words of consent had to be spoken in the present tense and not as a future promise. This simple act of exchanging vows forged a bond (*vinculum*) between a couple, a bond that could not be broken but could be annulled under certain conditions.

Although a marriage bond was made by simple exchange of vows, a marriage also had to be solemnized "in the face of the church" in order to make it legitimate. Ideally, the exchange of vows took place openly, in public, at the church door, and was followed immediately by a nuptial mass at the altar. But, as sometimes happened, marriage vows were exchanged at an earlier date before solemnization. For example, of 41 marriages found in a Canterbury deposition book for 1411-1420, 38 had taken place elsewhere, beyond the church door.[43] In such cases, allegedly valid marriages were not yet licit; and consummation of these marriages was not allowed until they had been solemnized. The problem for church authorities in an age without official enrollments of marriages in a parish register, of course, was to ensure that there were plentiful witnesses to a marriage; there must be some proof that vows actually had been exchanged.

In one rare instance, a man tried to argue in court that coitus rather than consent made a valid marriage. Thomas Richardson admitted in

42. See especially A. Esmein, *Le mariage en droit canonique*, 2 vols., 2nd ed. (Paris, 1929), for canon laws of marriage; and John T. Noonan, Jr., *Power to Dissolve*, for these same laws applied to real people. For a good history of court cases concerning marriage in late medieval England, see Richard Helmholz, *Marriage Litigation in Medieval England* (Cambridge, 1974), esp. pp. 26–31, for an excellent summary of the canon laws of marriage.

43. Helmholz, *Marriage Litigation*, p. 28.

court that he had exchanged marriage vows with Sibil Bethom but claimed that at the time he had already fathered a child by Agnes Wade. Coitus with Agnes Wade, he argued, constituted a previous marriage contract.[44] Perhaps behind Richardson's plea was the canonical view that a valid marriage could also be made if sexual intercourse followed vows of *future* consent.[45] This more subtle plea, however, does not appear in the record. Richardson, in fact, was grasping at straws. He was bound in marriage to Sibil Bethom by his exchange of vows with her, and this marriage was declared a valid one. For two centuries before this case appeared in a commissary court, canonists had decided that coitus neither made nor was essential for a valid marriage.

Plaintiffs usually appealed to the London commissary court to establish valid marriages, to force defendants to solemnize their vows, and to force cohabitation with their married partners. Questions of separation and "divorce" (annulment) were rarely at issue.[46]

Although few marriage disputes were brought to the commissary court, such suits were more frequent after the turn of the sixteenth century than in previous decades. Marriage litigation itself seems not to have increased in London; rather, marriage suits that formerly were heard in consistory court were now being heard more cheaply and quickly in commissary court. In the late fifteenth century, plaintiffs in marriage litigation in the commissary court were usually couples who complained of third parties (e.g., parents) impeding their marriages (these were not claims that the third party was married to one of the litigants), or wives whose husbands had expelled them from their homes. These were simple disciplinary cases that did not require rulings on the validity of marriages. After the turn of the sixteenth century, two types of marriage cases, new to the commissary court, made their appearances: cases in which two parties allegedly had made a marriage contract but one party refused to have it solemnized, and cases in which two parties claimed the same spouse. Both types of marriage litigation required court rulings on the validity of these marriages.

Questions of validity, in turn, usually meant that witnesses had to be summoned and depositions taken; these were procedures common to the higher consistory courts. But early in the sixteenth century, the new procedures found in defamation suits in the commissary court became

44. Acta correct., vol. 11, fol. 135r (date: 1513).
45. Helmholz, *Marriage Litigation*, p. 26.
46. Cf. ibid., p. 75.

available also in marriage litigation. Simple compurgation still was required of defendants, but plaintiffs could object to purgation and produce witnesses to give *viva voce* testimony in court. Thus, in 1502, a marriage contract was "proved" after witnesses were introduced in court: Margaret Heyn had bragged that she had contracted a marriage with Thomas Risley ("Margareta Heyn iactitat se matrimonium contraxisse cum Thoma Risley"). Margaret claimed that Risley had said, "if ye be willing to have me I plight you my trowth." Two witnesses supported Margaret but with ambiguous language: one witness, Richard Yeadley, heard one of the parties simply say "ther is a bargain." Thomas Risley in fact wished to be married to another woman, not Margaret Heyn. The judge ruled that Margaret's testimony did not suffice to impede a marriage between Thomas Risley and Ann Wedd; Risley then produced several witnesses of his own to prove his marriage to Ann Wedd the valid one.[47]

The use of witnesses to prove facts through *viva voce* testimony in open court was an entirely new procedure in commissary marriage suits. In other words, as the statistical table below shows, many marriage suits, like defamation suits, which formerly were heard in the consistory, from the 1490s now were tried in the lower commissary court.[48] The consistory lost much of its business, and litigants found quicker, cheaper justice in the commissary court.

	1471	1485	1493	1502	1511	1512	1513
Total marriage suits	8	3	15	14	29	29	25
1. *Disciplinary*	*7*	*2*	*7*	*5*	*6*	*6*	*6*
Secret marriage	0	0	0	0	1	0	0
Expulsion of wife	3	1	5	4	3	2	2
Impeding matrimony	4	1	2	1	2	4	3
2. *Validation of marriage*	*1*	*1*	*8*	*9*	*23*	*23*	*19*
Multiple spouse	1	0	2	4	11	13	12
Refusal to solemnize marriage	0	1	6	5	12	10	7

What is astonishing at first glance to a modern observer, living in an age when the marriage failure rate approaches fifty percent, is how infrequent were cases that questioned the validity of marriages. It is probable that some couples practiced informal divorces and simply lived apart or took up with new partners; numbers of these cases are impossible to determine. Some of the cases to validate marriage on the above table may in fact have been informal divorce cases from pre-

47. Acta correct., vol. 9, fol. 8r (fols. 5 and 6 are missing).

48. See Appendix B, pp. 155, 157–58, for examples of cases.

vious spouses. A historian's evaluation of another culture's acceptance of marriage is necessarily impressionistic; quantitative data is unyieldingly stingy in giving us evidence of sentiment. My impression of medieval London marriages is that for most couples acceptance of the institution of marriage for better or for worse was second nature. Couples in early Tudor London rarely challenged their marriage bonds. Church doctrine, of course, helped shape lay expectations of married life. Perhaps more important than church doctrine was a high death rate which made marriage necessarily "a transient and temporary association." As Lawrence Stone observes, "it looks very much as if modern divorce is little more than a functional substitute for death." [49]

In rare instances, marriage litigation in the commissary court revolved on questions of separation (not divorce or annulment). Joan Alpe, for example, complained to the court that her husband, William, refused to live with her. William Alpe in turn argued that his wife was insane ("Johanna est mente capte") and that he refused to live with her for fear of his life; he did promise, however, to pay her a small sum of 10s per year for her food and clothing if he could be separated from her. William's story was accepted by the court, seemingly without challenge from Joan; he swore an oath to pay the agreed sum and was dismissed from the court.[50] The records do not indicate if a "sanity" test of some sort was given to Joan; she seems to have been accepted as insane on William's testimony alone. Perhaps Joan also wanted a separation and took William to court to obtain a sort of pension. There was never a question of the validity of their marriage, nor was there an attempt to dissolve the bond that bound the couple together; according to the canons, only separation was possible for insanity that developed after the marriage bond was formed.[51]

Not all possible causes for separation were, or could be, contained in the canon law. Judges on occasion had to use their own judicial common sense to determine what constituted legitimate grounds for separation. Thus, although Andrew Peerson confessed that he had exchanged marriage vows one year earlier with Agnes Wilson, he refused to have his marriage solemnized, because Agnes proved to be such a great scold ("tanta objugatrix et scolda") that she was indicted by her ward as a scold. Neither Andrew Peerson nor the judge, Thomas Sewell, could deny that a marriage bond had been formed; but the com-

49. Lawrence Stone, *The Family, Sex and Marriage in England, 1500–1800* (New York, 1977), pp. 55–56.
50. Acta correct., vol. 11, fol. 237r.
51. X. 4.1.24 fol. 442r, gloss on "furore"; Decretum c. 32, q. 7, c. 26, col. 1147; Noonan, *Power to Dissolve*, pp. 148–50, 431 n. 47.

mon medieval cliché that marriage with a scolding wife is unbearable was a compelling argument to justify separation. In a Solomon-like decision, Sewell allowed a judicial separation (without solemnization of the marriage?) and ordered that neither party could marry again during the lifetime of the other.[52]

Secular authorities made virtually no inroads into canon laws of marriage. Marriage was a sacrament and, until the end of the seventeenth century when parliament began to grant divorces, was beyond the pale of secular jurisdiction.[53] Civic authorities in London, however, did have the right to require licenses of those who wished to marry orphans under their care. But if a person married an orphan without license, city officials could only fine the wrongdoer; they could not break the marriage bond.[54]

5. Nonobservance of Sundays and Feast Days

Complaints were few but persistent by parish authorities against parishioners who neglected to attend church or to observe feast days. Curates and churchwardens reported their neighbors who either spent Sundays drinking in taverns or were more industrious and opened their shops to sell goods on Sundays or feast days. Of the few types of people cited in court, shoemakers and poulterers stand out from the rest. But any such citations were so rare that we must not make too much of the rebellious nature of shoemakers and poulterers.[55] Most cases resulted in successful compurgation or were dropped in mid-proceedings. Rarely did a defendant confess his wrong. Among those who did confess, none was ever noted by the court scribe as having received punishment. Such a lack of information probably was not a

52. Acta correct., vol. 11, fol. 41v. Cf. Helmholz, *Marriage Litigation*, pp. 100–101: this presumably was a judicial separation, a divorce *a mensa et thoro*, for cruelty; however, in order to prove cruelty it was necessary to show physical injury or a threat thereof. In the end we do not know why a separation was granted.

53. Stone, *The Family*, pp. 30–41 (for sixteenth- through eighteenth-century marriages and divorces), and p. 38 (for late seventeenth-century divorces granted by parliament).

54. E.g., see Letterbook N, fol. 46r (date: 1517): a fine levied (and remitted) on Roger Aleyn, who married the orphan daughter of "Master Gray" without a license from the city.

55. Acta correct., vol. 5, fol. 172r; vol. 7, fol. 36v; vol. 11, fol. 56r–v. During the early nineteenth century, shoemakers, "because of their superior education," were often village radicals: see the superb study of the English agricultural revolt of 1830 by Eric Hobsbawm and George Rudé, *Captain Swing* (New York, 1968), pp. 63, 181–82.

mere scribal oversight, because this lacuna in the court record is peculiar only to this type of case. Guilty parties probably were admonished to observe Sundays and feast days and then dismissed from court.

One man cleverly used the collection of tithes by his curate to justify opening his own cobbler's shop on Sunday to make a living. When charged in court for selling goods on Sundays, James Cornelys defiantly declared, "I will kepe my shop opyn and sel my war as long as Master Vicar standeth takyng his offering."[56] There is in this statement the kind of bedrock anticlerical resistance to clerical wealth that was to prove so damaging to the clergy during the Reformation Parliament.

After the turn of the sixteenth century, prosecutions for nonobservance of Sundays and feast days shrank to only a trickle. Simple admonitions probably could be meted out by parish authorities just as effectively as by diocesan court officials. Sabbatarianism was much more peculiarly a Protestant, especially a Puritan, pose; respectful observance of Sunday was more tenaciously a part of Protestant conceptions of proper discipline for a Godly kingdom on earth. In fact, in a later "Protestant Age," during the especially tense year of November 1639 to November 1640, about eighteen hundred people were charged with some sort of crime in the court of the archdeacon of London, "three fourths of whom . . . were presented for tippling during Divine Service, breaking the Sabbath, and non-observance of Saints' Days."[57] Cases that numbered over a thousand in 1639 could be numbered on one hand before the Reformation.

	1471	1485	1493	1502	1512	1513	1514
Total nonobservance cases	11	18	18	8	2	1	1
1. Case dropped	8	5	2	1	0	0	0
2. Successful compurgation	1	5	10	6	2	0	0
3. Confession of guilt, penance?	0	0	2	1	0	1	0
4. Suspension, excommunication	0	3	1	0	0	0	0
5. No summons	2	5	3	0	0	0	1

6. Other Crimes

A smattering of crimes that were reported to the London commissary court are especially noteworthy for their low incidence. The

56. Acta correct., vol. 7, fol. 36v.
57. Hale, *Precedents*, p. liv.

crimes of heresy, witchcraft, usury, and infanticide, which have been of interest to modern researchers, seldom appear in commissary court records. Infanticide probably was rarely committed; usury probably was prosecuted in other courts; and contemporaries seem to have been indifferent to witchcraft and other forms of magic as criminal offenses.

Heresy, however, is a special case. Only scant information on heretics may be culled from commissary court records, but this does not indicate the absence of heresy or official indifference to it. Notorious heretics, such as Lollards, were usually tried elsewhere, before a committee of bishops or the bishop and his chief judges.[58] Consequently, although no more than six people were charged for heresy during the thirty-four years for which we have records, this does not mean that there were no heretics in London. Like the Chiltern Hills in Lincoln diocese, London was a haven for Lollards. Records of heresy prosecutions were kept elsewhere, apart from normal court records. The martyrologist John Foxe, for example, found records of heresy prosecutions in deposition books (some of which since have been lost) and bishops' registers.[59]

Based on surviving scraps of evidence, pre-Reformation London "heretics" appear to have been of three sorts. The first group probably were not heretics at all; these were the six men and women who in various years were charged in commissary court for heresy and ultimately released, usually after simple compurgation; they faced little threat of being burned at the stake. In one case, the court used a heresy charge to force a contumacious defendant to court: John Steward was charged with adultery and had been overheard (by the summoner?) to say contemptuously of the court, "I sett nothin by curse [excommunication], yff I be ones on horsse bake and my ffete within the stirroppis." These words brought him an additional charge of heresy from the "office" of the bishop ("detectus officio est de crimine heresis"); further opprobrious words brought him a contempt of court charge. Steward successfully purged himself of the original adultery charge and was "canonically corrected" for being in contempt of court (the punishment was not recorded). No further mention was made of heresy, which probably had been used only as leverage to force Steward to court.[60] In another case a heresy prosecution was begun but the charge strangely shifted to fornication: Saunder Goldsmith was charged with

58. For late fifteenth- and early sixteenth-century heresy trials, see J. A. F. Thompson, *The Later Lollards, 1414–1520* (Oxford, 1965), p. 92.
59. For example, see the Foxe Miscellany (a collection of folios removed from deposition books presumably by John Foxe) in British Library, Harl. MS 421.
60. Acta correct., vol. 5, fol. 142v.

heresy for having said contemptuously, "I had as leffe ther wer powrid a bottl of pisse uppon my hed as the hand of the Juge geving absolucion." He denied saying this but inexplicably confessed to fornication with many prostitutes; his penance was for fornication, not heresy.[61]

There was in London a second type of heretic, genuine Lollards who were an old nagging problem for English churchmen. Lollards comprised an amorphous sort of heresy that was marked especially by anticlerical and antisacerdotal attitudes. As people, they usually were the working poor. As heretics, they anchored their faith on the Bible alone, "Godes Law," which they interpreted with a devastating literalmindedness that mocked centuries of Catholic dogma and traditions. Lollardy had survived fifteenth-century persecutions, and from the 1480s had even enjoyed a revival. By the early sixteenth century, Lollardy again seemed, at least to churchmen, to be a serious menace. Heresy purges took place during 1510 and 1511 in the dioceses of London, Lincoln, and Coventry and Lichfield. Lollards who purged themselves in Coventry and Lichfield were older people, rather than "hotheaded young men" with imported "new-fangled notions." [62] London heretics in these same years appear also to have been part of an older Lollard tradition. It was sometime during the winter of 1510–1511 that the notorious Richard Hunne first began his running battle with church authorities by publicly defending the London Lollard Joan Baker.[63] Two London heretics were burned at Smithfield in 1511, but we do not have their court records and do not even know their names. Real heretics were much too important to go through the commissary court.

During 1527 and 1528, heresy trials in London brought to light a third and more ominous type of heretic. Their court records survive only in folios torn out of a now lost deposition book, presumably by John Foxe;[64] the court perhaps was the bishop's consistory. Unlike the

61. Ibid., vol. 6, fol. 35v.

62. J. Fines, "Heresy Trials in the Diocese of Coventry and Lichfield, 1511–12," *Journal of Ecclesiastical History* 14 (1963), 160–2; and Thompson, *The Later Lollards,* p. 238.

63. I am preparing an article that gives some new evidence on the Hunne case and which implicates the vicar-general of London in Hunne's murder. For the evidence and authorities in the Hunne case, see E. Jeffries Davis, "The Authorities for the Case of Richard Hunne, 1514–1515," *English Historical Review* 30 (1915), 477–88, supplemented by recent discoveries published by S. F. C. Milsom, "Richard Hunne's 'praemunire,' " *English Historical Review* 76 (1961), 80–82, and J. Fines, "The Post-Mortem Condemnation for Heresy of Richard Hunne," *English Historical Review* 78 (1963), 528–31.

64. British Library, Harl., MS 421, John Foxe Miscellany.

many barely literate men and women who swelled the ranks of the Lollards, the new heretics were young, university-trained men in English church livings clutching imported works of Martin Luther. Sebastian Harris, curate of Kensington parish, confessed that he received certain books of Luther from a friar, William Hechyn; and Robert Forman, professor of sacred theology and rector of All Hallows Honey Lane, also confessed that he possessed certain works of Luther.[65]

Fear of this new continental heresy was not confined to churchmen alone. One year before the trials of these firstborn sons of the Reformation, in October 1526, London civic authorities had initiated an examination of every parson in each alderman's ward to find certain unspecified books of heresy; they perhaps had in mind Luther's works or Tyndale's recent translation of the Scriptures, which was coming into circulation: "At this Court it is agreed that commyssions shall be made to every alderman that they shall examyn every person [commonly used for "parson"] in ther Warde for & concernyng certeyn bokes of heresy."[66] London clerics like Sebastian Harris and Robert Forman probably had been detected originally through investigations of aldermen. Michael Kelly's argument that the commons (lay people) feared the effectiveness of the church courts in heresy prosecutions ought to be taken with reservation for London. Successful heresy prosecutions were always a result of secular and ecclesiastical cooperation.[67]

Witchcraft and sorcery were of much less concern as crimes than heresy to Yorkist and early Tudor Londoners. Only a few people were ever charged for sorcery, and only one was ever punished with penance. Alianor Dulyn, for example, easily purged herself of a charge that she had contrived to kill her husband by certain arts of divination; she even brought countercharges of defamation against Anne Miller, who had circulated the gossip. And a certain "Mistress Heydon," who had been charged with having used sorcery and other evil incantations against the church, simply paid her dismissal fees and was released from court without even having to face compurgation.[68]

The constricted sensibilities that marked later Elizabethan persecu-

65. Ibid., fols. 11r–13r, 15r, 19r. In 1528 Sebastian Harris confessed that he had committed adultery with Joan Hylton of Kensington parish, that he had abducted her, and that he had neglected his cure (Colin A. McLaren, "An Early 16th Century Act book of the Diocese of London," *Journal of the Society of Archivists* 3 [1968], 339).

66. Repertories, vol. 7, fol. 140r; Letterbook O, fol. 17v.

67. Michael Kelly, "The Submission of the Clergy," p. 108.

68. Acta correct., vol. 9, fols. 56r, 57r; vol. 5, fol. 71r.

tors of witches are not evident in the pre-Reformation London church courts, whose officials looked upon sorcery, "white magic," and witchcraft with ambivalent indifference. Sorcerers, witches, soothsayers, and cunning men appear to have been common in London before the Reformation. As Keith Thomas reminds us, they were common throughout England until modern times, perhaps until the turn of this century.[69] In pre-Reformation London, diviners were looked to by their neighbors to solve life's simple problems: a woman who had some clothes stolen from her washline "sent to a soyth sayer to knowe yf they [her suspected neighbors] had take away clothes." [70] Such methods of tracing a loss of goods through "thief magic" were common—and effective if the thief also believes in the soothsayer's powers.[71] Another woman who had lost some money from her purse accused Richard Faques of theft because a "soothe sayer" told her that a man with "a blemyshe on his Face" stole it; Faques was the only man in her company with a blemish. And a widow, Margaret Geffry, gave her few miserable possessions to a man who promised to contact a sorcerer for her who would find her a husband through love magic. This was the one case in which a defendant was punished. It was not so much that the defendant Richard Lawkiston was a sorcerer—he had only offered to put the widow in touch with a cunning man for a fee—but that Lawkiston had perpetrated a fraud and delivered neither a sorcerer nor a love potion.[72] Sorcerers did not strike Londoners as particularly evil or heretical but rather as useful helpers to solve those sorts of problems for which there was little real help available. Authorities—civic and ecclesiastical—were neither eager nor willing to prosecute these practical magicians.

Usury was also a crime rarely prosecuted in commissary court. During thirty-four years of records, only five alleged usurers were reported to the court. None was actually tried, and only one summons was sent to a defendant who subsequently failed to appear in court.[73]

The responsibility of prosecuting usurers probably was left to civic authorities, who were especially watchful of usurious and fraudulent business deals. In 1488, for example, the mayor and aldermen issued a proclamation against "the foule and harrible vice of usurie and fals

69. Keith Thomas, *Religion and the Decline of Magic* (New York, 1971), p. 582.
70. Acta correct., vol. 11, fol. 158r.
71. Thomas, *Religion and the Decline of Magic,* esp. pp. 221–22.
72. Acta correct., vol. 5, fols. 29v–30r; also printed in Hale, *Precedents,* pp. 32–33. For more on "love magic" see Thomas, *Religion and the Decline of Magic,* pp. 233–34.
73. Acta correct., vol. 8, fol. 231r.

chevisaunce . . . by the meane of diverse unlawfull and ungodly contracts and unclene bargayn." If any person "of what astate degree or Condition" be cheated by a usurer, then

> let hym come to my said lord the mair and other commissioners assigned to here and determyne all such compleyntes uppon Moneday next commyng at ix of the Clocke before none [= noon] . . . and they shall have rightwisnes mynystered to them with all diligence accordyng to the laws and Custumes of this Citee in suche cases used.[74]

The mayor's court also allowed compensation to victims of usury.

Infanticide is perhaps the most surprising crime to find in church court records. Although infanticide meant that an infant was deliberately or accidentally slain, it seems not to have been punished as homicide in fifteenth-century England. Recent research into the problem of infanticide by Richard Helmholz has suggested that although infanticide was sometimes practiced in the fifteenth century, it was not considered a serious enough crime to be tried as homicide in royal courts; ecclesiastical penance was deemed punishment enough, and such penance was no different from penance for adultery or fornication.[75]

Although the evidence is slim, there is some indication that during the early sixteenth century the secular courts may have assumed jurisdiction from the church courts over infanticide. There appears in a Lincoln Audience Court Book for 1514–1520 a case in which an unwed mother suffocated her unwanted child and buried it under a pile of straw. Although the woman's suspicious neighbors reported her to ecclesiastical authorities, the bishop of Lincoln pointedly reserved her case for other, presumably secular, authorities; the bishop only charged her with failure to baptize the baby before she murdered it.[76] Also, no infanticide cases appear in London commissary court records after at least 1509. It may be that common law courts during the first decade of the sixteenth century appropriated this crime for themselves. Only a thorough investigation of secular court records will reveal an

74. Journals, vol. 9, fol. 169r. The proclamation itself is undated but was enrolled with a document dated 13 March, 3 Henry VII. Other civic acts against usury may be found in the Journals, vol. 7, fols. 12v, 23r.
75. Richard Helmholz, "Infanticide in the Province of Canterbury during the Fifteenth Century," *History of Childhood Quarterly: The Journal of Psychohistory* 2 (1975), 379–90; also Barbara A. Kellum, "Infanticide in England in the Later Middle Ages," *History of Childhood Quarterly: The Journal of Psychohistory* 1 (1974), 371–75.
76. Bowker, ed., *An Episcopal Court Book*, pp. xxi, 54.

answer; unfortunately no such records exist for years between 1408 and 1554 for the London sheriff's courts where such actions first would be taken.[77]

It was usually charged in court that an infant had been slain by suffocation in bed. Scribes used the words *oppressit* or *expressit in lecto* to indicate that a child had been suffocated. Accidental suffocations among swaddled infants were perhaps not uncommon. Evidence of actual infanticides in London, however, is difficult to interpret. The frequency of such prosecutions during the late fifteenth century was rarely more than one per year, although in 1488 four separate persons were charged; in some years infanticide was not charged at all. Of the few Londoners charged in court, none was ever found guilty.

Certain cases are worthy of mention specifically for the questions they raise about infanticide charges, and generally to show the inherent difficulty in penetrating behind the rapidly scribbled words in the court record to discover what really happened. One peculiar charge merely was noted in the court record with no indication that any action was taken against the accused: three women including the mother allegedly "tore away (?)" (distraxerunt) the baby of the mother and carried the infant to the Thames, where presumably it was drowned. "Cecilia Clyften, Agnes Bartylimewe, et Katerina Cranysende distraxerunt puerum predicte Katerine; et Cecilia portavit puerum ad tamesiam." [78] This case, if true, was certainly infanticide. But is abortion also implied in this baffling use of the verb *distrahere?* Or there is the case of John Russell. Russell allegedly struck Alice Wanten, who was pregnant; Alice then delivered a dead child. Killing the unborn, therefore, could be construed also as infanticide. John Russell denied the charge and purged himself successfully with six others, so we will never know if the charge was true.[79] Finally, there is the case of Alice Fort, who was charged with being the pimp of Agnes Lewes. Agnes became pregnant and delivered a baby in Alice's home. Alice, it was further charged, killed the baby, but made a likeness of the baby out of swaddling clothes and showed it to the mother saying that this was her child ("et post partum eadem uxor [Alice Fort] occidit puerum et postea fecit quendam puerum cum pannis et dixit matri hoc est puer tuus").[80]

77. Philip E. Jones and Raymond Smith, *A Guide to the Records in the Corporation of London Records Office and the Guildhall Library Muniment Room* (London, 1951), p. 66.

78. Acta correct., vol. 2, fol. 99r.

79. Ibid., vol. 5, fol. 58v (62v in pencil).

80. Ibid., vol. 7, fol. 62v.

Was Alice taunting the mother or was she indulging in some sort of sympathetic magic? Alice Fort, in any case, denied the charges and her case disappears from the court records.

Because of the importance of "mortuary" in the Reformation Parliament, a few words must be said concerning its litigation in the commissary court. Mortuary was a payment usually of a deceased person's best personal article to a local church or altar. In practice the officiating curate received the article.[81] The Reformation Parliament ultimately regulated by statute the amount owed for mortuary (21 Henry VIII, c. 6). Only rarely do disputes over mortuary appear in the commissary court record. In 1502, for a rare example, the vicar of All Hallows Barking had refused to bury the body of James Jonson until he received mortuary. The heirs of Jonson claimed that they owed nothing according to the customs of the city of London ("nullum in hoc casu sibi debeatur iuxta consuetudinem in Civitate Londoniensi").[82] We do not know which customs of London the heirs specifically were referring to. It was perhaps common to claim "custom" as a defense, even if that custom existed only in the minds of particular defendants. Canon law recognized that payments to a church could be regulated by local custom so long as it did not violate the *ius commune* of the church.[83]

Nothing appears in the court records touching mortuary around the time of the notorious Hunne affair: Richard Hunne was the defendant in a mortuary suit in 1512, but the case was heard by the archbishop's official at Lambeth. Mortuary, in any case, was only incidental, I believe, to Hunne's quarrel with London's clergy that led to his eventual murder.[84]

The London commissary court heard other cases, mostly petty, private disputes: there were wrangles over rights to pews, physical fights with priests, disputes over salaries owed to proctors and parish clerks, and attempts by confraternities to force members to obey their stat-

81. Heath, *The English Parish Clergy*, p. 153.
82. Ibid., vol. 9, fol. 36v; also in Hale, *Precedents*, p. 75.
83. X, 3.30.18, fol. 378r, gloss "ad consuetudinem"; X, 1.31.16, fol. 129v, gloss "Mortuariorum"; Lyndwood, *Provinciale* 1.3.1, p. 22, gloss "Consuetudine laudabili."
84. The Hunne affair is too complex to explain here, and not really relevent to this treatment of the London commissary court. In an article now in preparation I will argue that the problem of mortuary was only incidental to Hunne's fight with London's clergy.

utes.[85] Such cases do not occur in the records with regularity. Often a court case gives us a lively view of sixteenth-century London: the churchwardens of St. Mildred's Breadsteet, for example, complain that at night a mad hermit sneaks into their parish church, breaks pews and fixtures, and overturns anything movable. Or a wife complains to the court about her husband, who loses money at dice and cards ("in illicitis ludis expendit pecunias viz. at the dice and the kardis").[86]

More important than isolated cameos of medieval life found in court records are patterns of litigation of common disputes. Which courts did Londoners seek out to find justice? To which public authorities did they habitually entrust their loyalty and confidence to solve their problems? What were court sanctions and were they effective in London society? These are social questions that must be asked of legal documents. The documents are not always generously yielding. But answers to these questions, even partial answers, give us important information touching that generation of Londoners who lived before and during the Henrician Reformation.

85. For a list of types of office and instance cases commonly heard in church courts see F. S. Hockaday, "The Consistory Court of the Diocese of Gloucester," *Transactions of the Bristol and Gloucestershire Archaeological Society* 46 (1925), 199–200.
86. Acta correct., vol. 11, fol. 145r; vol. 4, fol. 251r.

BLANK PAGE

Conclusion

Any analysis of pre-Reformation English church courts ultimately must make some reference to the Reformation Parliament. During seven sessions, sitting from 1529 through 1536, parliament broadly attacked ecclesiastical jurisdiction and effectively legislated the English Reformation. The decisions of this parliament concerning landholding, church administration, and royal power resounded for centuries in English society.

When the commons first assembled in November 1529, they came to correct, among other things, what they felt to be abuses by the clergy. The mayor and aldermen of London had polled London's leading companies for legislative proposals that they could send to the parliament with London's four representatives. In response, the Mercers' Company, among others, submitted grievances for redress: four articles dealt with trade and one was a bitter attack on a rapacious clergy. The Mercers' Company program is a good source for opinions of many London lay elites pertaining to lay-clergy relations, notably in the church courts.

> Item, to have in remembrans howe the kynges poor subgiectes, pryncipally of London, have been polled and robbed without reason or conscience by th'ordenarys in probatyng of testamentes and takyng of mortuarys and also vexed and trobled by citacions with cursyng oon day and absoilyng the next day, *et hec omnia pro pecuniis.*[1]

The Mercers' petition had a sympathetic audience in the commons. Edward Hall, the chronicler and also a member of parliament, recollected that when the subject of church probates arose in debate, many members told of their unpleasant experiences in church probate courts. Sir Henry Guilford, among others, complained that he and the

1. Quoted from Helen Miller, "London and Parliament in the Reign of Henry VIII," *Bulletin of the Institute of Historical Research* 35 (1962), 144, from Mercers' Company Acts of Court, fol. 25v. For London members to parliament see also Lehmberg, *The Reformation Parliament*, pp. 20–21, 81–84. The senior member of parliament from London was Thomas Semour (Semer), formerly warden of the Mercers' Company and mayor of London.

executors of the will of Sir William Compton had to pay to Archbishops Wolsey and Warham over 1,000 marks for probate alone.[2]

The commons consequently drew up a six-point program against the clergy. Excessive exactions for probates and mortuaries—major complaints of the Mercers' Company—were the first two items on their program. Corrective statutes concerning both subsequently received royal assent (21 Henry VIII, c. 5 and c. 6). Thus, Londoners directly benefitted from the Reformation Parliament. Both mortuaries and church probate fees were reduced and regulated by statute, although probate in earlier years already had come under some regulation by the city.[3] And with an anticlerical commons at its back, city officials intimidated the clergy in 1530 to retain established tithe rates; these rates were even reduced in 1534 and the lower rates were given the sanction of parliamentary statute in 1536 (27 Henry VIII, c. 21). Parliamentary statute, in other words, capped a trend in London of secular control over some ecclesiastical matters—a trend which had begun a generation earlier.

Included also in the Mercers' Company petition was a complaint that church courts too freely handed out sentences of suspension and excommunication. Judged from commissary court evidence, this complaint was only partially true. If a defendant failed to appear in court, he was suspended *ab ingressu ecclesie;* a second failure to appear brought a sentence of excommunication. Forcing defendants into court is a serious problem for any court system; plaintiffs, in fact, had often been attracted to sue their cases in a church court because of its *sub poena* powers over defendants. In any case, neither suspension nor excommunication of a contumacious defendant seems to have been frequently used in London unless a promoter of a suit was willing to step forward and press his case. Perhaps this is where the Mercers ought to have directed their complaint: to promoters of suits rather than to the courts. In fact, many suits in the London commissary court failed to reach any conclusion because accusers themselves failed to appear in court; charges against defendants were then dropped without sentence of excommunication.

The Mercers had objected to fees charged for absolution from sentences of suspension and excommunication. In London the fee for absolution from suspension alone was 9d and from excommunication a further 9d (or 18d total). Technically these fees may have been for the preparation of scribal documents rather than for absolution *per se.* London fees were below those alleged in the 1532 "Supplication of the

2. *Hall's Chronicle,* p. 765.
3. See above, pp. 115–17.

Commons," in which the commons complained that 20d was charged by the scribe alone for absolution.[4] Fees for absolution rarely were challenged in open court, although the Mercers' Company petition itself is testimony of some hostility in London to the fees. The one case that we possess in which this fee was contested resulted in the court's dropping the fee altogether: Joan Bayly was charged with defamation, failed to appear in court, and was suspended from entering church; she later denied the defamation charge and outright refused to pay for absolution: "I wil never pay on peny for itt [absolution] as long as I lyve for I am not gylty." After purging herself of the defamation charge, Joan Bayly was required to pay only 8d in dismissal fees—not the 9d for absolution.[5]

It is surprising that the Reformation Parliament—and most defendants like Joan Bayly—did not complain about dismissal fees. Of any church court fees, surely these were most patently unfair. Before any case was discharged from London's commissary court, a defendant, whether innocent or guilty, was required to pay a *feodum dimissionis*. The court charge varied from 6d to 20d, but most fees were either 12d or 14d. From this sum the apparitor seems to have taken about 8d and the court scribe the remainder. Only legitimate paupers were excused from paying dismissal fees.[6] It is true that the dismissal fee served the "social function" of punishing those people who were guilty but who easily had acquitted themselves by compurgation. But it was still an indiscriminate fee charged to innocent folk as well as guilty. The "social function" that this fee perhaps performed does nothing to exculpate the court of its injustice to innocent defendants.

What especially vexed Londoners, however, was not the system of fee assessment, but rather the court officers who collected the fees. Obviously to many people in pre-Reformation London clerics and court officers were more willingly despised than an abstract "system" or abstract "church."[7] Later generations who had been led through the conflagration of Reformation were pushed over the twilight zone where the system itself became the enemy. A Roman church or an episcopal church had to be abstracted from a Christian church before critical minds found evil in Roman or episcopal systems and their systems of law enforcement.

Consequently, dismissal fees apparently were not regarded by Londoners as inherently offensive; but evil, malicious accusers and court officers were. The problem, Londoners and the commons thought, was

4. C. H. Williams, ed., *English Historical Documents* (Oxford, 1967), 5:734.
5. Acta correct., vol. 6, fol. 106v.
6. See above, pp. 54–55.
7. Cf. Ferguson, *The Articulate Citizen*, pp. 15–16.

one of court officers, not of a flawed system of fees. This same system of dismissal fees meant that the livelihoods of court officers depended on misfortunes of others; court officers naturally appeared rapacious to those who were summoned before London's commissary court.

The remedy for unjust dismissal fees is a court supported by public funds. If people were to be charged by the public voice then the public should pay the costs of prosecution. But such a suggestion was quite beyond the comprehension of early-sixteenth-century churchmen or members of parliament. If a revision of the church court system had been contemplated in the Reformation Parliament, it was premature, just as the actual proposal was premature that vagabonds ought to be put to work on public works projects.[8] Reform of church court fees by members of the commons required that they make a mental leap from denouncing seemingly unjust court officers to denouncing an abstract world of a flawed fee system.

Thus, the commons in 1529 lashed out at evil church court officers: summoners "being light and indiscreet persons," [9] and ecclesiastical judges, "a sorte of ravenous woolvys nothing elles attending but there onelie pryvate lucres and satisfaction of the covetous and insaciable appetites of the said prelatis and ordynaries." [10]

But was the problem raised by parliament in 1529 really one of rapacious court officers? If this was the problem then the members of the Reformation Parliament failed to specify who exactly was being rapacious. Evidence from London church court records does not support parliament's attack—nor does evidence from, say, Lincoln.[11] We must not assume that parliamentary charges were necessarily well founded; they may have been nothing more than commonplace anticlerical clichés.

Was the problem in 1529 then one of fear of the efficiency and effectiveness of the church courts, especially in heresy prosecutions, as Michael Kelly and Margaret Bowker have argued?[12] Again, London evidence points to an opposite conclusion; civic authorities in the late 1520s were as zealous as church officers in tracking down heretics; and London's commissary court—the primary court of correction in London—was largely ineffective and inefficient.

8. See Lehmberg, *The Reformation Parliament,* p. 121, and G. R. Elton, *Studies in Tudor and Stuart Politics and Government,* 2 vols. (Cambridge, 1974), 2:141.

9. Lehmberg, *The Reformation Parliament,* p. 85. Most of this passage ultimately was deleted by Cromwell.

10. A full discussion of this draft petition against the ordinaries is in ibid., p. 85.

11. Bowker, ed., *A Episcopal Court Book,* introduction, pp. xxi–xxii.

12. See above, Introduction, n. 10.

Rather, between the 1490s and 1529, a subtle process was taking place in London which seems to have had little to do with the commons' complaints but which nevertheless left an imprint on the Reformation Parliament. From the 1490s in London, litigants began to drift away from church courts and to seek justice in secular city courts. Creditors in petty debt suits found more severe justice in civic courts, and they abandoned London church courts altogether. Prosecutions of sexual offenders, notably of prostitutes and pimps, declined in London's commissary court and increased in the mayor's court; civic officials had better success in policing sexual mores than did church officials. Londoners who were dissatisfied with their curates' increased tithe demands appealed to civic authorities for help; and they received it. And some plaintiffs, notably creditors of deceased persons, encouraged city officials to control church court probates. In other words, litigants in search of courts favorable to their causes (i.e., courts that would respond according to their expectations) gradually abandoned church courts. Their motives were both for personal gain (as with creditors seeking debts owed them) and for more broadly moral ends (as with prosecutions of sexual offenders). The result was the same: many formerly "spiritual" matters came under secular control.

This process was part and parcel of the secularization of society in the late medieval world. By secularization I mean that there was an assumption among many or most Londoners that secular authorities can and ought to solve certain legal problems which formerly had been ecclesiastical problems. Secularization is not necessarily antireligious or nonreligious. It may show, as I suspect it does for the early sixteenth century, an intensely religious, reforming attitude on the part of laypeople. It may represent the desire to make the state a more active partner within the Christian body to enforce Christian norms. At work among various peoples throughout pre-Reformation Europe was a dynamic social myth: an age-old frenetic desire to return to ideally remembered days of Apostolic purity, a desire to "re-form" society and the personal spirit into a primitive Christian mold. The prevailing sentiment among sensitive men and women was to cleanse society of its corrupted practices; the gap between the ideal world of Christian memory and the real world of Christian society must be closed; the world as it *is* should more closely approximate the world as it *ought* to be.[13]

13. Parts of this paragraph have been influenced especially by Owen Chadwick's chapter, "The Cry for Reformation," in his *The Reformation*, Pelican History of the Church (Baltimore, 1964), pp. 11–39. During the 1490s there were, increasing in

What I have done in this monograph is to show how this secularization process took place in one crucial area: ecclesiastical jurisdiction in the city of London. From London court records, two clear facts emerge. First, there was from the 1490s a precipitous decline in suits brought to London church courts. Second, in all types of suits there was an extremely low enforcement rate (or high acquittal rate). These two quantitative facts require interpretation. I have suggested that the expectations of plaintiffs and claimants were not being met in London's church courts; that from the 1490s there were in London changing expectations or changing attitudes about justice in which plaintiffs and claimants began to demand stricter enforcement of norms. Expectations were not met because the London commissary court had such a low enforcement rate. This low rate, I have argued, was due primarily to the inherent weaknesses of a rural "trial" system, that is, compurgation, in an urban setting. Such a system apparently was effective and efficient in rural Lincoln, which in retrospect makes the courts appear effective and efficient. But in London much of village social cohesiveness–the foundation of a compurgation system–was lost. London, in fact, was a honeycomb of small groups. Thus, people such as churchwardens wishing to discipline wayward members of the parish reported their neighbors in great numbers to the church courts of correction; but those same neighbors belonged to other groups in London and easily found compurgators to free them of criminal charges. So long as plaintiffs did not expect higher enforcement rates from their courts, they would continue to flood the courts with charges as they did during the 1470s and 1480s. From the 1490s, Londoners' expectations changed, and their apparent dissatisfaction with church court justice led them to seek justice elsewhere.

Where then did people go to find justice? They went to the civic, secular courts. The mayor and aldermen of London attracted much legal business from the church courts, but they did so in default of church courts to enforce certain norms.

What could secular courts offer that church courts lacked? Effective sanctions. Throughout the medieval centuries, the church had provided rules of behavior that seem to have been widely accepted, and a court system to enforce those rules. What church courts lacked was compelling sanctions. The ultimate sanction was excommunication. But community ostracism (i.e., excommunication) was ineffective

intensity, millenarian expectations especially in Italy: see Marjorie Reeves, *Joachim of Fiore and the Prophetic Tradition* (London, 1976; repr. New York, 1977), pp. 83, 89–90.

against the professional wrongdoer, say, a pimp; he lives by illegal acts and thus has already ostracized himself by his own actions. Ostracism is effective only against the law-abiding citizen temporarily gone wrong. Weak sanctions, therefore, failed to elicit fear in the "bad man" to compel him to conform to accepted rules; and weak sanctions dissatisfied the sense of justice of the "good man" by showing him that valid norms could not be maintained by church authorities. London civic officers knew as well as church officers that certain norms ought to be maintained, that pimps and prostitutes should be severely punished, that debtors should be compelled to pay their debts, that wills should be scrupulously proved, that heretical literature should be confiscated. There was complete agreement between temporal and spiritual authorities over accepted norms. Londoners, then, turned to secular, civic officers to find the justice—the enforcement of norms—that was lacking in church courts. Tough, civic authorities, it was perhaps perceived by those seeking justice, could make the world-as-it-is more closely resemble the world-as-it-ought-to-be.

A final question arises. Why did not the church courts respond more forcibly to increase the enforcement rates as litigants presumably wanted and expected? Some procedural changes, indeed, were allowed in the commissary court in the early sixteenth century: witnesses were allowed to testify in defamation and marriage suits. But these changes seem to have been instigated by litigants themselves, not by the courts. Such court reforms, in any case, still were too minor to stop the drift of litigants away from London church courts.

Much of the responsibility to increase enforcement rates and make necessary procedural changes should have belonged to London's church court judges. They alone had enough discretion in courtroom procedure to increase enforcement rates. But they were, I have argued, specially trained in notions of canonical equity. This training, I believe, gave them a unique view of justice, one that was not unlike that of a just, merciful God: each case should be decided on its own merits; cases ought to be judged according to the spirit of the law, not the harsh letter of the law; mercy and leniency should be shown to penitent sinners. Other personal factors may also have entered into the behavior of London judges, but the end result, nevertheless, was the same: they behaved leniently toward defendants of all types, that is, they behaved according to the precepts of canonical equity as forgiving, merciful churchmen. Equitable notions and lenient behavior, it appears, were out of step with what many Londoners began to expect from their courts; they wanted sterner justice. And from the 1490s they began to seek justice from secular authorities. The secularization of London society was in progress.

BLANK PAGE

Appendix A

Tables

The following tables give a statistical picture of the disposition of cases brought before the commissary court of London. I have chosen from the surviving court books a select few of the best-documented years during each decade from 1470 through the 1510s to illustrate general trends. The numbers do not represent defendants, some of whom were charged for multiple offenses. For example, a defendant charged with pimping, prostitution, and defamation is counted as three cases, because he had to clear himself of all three charges. Persecutions against one person for multiple offenses, however, represent only a small minority of cases.

TABLE 1

Disposition of Defamation Suits in the London Commissary Court

	1471	1472	1484	1485	1492*	1493	1502	1503*	1512	1513	1514
Total cases in commissary court	980	1305	764	351	727	1061	547	221	294	303	328
Defamation cases	227	405	171	97	183	211	160	54	129	110	149
% of defamation cases	23%	31%	22%	28%	25%	20%	29%	24%	44%	36%	45%
1) No citation issued	12	19	18	4	42	58	10	2	18	7	16
%	5%	5%	10%	4%	22%	27%	6%	3%	14%	6%	11%
2) Acquittal											
Compurgation	57	151	37	6	58	38	31	15	1	3	1
Simple dismissal	46	55	41	19	18	14	46	11	20(3)	15(3)	25(4)
% (total)	45%	51%	46%	27%	42%	25%	48%	41%	16%	16%	17%
3) Case dropped	75	122	34(1)	16	22	32	43	9	43(17)	35(8)	51(18)
%	34%	30%	20%	16%	12%	15%	27%	14%	33%	32%	34%
4) Outside agreement											
Arbitration	2	11	14	26	5	3	1	3	1(1)	4	2(1)
Concord	9	14	11	6	15	14	7	5	16(3)	12(1)	20(1)
% (total)	5%	6%	15%	33%	11%	8%	5%	12%	13%	15%	14%
5) Confession											
"Penance"	3	2	0	2	4	19(3)	9	2	18(4)	13(6)	18(7)
Penalty unknown	0	5	0	0	2	1	2	0	0	0	0
% (total)	1%	2%	0%	2%	3%	9%	7%	3%	14%	12%	12%

6) Contumacy											
Suspension	13	20	13	18	9	21	3	2	6	12	12
Excommunication	2	2	1	0	1	0	0	0	8(2)	8(2)	3(1)
% (total)	7%	5%	8%	19%	5%	10%	3%	3%	11%	18%	10%
7) Sent to Consistory	1	2	0	0	6	11	6	5	0	0	0
8) Other	7	2	0	0	1	0	2	0	0	1	1

* Data exists for six months only.
Figures in parentheses indicate cases in which witnesses were introduced.

TABLE 2

Disposition of Adultery Cases in the London Commissary Court

	1471	1472	1484	1485	1492*	1493	[1497	1498]	1502	1503*	1512	1513	1514
Total cases in commissary court	980	1305	764	351	727	1061	224	142	547	221	294	303	328
Adultery cases	224	282	236	68	255	348	42	22	160	64	44	70	70
% of adultery cases	23%	22%	31%	19%	35%	33%	19%	15%	29%	29%	15%	23%	21%
1) No citation issued	72	80	74	18	78	77	8	0	8	2	2	10	9
%	32%	28%	31%	26%	31%	22%	19%	0%	5%	3%	5%	14%	13%
2) Acquittal													
Compurgation	68	112	67	19	98	116	12	4	40	19	9	16	19
Simple dismissal	2	17	9	2	6	23	2	2	19	12	8	13	7
% (total)	31%	46%	32%	31%	41%	40%	33%	27%	37%	48%	39%	41%	37%
3) Case dropped	37	28	45	18	23	67	8	5	46	9	11	7	6
%	17%	10%	19%	26%	9%	19%	19%	23%	29%	14%	25%	10%	9%
4) Confession													
"Penance"	14	10	7	2	15	27	6	6	33	11	3	10	15
Penalty unknown	3	6	6	0	3	1	0	0	0	0	0	0	0
% (total)	8%	6%	6%	3%	7%	8%	14%	27%	21%	17%	7%	14%	21%
5) Contumacy													
Suspension	17	26	22	8	12	27	6	4	5	5	5	5	7
Excommunication	3	1	2	0	6	0	0	0	3	2	2	2	2
% (total)	9%	10%	10%	12%	7%	8%	14%	18%	5%	11%	16%	10%	13%
6) Other	8	2	4	1	13	9	0	1	6	4	4	7	4

* Data exists for six months only

[ ] Data for deaneries of Middlesex and Barking only.

TABLE 3

Disposition of Fornication Cases in the London Commissary Court

	1471	1472	1484	1485	1492*	1493	[1497	1498]	1502	1503*	1512	1513	1514
Total cases in commissary court	980	1305	764	351	727	1061	224	142	547	221	294	303	328
Fornication cases	95	171	89	34	103	160	9	8	79	26	58	48	35
% of fornication cases	10%	13%	12%	10%	14%	15%	4%	5%	14%	12%	19%	16%	11%
1) No citation issued	10	19	28	11	24	46	1	0	8	1	6	9	5
%	11%	11%	31%	32%	23%	29%			10%	4%	10%	19%	14%
2) Acquittal													
Compurgation	19	41	21	9	36	39	3	0	12	7	7	8	3
Simple dismissal	8	13	6	1	6	12	0	1	11	10	5	8	5
% (total)	28%	32%	30%	29%	41%	32%			29%	65%	21%	33%	23%
3) Case dropped	26	43	12	2	3	19	1	5	23	2	15	3	5
%	27%	25%	13%	6%	3%	12%			29%	8%	26%	6%	1%
4) Confession													
"Penance"	7	12	2	1	16	25	4	1	21	5	19	10	11
Penalty unknown	5	7	2	2	2	3	0	0	0	0	0	1	0
% (total)	13%	11%	4%	9%	17%	18%			27%	19%	33%	23%	31%
5) Contumacy													
Suspension	16	24	11	6	7	11	0	0	2	0	2	4	3
Excommunication	2	2	5	1	3	2	0	1	0	0	3	1	1
% (total)	19%	15%	18%	21%	10%	8%			3%	0%	9%	10%	11%
6) Other	2	10	3	1	6	3	0	0	2	1	1	4	2

* Data exists for six months only.
[ ] Data for deaneries of Middlesex and Barking only.

TABLE 4

Disposition of Pimping Cases in the London Commissary Court

	1471	1472	1484	1485	1492*	1493	[1497	1498]	1502	1503*	1512	1513	1514
Total cases in commissary court	980	1305	764	351	727	1061	224	142	547	221	294	303	328
Pimping cases	191	248	140	48	93	112	33	18	65	33	8	20	24
% of pimping cases	19%	19%	18%	14%	13%	11%	15%	13%	12%	15%	3%	7%	7%
1) No citation issued	43	47	31	12	21	32	6	1	6	2	0	4	0
%	23%	19%	22%	25%	23%	29%	18%	5%	9%	6%	0%	20%	0%
2) Acquittal													
Compurgation	71	121	58	21	48	43	14	6	21	13	1	7	10
Simple dismissal	14	21	10	1	4	8	4	2	27	10	5	4	6
% (total)	45%	57%	49%	46%	56%	46%	55%	44%	74%	70%	75%	55%	67%
3) Case dropped	39	34	27	10	8	15	9	7	7	3	2	2	3
%	20%	14%	19%	21%	9%	13%	27%	39%	11%	9%	25%	10%	12%
4) Confession													
"Penance"	2	2	0	0	0	1	0	0	2	0	0	0	0
Penalty unknown	0	0	0	0	0	0	0	0	0	0	0	0	0
5) Contumacy													
Suspension	16	21	13	3	6	9	0	2	1	3	0	2	4
Excommunication	0	1	0	0	1	2	1	0	0	0	0	0	1
% (total)	8%	9%	9%	6%	8%	10%	3%	10%	2%	9%	0%	10%	20%
6) Other	6	1	1	1	5	2	0	0	1	2	0	1	0

* Data exists for six months only.

[ ] Data for deaneries of Middlesex and Barking only.

TABLE 5

Disposition of Prostitution Cases in the London Commissary Court

	1471	1472	1484	1485	1492*	1493	[1497	1498]	1502	1503*	1512	1513	1514
Total cases in commissary court	980	1305	764	351	727	1061	224	142	547	221	294	303	328
Prostitution cases	77	65	42	10	54	61	10	2	28	8	1	5	14
% of prostitution cases	8%	5%	5%	3%	7%	6%	4%	1%	5%	4%	.3%	2%	4%
1) No citation issued	14	11	7	1	20	13	0	0	2	1	0	1	1
%	18%	17%	17%	10%	37%	21%			6%				
2) Acquittal													
Compurgation	21	18	12	2	21	21	2	0	7	2	1	1	1
Simple dismissal	2	8	1	1	4	2	1	1	9	3	0	1	3
% (total)	30%	40%	31%	30%	46%	38%			57%				
3) Case dropped	22	15	12	2	2	12	4	1	7	1	0	1	4
%	29%	23%	29%	20%	4%	20%			25%				
4) Confession													
"Penance"	3	0	0	0	0	0	1	0	2	0	0	0	1
Penalty unknown	1	0	1	0	0	0	0	0	0	0	0	1	0
5) Contumacy													
Suspension	12	13	9	4	3	9	2	0	1	0	0	0	3
Excommunication	0	0	0	0	1	0	0	0	0	1	0	0	1
% (total)	16%	20%	21%	40%	8%	15%			4%				
6) Other	2	0	0	0	3	4	0	0	0	0	0	0	0

* Data exists for six months only.
[ ] Data for deaneries of Middlesex and Barking only.

Appendix B

Sample Folios from the "Acta quoad correctionem delinquentium"

Below are sample folios taken from various volumes of the "Acta quoad correctionem delinquentium," now located in the London Guildhall Library (MS 9064 series). I have chosen two folios each from five different volumes. The folios were produced at roughly ten-year intervals and show, I think, the evolutionary nature of the commissary court. I have chosen these particular folios because they are especially typical of the volumes in which they appear. I have tried as well to find folios with cases that illustrate legal or procedural changes in the court. These samples, I hope, will give some sense of the richness of church court records, as well as their limitations.

All court books are in paper. A scribe seems to have had before him, when a new court record began, a blank, bound notebook. Notebooks were bound in sections, each section consisting of six sheets of paper, folded once to form twelve folios or twenty-four pages.

In the left-hand margin of the court record, scribes first placed the name of the defendant's parish, then the initial or name of the summoner in the case. When a case was completed, the scribe scratched it out by placing a large "X" in the left-hand margin or over the case itself. For ease of typesetting I have placed the parish and the summoner's initial or name in italics at the beginning of each case.

Throughout I have silently extended abbreviated words and added only punctuation that I felt necessary to make the entries comprehensible; the originals contain no punctuation. I have modernized the use of "u" and "v," except in volume 9, in which the scribe himself usually made the modern distinction. Note the form of *purgare sese:* one "se" is often separated from the other "se"; the second "se" has not been misread for "cum."

I. MS 9064/1, fol. 64r–64v (1471)

The entire manuscript of volume 1 is badly water damaged, especially the bottom portions of all folios. Parts of many entries, therefore, are illegible. Each folio was lined before any entries were made and space was alloted on each folio side for eight to ten case entries. Scribes did not anticipate long, involved cases, but rather expected many short, routine cases—that is, cases not using more than one or two lines of folio space.

Summoners were noted in the original manuscript only by their initials. They were noted presumably so the scribe could give them their fees when a case was concluded and the *feodum dimissionis* was paid.

Note the two entries from the parish of St. Andrew by Baynard Castle. The words *indictata est* suggest that the cases originated in wardmoot.

[Vol. 1, fol. 64r]

Omnium Sanctorum [*Bar*]*kyng* *v:* Pyl James operabatur in die sancti pauli.

[illegible]: [illegible] Basset[1] aldermanus s [*sic*] adulteravit cum margeria famula sua.

Christoferi *v:* Johanna at Wode pronuba Amye commoranti secum. partes comparuerunt, negaverunt articulum; in die lune uterque purgare se se 3. illo die Johanna purgavit se et dimittitur et amya purgavit se similiter.

Andre Baynard *T:* Elizabeth Sterndayll meretrix et indictata est pro eodem crimine. mulier citata ad x diem Januarii. [ad] primum diem Februarii quia non comparuit suspensa. recessit.

Andre Baynard *T:* Margareta Foster meretrix et indictata est pro eodem crimine. recessit.

Marie Magdelene in veteri piscaria *T:* Johanna Andwort meretrix et indictata est pro eodem crimine in Westminster.

Marie veteri piscaria *v:* Ricardus Mairtoun paterfamilias apud le cardenallyshate suscitavit prolem super Agnetem servientem suam. vir citatus ad 1 diem Februarii. quia non comparuit suspensus.

[*Mary*] *Abchurch* *B:* Johannes Thomas diffamavit vicinos. vir comparuit xxx die Januarii. gratis.

Martin Vintry *v:* Adam Wellys suscitavit prolem super margeriam hwys. vir comparuit xxix die Januarii, fatabatur articulum; et continuatur ad diem veneris; et iudicatur sub [pena] excommunicationis quod non solempniset matrimonium pendens causa in [consistoria (?)]. [quia] non comparuit suspensus. citatus per litteram [viis et modis] ad [?] Februarii. quia non comparuit suspensus. [?] Februarii canonice corrigitur.

[Vol. 1, fol. 64v]

Mary Magdelene Milkestrete *t:* Willielmus Rowthe adulteravit cum Johanna Feloes et margareta commorantibus in le seler sub magna schopa sutoris. commorant infra prescinctum sancti martini. vir citatus ad 4 diem Februarii. quia non comparuit suspensus. 23 die Februarii Willielmus purgavit se coram commissario.

Marie Magdelene in veteri piscaria *B:* Elena hyway fregit fidem Phillippo Barker clerico in ecclesia sancti pauli pro [deleted: certa summa pecunie] xi^{s}.

Botophi Algate *T:* Agnes Wellys diffamatrix vicinorum [deleted: vocando] et specialiter uxoris Roberti Carter dicendo quod illa intoxicaret infantes. mulier citata ad comparendum 30 die Januarii. quia non comparuit suspensa. Agnes et Robertus comparuerunt; propter testimonium quod [several words deleted:

1. The alderman is Richard Basset. See Thrupp, *The Merchant Class*, p. 323.

illegible]. citatur die martis proximo; et continuatur ad illum diem. illo die continuatur ad diem Jovis. quo dies [*sic*] partes comparuerunt et Agnes Wellys peciit veniam et dimittitur. pro muliere sed non pro viro.

Katerine Colman *b:* Dominus Willielmus Flete extinxit candelam cuiusdam mulieris venientis ad purificacionem et hoc fecit apud hostium ecclesie et quando lavavit manus suas tempore misse dixit aperte Kessetes in anglice, "Kessetes it is a fair joy that we most tend to you for a candel a peny and a clowte" [2] et publicat confessiones parochianorum suorum. capellanus comparuit 5 die Januarii, negat articulum et continuatur ad diem veneris.

[*illegible*] *m:* Phillippus Taylor est pronoba [*sic*] et specialiter cuidam viro, mulieri, et cuidam sacerdoti. vir citatus ad primum diem Februarii.

Trinitatis *R:* Uxor magistri Clementi pronoba [*sic*] marione wynter et coco domini de northfolke qui quidam cocus adulteravit cum ea in le heylawth. mulier citata primo die Februarii; continuatur ad diem lune ix die Februarii. dimittitur.

Mary at Hyll *v:* Johannes Gaskall et uxor diffamatores vicinorum. xxxi die Januarii dominus dimisit eos.

[*illegible*] *T:* Johanna Redyng diffamatrix vicinorum. 4 die Februarii dimittitur per commissarium.

II. MS 9064/2, fol. 68r–68v (1484)

As in volume 1, the scribe has lined the folios of his book to allow eight to ten entries on each page. Cases still were expected to be summarily uncomplicated.

Note the method of purgation: often a defendant seems simply to have appeared in court with his neighbors and then been summarily dismissed without formal purgation (*comparuit cum vicinis et dimittitur*).

[Vol. 2, fol. 68r]

Stephani Colmanstrete *R:* Margeria Hill citata ad xvii diem Maii ad reddendum compotum et quia non solvit iii solidos et quatuor denarios legatos vicario ibidem. quia non comparuit ideo suspensa.

Marie at Ax *bl:* Matildis [*sic*] Warner communis pronuba et diffamatrix vicinorum suorum. Mulier citata ad xxii diem Maii. illo die maritus comparuit, negavit articulum; die lune proximo purgare se se 4. quia non comparuit ideo suspensa. ultimo die Maii mulier comparuit cum vicinis et dimittitur.

Sepulcri *bl:* Thomas Purchase fornicavit cum Johanna Schawe. citacio in viis et modis. vir comparuit xxv die Maii, negavit articulum; die mercurii proximo post viii dies [understood: purgare se].

Omnium Sanctorum Berkyng *bl:* Johanna Eliot pronuba filie sue. mulier citata ad xxii diem Maii. illo die mulier comparuit, negavit articulum; die lune

2. "Clowte" is a piece of cloth. See *O.E.D.*, S.V. "clout."

proximo purgare se se 4. illo die mulier comparuit cum vicinis et dimittitur.

Botolphi Bisshop[gate] *C:* Amea Stokys diffamavit Johannam Jesope vocando eam pronubam. citacio in viis et modis. primo die Junii partes comparuerunt et compromiserunt in Johannem Smyth wheler et Willielmum Scheter barber ita quod ferant laudum citra dominicam post festum Corporis Christi proximum futurum. x die Julii dimittitur quia pax.

Benedicti Powlis[wharf] *C:* Amea Pore pronuba Johanne manenti cum ipsa Johanna [*sic,* read: Amea]. citata ad xxii diem [M]aii. mulier comparuit xxviii die Maii cum vicinis et dimittitur. [deleted in margin: debet feodum]

Laurencii Pountteney *bg:* Henricus Hunderpounde fornicavit cum Felicia Abot et Elizabeth Good. citacio in viis et modis.

Michaelis Quinhith *B:* Elizabeth Williames communis meretrix et communis pronuba. mulier citata ad xx diem Maii.

[Vol. 2, fol. 68v]

Andree Estchepe *C:* Nicholaus [blank] Bruer diffamavit Robertum Tut Turner vocando eum nenerum[3] vicinorum. citatus ad xxiiii diem Maii. [in margin: debet]

Petri Powliswharf *C:* Johanna Eldergar communis meretrix et communis pronuba. mulier citata ad xxiiii diem Maii. illo die mulier comparuit, negavit articulum; die veneris proximo purgare se se 4. illo die mulier comparuit cum vicinis et dimittitur. [in margin: debet feodum]

Albani Wodstrete *C:* Elizabeth Deynes diffamavit Willielmum Wistowe dicendo quod ipse adulteravit cum Agnete Cowper. mulier comparuit xxviii die Maii et continuatur ad diem mercurii.

Sepulcri *BL:* Johanna Hunt pronua [*sic,* read: pronuba] servientibus suis. Johanna citata ad xxv diem Maii. quia non comparuit ideo suspensa. primo die Junii mulier comparuit, negavit articulum; die veneris proximo purgare se se 4. et postea allegat previncionem [*sic,* read: prevencionem].

Sepulcri *BL:* Johanna Draper communis meretrix.

[*Blank*] *:* Johanna Pekeryng communis meretrix. mulier citata ad xxv diem Maii.

Michaelis Quern *bl:* Johannes Persemer adulteravit cum Alicia serviente sua. vir citatus ad xxviij Maij. illo die vir comparuit, negavit articulum; die lune proximo purgare se se 4. illo die vir comparuit cum vicinis et dimittitur.

III. MS 9064/6, fol. 74r–74v (November 1494–January 1495)

By the 1490s cases in the commissary court had become more complex. Scribes, therefore, anticipated longer court book entries by allowing room on each page only for four or five cases.

3. This is not a misreading. "Nenerus" seems to be a noun form of the verb *nenior* ("to babble").

The first case concerning Robert Serle is noteworthy because it involves nonpayment of a debt over 40s. The case was sent to consistory for resolution.

Note also the final case of alleged fornication between Phillip Bocher and Alice Mathew. Their defense was that they had already exchanged marriage vows. The case was sent to consistory court. By the 1500s, similar marriage suits were heard regularly in commissary court.

[Vol. 6, fol. 74r (73r in pencil)]

[*Katherine*] *Kri Colman* [*street*] *M*[*?*]: Robertus Serle communis violator fidei et presertim violavit Fidem Johanni Finche haberdassher in non soluto eidem iii^{li} iii^{s} pro quibus fideiussit coram testibus fidedignis. 4to decembris comparuit, et negavit, et habet die sabbati proximo ad comparendum. quo die comparuit et dominus sedens judicialiter in curia audita causa remisit illam in locum consistorii, et decrevit Johannem Martyn partem citare ad comparendum in predicto loco die Jovis proximo futuro viz. xi die decembris.[4]

Omnium Sanctorum Stanyng HK: Johanna Ady violavit Fidem Jacobo Dalby et debet eidem Jacobo ut liquet pro compotum vi^{s}. xvi Januarii comparuit Thomas Heyward et deposuit virtute juramenti sui in anglice verbis viz. "First my master send unto her a barell of goodale which she pad for or [i.e., before] she Receyvid it, and whan she receyvid it she refusid it and set it home ageyn for it was not good. than immediately or she departid unto the north she had iii kilderkyns[5] of good ale and therefor paid her husband unto Janis dalby; and then after she came out of the north she had iii kilderkyns of goodale which she hath not paid for." et hoc dicit ex scientia quia deliberavit et virtute sui Juramenti sic deposuit. xi Februarii comparuit et promisit fide sua solvere iiii^{s} immediate et stare ideo paci. et solvit.

Omnium Sanctorum Major hk:[6] Johanna Norbery fornicavit cum Humfrido Hogg. citata ad xi novembris et fatebatur crimen et dominus iniunxit sibi penitenciam publicam etc. comparuit vir et solvit pro redemptione penitentie ut sequitur:

Humfridus Hogg fornicavit cum Johanna Norbery. xii Novembris comparuit et fatebatur crimen et dominus iniunxit penitenciam publicam viz. dominica proxima nudis pedibus etc. ad modum penitentis. comparuit et solvit pro redemptione penitentie iii^{s}.

Petri Powliswharff g: Katherina Archer adulteravit cum Johanne Brawne. xvii novembris comparuit, et negavit, et purgavit se, et dimittitur.

[Vol. 6, fol. 74v]

Michaelis Quenhith k: Ricardus Stone fornicavit cum Isabella Wright. ultimo novembris comparuerunt et purgaverunt se vicinis, et dimittuntur ex gratia quia pauperes.

4. The words "Martin . . . comparendum" are badly smudged in the MS. I have reconstructed the words from similar entries in other parts of this court book.

5. A kilderkyn is a cask containing half a barrel of liquid.

6. The two cases are joined by a bracket in the MS.

Clementis extra Barras g: Nicholaus [blank] chaundeler communis violator sabbati eo quod diebus dominicis et festivis ostendit venalia publice prout in ceteris diebus. citatus ad viii novembris. non comparuit ideo suspensus. habet ad purgandum die lune se 3^a manu. quo die comparuit et purgavit se vicinis et dimittitur.

Martini at Well with ii bokkettis [*buckets*] [*no initial*]: Robertus Thruggod communis diffamator vicinorum et seminator discordiarum et defector virorum veridicorum et proborum. xvi novembris comparuit et offertat de consensu purgare se vicinis. [Dixit] "men be pald [=polled] hidder. I will nat say that ye do me no wrong but [rather] they that caused me to be callid hidder." quia non comparuit ideo suspensus.[7]

Katherine Cri W: Phillippus Bocher fornicavit cum Alicia Mathew [deleted: Bocher]. citati ambo ad xiiii Novembris. non comparuit mulier ideo suspensa. xv novembris comparuerunt se, negarunt crimen quia precontractu. dominus remisit causam in locum consistorii, et decrevit Willielmum Jamys apparitorem ad citandum eosdem quod compareant et uterque compareat proximo die Jovis ex tunc sequente.

IV. MS 9064/7, fol. 70r–70v: from the circuit court of Middlesex and Barking (December 1496)

Cases were expected to be complex and, thus, room for only three or four entries was allotted to a page.

Note the number of "hands" ordered to free a defendant and the actual number allowed. A defendant's own oath was counted as a hand; and in the case of William Salman, he was successfully purged even with one less hand than ordered.

[Vol. 7, fol. 70r]

Dukenham [*no summoner initial*]: Willielmus Gerves communis diffamator vicinorum suorum presertim diffamavit Thomam Clerke et eius filium dicendo in anglice "Thomas Clerke and his son be ii stronge theves and false harlettes." citatus ad xxi diem mensis Novembris. quo die comparuit, et negavit articulum; tunc habet ad purgandum se isto die ad quindenam se iii manu. quo die non comparuit ideo suspensus. comparuit et allegavit infirmitatem; tunc dominus eum absolvit; et nichil solvit pro [absolutione]; habet ad solvendum dimissionis die lune proximo post Epiphaniam proximo. comparuit et dimittitur ex gratia.

Lune ix Decembris

Iseldon tk: Helena Geffrey notatur in adulterio cum domino Thome Gore vicarius [*sic,* read: vicario] ibidem dum vixit nuper defuncti. citata mulier ad diem Jovis proximo. comparuit et fatebatur articulum et juratus [*sic*] est ad penitenciam, et habet ad recipiendum citra diem Lune proximum post Festum Epiphanie proximum. composuit et solvit domino iii^s iiii^d.

7. The final phrase, "quia . . . suspensus," is in a later hand.

Iseldon tk: Henricus Colett notatur officio quod est communis pronuba presertim inter dictum dominum Thomam et Helenam. citatus ad diem Jovis proximum. comparuit et negavit articulum; tunc dominus indixit sibi ad purgandum se die marcurii proximo se iiii manu. purgavit se Johanne Oluffe, Johanne Ben, et Willielmo Kynnalton; solvit feodum et dimittitur.

[Vol. 7, fol. 70v]

Iseldon tk: Dominus Willielmus Salman Curatus ibidem notatur in adulterio cum Agnete Garner de parochia Sancti Botolphi extra Bishopgat. citatus ad diem Jovis proximum. comparuit et negavit articulum; tunc dominus indixit sibi purgare die marcurii proximo se v manu, viz. ii presbiteris et ii laicis. quo die non comparuit ideo suspensus in scriptis. postea comparuit, et absolutus est, et purgavit se domino Roberto Kyde, domino Edwardo Weke et Ricardo Steven; solvit feodum et dimittitur.

Fyncheley Fox: Johannes Parkman communis diffamator vicinorum suorum presertim diffamavit Thomam Bygmor vocando eum in Anglice "Thow art a false theve and an horeson and a chorled horeson." citatus ad diem Jovis proximum. comparuit et negavit articulum; tunc habet ad purgandum se die marcurii proximo se iiii manu.

Iseldon [*no summoner initial*]: Dominus Willielmus Salman, Henricus Colett, et Helena Geffrey xii die decembris comparuerunt, quos dominus Jurare fecerunt [*sic*, read: fecit] de ostendendo omnia bona domini Thome Gore, etc., Ricardo Nore executori dicti defuncti et appreciatoribus domini in eorum custodia remanentia, et de revelando alia que venient ad ipsorum noticiam etc.

V. MS 9064/9, fol. 42r–42v (June 1502)

Pages generally were allocated space for only three cases—sometimes for only one or two cases. Court days are usually noted by a specific date before cases were entered in the record. The court by 1502 was meeting less frequently than in the late fifteenth century.

Court records were becoming more complex and more self-consciously precise. This is not a peculiarity of a specific scribe. Scribes changed, but the complexity of the cases remained. We now find, for example, common use of the phrase *notatur officio fama publica referente* to designate the origin of a charge.

By 1502 there were few "easy" cases, unlike in earlier decades. The first case of Bartholomew Capper, an accused adulterer who used marriage as a defense, was heard only in the commissary court rather than sent to consistory.

[Vol. 9, fol. 42r]

Albani in Wodstrete tk: Bartholomeus Capper notatur officio fama publica referente quod diu vixit in adulterio cum quadam Elena quam tenuit ut vir et uxor hiis annis et plures ab eadem suscitavit. citatur per Kemp die Sabbati iiii^{to} Junii ad decimum diem eiusdem. quo die comparuit, et asseruit se dictam Elenam in uxorem duxisse xii Annis elapsis et ultra in Manchestir; et habet ad exhibendum testimoniale citra festum sancti iacobi proximum.

Benedicti Fynk tk: Dominus Nicholaus Couper Senescallus Sancti Antoni notatur officio fama referente quod adulteravit cum quadam Elizabeth Makerel de parochia sancti Clementis Dacorum. citatur vir ix° die Junii in parochia Sancti Benedicti Fynk ad xv diem eiusdem. quo die comparuit et negavit articulum et habet ad purgandum se die veneris proximo se iiii^{ta} manu. quo die comparuit et dominus monuit eum ad comparendum coram eo die mercurii ad allegandum causam quare non debeat pro convicto declarari pro eo quod defecit in purgatione [deleted: super causa ista]. ipse allegans se privilegiatum[8] [deleted: et habet ad ostendendum huiusmodi privilegium eodem die].

Clementis in Estchepe Foster: Willielmus Sevill aquebaiulus ibidem notatur officio quod vilipendit et adnichilavit ac diffamavit dominum Thomam Warde sic maliciose dicendo "goo forth fole and set a Cockis combe on thi crowne" sacerdotalem ordinem nequiter contempuendo. citatur xi^{mo} die Junii in domo sua infra eandem parochiam. ad comparendum xiii° die eiusdem. quo die comparuit et dimittitur quia concordati sunt etc.

[Vol. 9, fol. 42v]

Petri Paupertatis F: [Name: blank] Curatus ibidem notatur officio quod est communis Rixator et presertim cum [name: blank] cantario [cantarista?] in ecclesia Sancti Benedicti Fynke qui evaginavit cultellum ad interficiendum eum. citatur ad decimum diem Junii. quo die comparuit, dimittitur.

Benedicti Fynk F: Dominus Thomas Browne Cantarius [Cantarista?] ibidem notatur super dicto Articulo. Citatur ad eundem diem. comparuit et dominus monuit eum quod concordantur ambo citra diem Sabbati Sabbati [*sic*] proximum, sin autem ad comparendum eodem coram eo ad allegandum causam quare non debeant puniri in debita juris forisfactura.[9]

Benedicti Poulliswharf tk: Edwardus Newton et Margareta uxor eius notantur officio fama publica referente quod sunt communes pronube diversis meretricibus de Stewis cum quibusdam presbiteris et laicis, prout nonnulli circumvicini et alii referunt. citatur vir x^{mo} Junii ad comparendum xiii° die eiusdem. xi^{mo} die eiusdem comparuit et negat articulum cuidam dominus indixit ad purgandum se die lune se vi^{ta} manu honesta vicinorum suorum. quo die comparuit et dominus monuit eum ad purgandum se ut supra die mercurii xv die eiusdem. eodem die continuatur usque in crastinum. xvi die eiusdem comparuit et purgavit se et dimittitur.

VI. MS 9064/10, fol. 38r–38v (September 1509)

Note the new procedure available to plantiffs in defamation suits (*Nicholas Scott* vs. *Agnes Willyams*). Plaintiffs now could prove their charges with *viva*

8. He perhaps is alleging that he is a "privileged tenant," i.e., that he is within the jurisdiction of another court.
9. The word in the MS is "for^{w}." The combination of words, therefore, is not *juris fori* (i.e., secular law), but most likely *in debita juris forisfactura* (according to the due penalty of the law).

voce testimony of witnesses, in which case, defendants no longer could easily free themselves with oath-helpers but could only cross-examine witnesses. The same procedure was available in marriage suits (*Roger Wadd* vs. *Alice Luca and John Denyse*). Marriage suits now were heard regularly in commissary court.

[Vol. 10, fol. 38r]

Marie Wolnos [*i.e., Wolnoth*] *Kemp:* Willielmus Amadas Junior notatur officio ad instanciam domini Willielmi Powell in quadam causa fidei lesionis et periurii. citatus fuit ad comparendum die veneris xiiii Septembris. non comparuit ideo suspensus.

Brigite Mathue: Agnes Willyams notatur officio quod est communis diffamatrix vicinorum suorum et seminatrix discordiarum inter eosdem et presertim diffamavit Nicholaum Scott vocando eum Cockcold. Citata fuit ad comparendum die mercurii proximo xii die Septembris. comparuit prefata Agnes, et negavit articulum; tunc dominus assignavit Scott ad producendum testes die Sabbati proximo et prefate Agnete ad interessendum eodem die. quo die produxit Margaretam Felton et Elizabethem Pingeon [?]. xv° die Septembris comparuit et submisit se correctioni cui Curatus dominus Iniunxit penitenciam sequentem quod precedat coram processione [deleted: nudis tibiis et pedibus], baiulans unum cereum valoris 5s, et par precularum [in manu sinistra] [10] etc.; quam penitenciam peragere expresse negavit. tunc dominus reputavit ipsam contumacem, et in pena contumacis ipsam excommunicat.

Omnium Sanctorum Barkyng Philipp: Margareta Wyndalle notatur officio quod est gravis [diffamatrix] vicinorum suorum et seminatrix discordiarum inter eosdem; et presertim diffamavit Elizabethem Farrore vocando eam hore et quod habuit [quod] pueri sui sunt illegitime nati. citata fuit ad comparendum die mercurii v° Septembris.

Katerine Cristchurche Kirkman: Christoferus Browne fama publica referente quod vivit in adulterio cum Elizabethe FithzJohn. citatus fuit ad comparendum die veneris vii die septembris. septimo die Septembris comparuit et negavit articulum, cui dominus assignavit ad purgandum se die mercurii. quo die produxit Rogerum Aysnewall, Robertum Versteyke, Alexandrem Arstride, et Willielmum Sudbery. fuit proclamatus, dominus admisit eum sine voce sine [*sic*].

Katerine Cristchurche Kirkman: Elizabethe [*sic*] FithzJohn fama publica referente quod vivit in adulterio cum Christofero Browne. citata fuit ad comparendum die veneris vii° die septembris.

[Vol. 10, fol. 38v]

Anno domini Millesimo quingentesimo [deleted: X] Nono

Marie Axe Kirkman: Alicia Lucas fama publica referente quod vivit in adulterio cum Rogero Wadd serviente magistri Milles et contraxit matrimo-

10. The phrase in brackets appears in vol. 11, fol. 25r; the penitent is to hold a rosary in her left hand, "etc."

nium cum prefato [name: blank] ac cum Johanne Denyse pynner. citata fuit ad comparendum die Veneris vii° Septembris. Comparuit prefata Alicia et fatebatur quod contraxhit cum Denysse sed dixit quod precontraxhit cum Rogero Wadd. Tunc dominus assignavit prefatum Wadd ad producendum testes super contractu huiusmodi et prefatum Denysse ad interessendum productioni huiusmodi die Mercurii proximo. quo die in pena contumacie dominus decrevit testes producendos Johannem Hawkyns, Willielmum Pyrry quos dominus oneravit.

Marie Magdelan Charles: Leticia Johnston notatur officio quod est communis diffamatrix vicinorum suorum et seminatrix discordiarum inter eosdem, et presertim diffamavit Aliciam Backe vocando eam harlott et hore. citata fuit ad comparendum die veneris vii° Septembris.

Sancte Fidei Kemp: Petrus Turnor notatur officio quod negat solvere stipendium clerico parochiali per gardianos et eiusdem ecclesie parochianos taxatum, licet per gardianos eiusdem fuerit diversis vicibus requisitus; et subtraxhit huiusmodi stipendium per tres annos summam viz. iiii^{or} solidos. quinto die Septembris comparuit, quem dominus monuit ad solvendum gardianis citra istum diem ad octavum sub pena Juris et ad certificiendum die mercurii proximo post festum omnium sanctorum proximum. quo die certificavit se satisfecisse dictum monitum, quem dominus dimisit.

Sancti Andree Barnardcastell Bewys: Alicia Persy notatur officio quod est gravis vicinorum suorum diffamatrix et presertim diffamavit Johannem Draper vocando eum strong theyff et Johannam eius uxorem strong prestys hoor and bawde. quinto die Septembris comparuit et negavit articulum; tunc dominus assignavit parti Draper ad producendum testes super prolatione verborum die lune proximo. quo die produxit Robertum Lytill in presencia Persy quem dominus oneravit de fidelitate. xii° die Septembris prefatus Draper produxit Aliciam Samson in testem quam dominus oneravit etc. quinto die Octobris prefata Alicia fatebatur quod [entry ends]

VII. MS 9064/11, fol. 322r (4 July 1516), fol. 327r (19 July 1516)

From fol. 293r (28 February 1516) to the end of the court book on fol. 329v (30 July 1516) the nature of court book entries changes significantly. Included among normal commissary court cases are now found cases presumably from the consistory court. The new style of entry is identical with the style of the consistory court book, the "Liber assignationum" (Greater London Record Office, DL/C/1): in the margin appears the names of litigants and their proctors; and a new entry is made for each court appearance. Thus, in the new style, a case is spread out over several folios, rather than contained in a single entry.

The significance of the new types of cases is that the upper and lower courts, the consistory and commissary, presumably were joined into a single court. This merger seems to have been a practical solution to the real problem of declining business in both courts. Until the lost court books for the 1520s reappear we have no way of knowing if this merger was a temporary expedient or a permanent solution.

[Vol. 11, fol. 322r]

Omnium Sanctorum Minorum Jo Bo [*John Bottell*]: Johanna mylner notatur officio etc. quod vivit et vixit in fornicatione cum quodam Johanne Robynson. iiii^to^ Junii comparuerunt coram domino commissario in domo habitacione eiusdem, et confessi sunt articulum. et dominus assignavit eidem Johanni ad recipiendum penitenciam die mercurii et mulieri ad recipiendum penitenciam die martis proximo.

Johanna (Emerson) Lytylton contra Thomam Gilbert in causa matrimoniali tw: quo die [4 July] comparuit Webbe et certificavit se citasse eundem Thomam ad hos diem et locum eidem Johanne in huiusmodi causa responsurum; quem preconizatum et non comparentem dominus suspendit in scriptis.[11]

Die martis 8vo Julii

Leonardi Shordych: Dominus Thomas [blank] curatus ibidem habet ex assignacione iudiciali ad videndum testes produci super fama. quo die comparuit et dominus assignavit ei ad idem, die lune proximo.[12]

Officium domini contra Margaretam Potter: Potter habet ad certificandum super factione penitencie alias sibi iniuncte. quo die non comparuit neque certificavit; quam dominus ab ingressu ecclesie suspendit in scriptis.[13]

[Vol. 11, fol. 327r]

Gryffyth contra Rogers; Talkarum, Crame:[14] quo die Crame dedit responsum in scedula in presentia Talkarum; et dominus ad peticionem eiusdem Talkarum assignavit eidem ad secundo producendum iiii^to^ [die post festum Sancte] Margarete proximum in presentia Crame et in parte eiusdem Termini. Idem Talkarum produxit Johannem Botell et Robertum Ides in testes,[15] quos dominus admisit et Jurari fecit in presentia crame protestantis de dicendo contra dicta, et depositi se etc., et petentis terminum ad ministrandum, cui dominus assignavit citra meridiem diei lune proximum.

Rogers contra Gryffyth; Crame, Talkarum: quo die Talkarum mutatis nominibus dedit consiliare responsiones sine scriptis. et dominus ad peticionem crame assignavit eundem ad secundo producendum iiii^to^ [die post festum Sancte] Margarete proximum.

Winbush contra Colbrand; Talkarum, Crame: quo die Talkarum dedit libelum in presentia crame, cui dominus assignavit ad respondendum iiii^to^ [die post festam Sancte] Margarete proximum. quo die Thomas Farebary exhibit

11. This is the first entry of *Lytylton* vs. *Gilbert*.
12. This case is continued from an earlier entry on fol. 321v.
13. On the previous court day (4 July) Potter failed her purgation for adultery, and was ordered to perform penance.
14. The proctors are William Crame and John Talkarum, both of whom also were proctors of the court of Arches. The case is a continuation from the previous court day, 14 July.
15. This may be John Botell the apparitor, and Robert Ides a proctor in the court.

procuratorium originale apud acta et [deleted: offert] obtulit se promptum ad respondendum si partem adversum habeat presentem.[16]

Andree Undershafte TC: Johanna Yvers notatur officio ad promocionem walteri lawlys eiusdem parochie quod est communis et gravis diffamatrix et presertim eiusdem Walteri vocando eundem pronubam et dicendo de eodem quod fovit lenocinium in domo sua inter simonem barber et aliciam servientem suam. quo die comparuit Yvers et articulum objectum negavit in presentia lawlys, cui dominus assignavit ad probandum iiii^{to} [die post festum Sancte] Margarete et Yvers ad videndum testes produci eadem die. quo die Lawlys in presencia Yvers produxit Johannem Glover in testem, quem dominus Juramento oneravit et monuit eum ad subeundum examem citra proximam curiam viz. diem mercurii proximum; et assignavit Lawlys ad precise probandum eodem et Yvers ad sic probari videndum eodem die. deinde facta fide per Lawlys quod requisivit Johannem Yvers testem necessarium, quem dominus monendum fore decrevit ad iii^{cium} post si etc. testimonium veritati perhibiturum.

16. This case is a continuation from the previous court day, 14 July.

Bibliography of Manuscript Sources

My research has been centered around two court systems in pre-Reformation London, the church courts and the secular courts. There survives an abundance of court records for one London church court, the commissary court. Evidence from secular judicial courts in London is not nearly so rich. Below is a list of manuscript sources in London that I have consulted.

The largest group of manuscripts and consequently the one most important to my research is the series of act books for the commissary court of London: the "Acta quoad correctionem delinquentium," now in the Guildhall Library Muniment Room, MS 9064 series. The correct dating of these volumes is noted below. I have marked with an asterisk (*) those volumes which archdeacon Hale knew of in 1847 and which have since been lost; and I have marked with a dagger (†) those volumes of whose existence he apparently was unaware. I have reckoned the year as beginning on 1 January rather than 25 March, as in the court books.

†9064/1, May 1470–March 1473
†9064/2, March 1483–July 1489
9064/3, May 1480–March 1483; October 1475 (from fol. 188r)–December 1477
9064/4, November 1489–December 1491
9064/5, October 1492–February 1494
9064/6, May 1494–February 1496
9064/7, Middlesex and Barking Deaneries, November 1496–September 1500
9064/8, November 1496–March 1501
9064/9, January 1502–July 1503
9064/10, January 1509–February 1511
†9064/11, July 1511–July 1516
*———, 1518–1526
*———, 1526–1529

Another rich source of commissary court records is the series of "Acta testamentorum" (probate records) kept in the Guildhall Library Muniment Room. The first eight volumes (MSS 9168/1–8) cover the years 1496 to 1526. See also the Registers of Wills (MSS 9171/6–9) that cover the years 1467 to 1521; and MSS 952/Box 1, original wills from the archdeacon's court, 1524–1603.

Extant records from the consistory court are much less prolific. There is one act book, the "Liber assignationum," now in the Greater London Record Office, MS DL/C/1 (fols. 1r to 11v are for 1496; from fol. 14r, the records cover May 1500 to October 1505). Five deposition books survive: four in the Greater London Record Office (DL/C/205–208: 1467–1533); and one in the Guildhall Library (MS 9065: 1487–1494).

Secular judicial records for pre-Reformation London are spotty at best. Actual judicial records for pre-Reformation London–i.e., the Court of Aldermen, the Sheriff's Court, the Hustings, the Court of Orphans–do not survive at all. What survives in abundance are minutes and records of proclamations of the meetings of the mayor and aldermen, and of the common council. The mayor and aldermen acted as a judicial court when they sat as the Court of Aldermen in the Inner Chamber, but records of their judicial activities do not, to my knowledge, exist (see P. E. Jones and R. Smith, *A Guide to the Records in the Corporation of London Records Office and the Guildhall Library Muniment Room* [London, 1951], pp. 29 seq.). Very little work has been done on pre-Reformation secular London courts, no doubt because of the paucity of records. I have begun research for a larger study of London during the Reformation; I hope to find more evidence of, or at least to put together a comprehensible picture of, civic judicial activities. Valuable for my work on pre-Reformation London have been the Journals (minutes of the court of the Common Council), Repertories (minutes of the court of the mayor and aldermen when they sat in the Outer Chamber as the Mayor's court–largely administrative), and Letterbooks (the official record of proclamations, documents, and the like): all are kept in the Corporation of London Records Office. The Repertories especially give some evidence of the judicial activities of the Court of Aldermen because some judicial problems were taken by the aldermen out of the Inner Chamber and discussed in the Outer Chamber. The Journals begin in 1416 and the Repertories in 1495.

Other secular courts that perhaps acted as alternatives to ecclesiastical courts were the king's courts at Westminster, records of which survive in abundance. These courts, however, were much too important to act as a rival judicial system to the petty commissary court of London. Compare, for example, the few defamation cases heard in King's Bench with the types and huge numbers heard in commissary court (cf. John Baker, ed., *The Reports of Sir John Spelman,* Selden Society 94 [London, 1978], p. 242). Rather, petty matters of prostitution, pimping, tithes, and the like ultimately were taken to one of the city courts–probably the Court of Aldermen or the Sheriff's Court–for which we have no records.

A list of other especially useful manuscripts that I have consulted is as follows:

British Library:
- Harl. 421. John Foxe, Miscellaneous Papers
- Harl. 2179. Fifteenth-Century Formulary Book
- Reg. MS 11. A. xi. Legal Formulary
- Reg. MS 11. A. xv. Tracts on Canon Law Legal Procedure

Corporation of London Records Office:
- Ward Presentments. Portsoken Ward, MS 242A
- Letterbook M, 1497–1515
- Letterbook N, 1515, 1526
- Letterbook O, 1526–1532

Guildhall Library Muniment Room:
- MS 9537/2. Visitation Book, 1561
- MSS 9531/1–. Bishop's Registers
- Pre-Reformation Churchwarden Account Books (an extraordinarily rich and largely untapped source of information of local London life):
  - MS 4956/1. All Hallows Staining
  - MS 1279/1. St. Andrew Hubbard
  - MS 1454. St. Botolph Aldersgate
  - MS 4887. St. Dunstan in the East
  - MS 2968. St. Dunstan in the West
  - MS 4570/1. St. Margaret Pattens
  - MS 959/1. St. Martin Orgar
  - MS 6842. St. Martin Outwich
  - MS 1239/1–2. St. Mary at Hill
  - MS 2596. St. Mary Magdelen Milkstreet
  - MS 4071/1. St. Michael Cornhill
  - MS 2895/1. St. Michael le Quern
  - MS 645/1. St. Peter Westcheap
  - MS 593/1. St. Stephen Walbrook
  - MS 4457/1. St. Stephen Colmanstreet

Lambeth Palace:
- Register Morton, I

Public Record Office:
- Significations of Excommunication. C 85/125
- Probate. Prob. 11/–

0123456

AIIM SCANNER TEST CHART #2

654321
A4 Page 6543210

Spectra
4 PT ABCDEFGHIJKLMNOPQRSTUVWXYZabcdefghijklmnopqrstuvwxyz;:",./?$0123456789
6 PT ABCDEFGHIJKLMNOPQRSTUVWXYZabcdefghijklmnopqrstuvwxyz;:",./?$0123456789
8 PT ABCDEFGHIJKLMNOPQRSTUVWXYZabcdefghijklmnopqrstuvwxyz;:",./?$0123456789
10 PT ABCDEFGHIJKLMNOPQRSTUVWXYZabcdefghijklmnopqrstuvwxyz;:",./?$0123456789

Times Roman
4 PT ABCDEFGHIJKLMNOPQRSTUVWXYZabcdefghijklmnopqrstuvwxyz;:",./?$0123456789
6 PT ABCDEFGHIJKLMNOPQRSTUVWXYZabcdefghijklmnopqrstuvwxyz;:",./?$0123456789
8 PT ABCDEFGHIJKLMNOPQRSTUVWXYZabcdefghijklmnopqrstuvwxyz;:",./?$0123456789
10 PT ABCDEFGHIJKLMNOPQRSTUVWXYZabcdefghijklmnopqrstuvwxyz;:",./?$0123456789

Century Schoolbook Bold
4 PT **ABCDEFGHIJKLMNOPQRSTUVWXYZabcdefghijklmnopqrstuvwxyz;:",./?$0123456789**
6 PT **ABCDEFGHIJKLMNOPQRSTUVWXYZabcdefghijklmnopqrstuvwxyz;:",./?$0123456789**
8 PT **ABCDEFGHIJKLMNOPQRSTUVWXYZabcdefghijklmnopqrstuvwxyz;:",./?$0123456789**
10 PT **ABCDEFGHIJKLMNOPQRSTUVWXYZabcdefghijklmnopqrstuvwxyz;:",./?$0123456789**

News Gothic Bold Reversed
4 PT **ABCDEFGHIJKLMNOPQRSTUVWXYZabcdefghijklmnopqrstuvwxyz;:",./?$0123456789**
6 PT **ABCDEFGHIJKLMNOPQRSTUVWXYZabcdefghijklmnopqrstuvwxyz;:",./?$0123456789**
8 PT **ABCDEFGHIJKLMNOPQRSTUVWXYZabcdefghijklmnopqrstuvwxyz;:",./?$0123456789**
10 PT **ABCDEFGHIJKLMNOPQRSTUVWXYZabcdefghijklmnopqrstuvwxyz;:",./?$0123456789**

Bodoni Italic
4 PT *ABCDEFGHIJKLMNOPQRSTUVWXYZabcdefghijklmnopqrstuvwxyz;:",./?$0123456789*
6 PT *ABCDEFGHIJKLMNOPQRSTUVWXYZabcdefghijklmnopqrstuvwxyz;:",./?$0123456789*
8 PT *ABCDEFGHIJKLMNOPQRSTUVWXYZabcdefghijklmnopqrstuvwxyz;:",./?$0123456789*
10 PT *ABCDEFGHIJKLMNOPQRSTUVWXYZabcdefghijklmnopqrstuvwxyz;:",./?$0123456789*

Greek and Math Symbols
4 PT ΑΒΓΔΕΞΘΗΙΚΑΜΝΟΠΦΡΣΤΥΩΞΨΖαβγδεξθηιφκλμνοπφρστυωχψζ≥±",./≤=≠°><≡
6 PT ΑΒΓΔΕΞΘΗΙΚΑΜΝΟΠΦΡΣΤΥΩΞΨΖαβγδεξθηιφκλμνοπφρστυωχυζ≥±",./≤=≠°><≡
8 PT ΑΒΓΔΕΞΘΗΙΚΑΜΝΟΠΦΡΣΤΥΩΞΨΖαβγδεξθηιφκλμνοπφρστυωχψζ≥±",./≤=≠°><≡
10 PT ΑΒΓΔΕΞΘΗΙΚΑΜΝΟΠΦΡΣΤΥΩΞΨΖαβγδεξθηιφκλμνοπφρστυωχψζ≥±",./≤=≠°><≡

0123456

White

Black

Isolated Characters

e	m	1	2	3	a
4	5	6	7	o	n
8	9	0	h	l	B

654321
A4 Page 6543210

MESH HALFTONE WEDGES

65
85
100
110
133
150

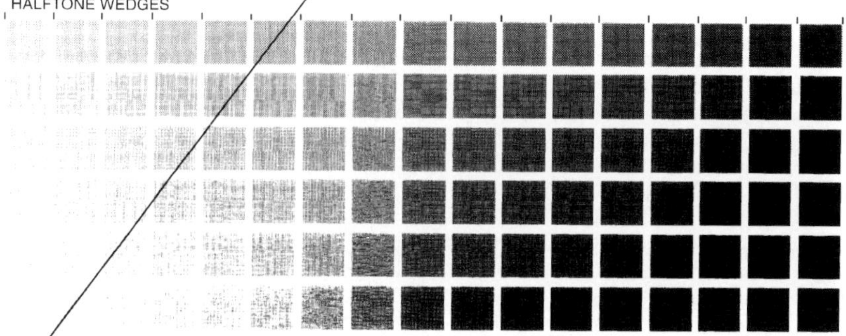

A4 Page 6543210

0123456

654321

18384648R00101

Printed in Great Britain
by Amazon